The Language of Power in the
Simile "Like a Caged Bird"

The Language of Power in the Simile "Like a Caged Bird"

A Critical Discourse Analysis of the Assyrian Royal Lion Hunt and Sennacherib's Military Campaign Against Hezekiah of Judah

Woo Min Lee

PICKWICK *Publications* • Eugene, Oregon

THE LANGUAGE OF POWER IN THE SIMILE "LIKE A CAGED BIRD"
A Critical Discourse Analysis of the Assyrian Royal Lion Hunt and Sennacherib's Military Campaign Against Hezekiah of Judah

Pickwick Publications
An Imprint of Wipf and Stock Publishers
199 W. 8th Ave., Suite 3
Eugene, OR 97401

www.wipfandstock.com

PAPERBACK ISBN: 979-8-3852-3528-5
HARDCOVER ISBN: 979-8-3852-3529-2
EBOOK ISBN: 979-8-3852-3530-8

Cataloguing-in-Publication data:

Names: Lee, Woo Min [author].

Title: The language of power in the simile "like a caged bird" : a critical discourse analysis of the Assyrian royal lion hunt and Sennacherib's military campaign against Hezekiah of Judah / by Woo Min Lee.

Description: Eugene, OR: Pickwick Publications, 2025 | Includes bibliographical references and index.

Identifiers: ISBN 979-8-3852-3528-5 (paperback) | ISBN 979-8-3852-3529-2 (hardcover) | ISBN 979-8-3852-3530-8 (ebook)

Subjects: LCSH: Sennacherib, King of Assyria, –681 B.C. | Jerusalem—History—Siege, 701 B.C. | Siege of Jerusalem—(Jerusalem : — 701 B.C.). | Metaphor in the Bible. | Assyro-Babylonian religion—Relations—Judaism. | Judaism—Relations—Assyro-Babylonian religion. | Cuneiform inscriptions, Akkadian. | Relief (Sculpture), Ancient—Assyria. | Assyria—History. | Civilization, Assyro-Babylonian. |

Classification: DS73.83 L44 2025 (paperback) | DS73.83 (ebook)

VERSION NUMBER 10/30/25

To my wife, Sang Mee Lee, and our children,
Rael, Hael, and Dael Lee

Contents

List of Figures | ix
Acknowledgments | xv
Abbreviations | xvii

CHAPTER ONE: Introduction: A Critical Analysis of Relevant Sources with Further Questions | 1
CHAPTER TWO: Theory and Methodology: A Relational Theory of Form Criticism and Critical Discourse Analysis in Ancient Texts | 43
CHAPTER THREE: Assyrian Royal Lion Hunting | 57
CHAPTER FOUR: Assyrian Military Campaign Strategies and Sieges | 96
CHAPTER FIVE: A Caged Bird Versus Yhwh's Protected City | 158

Conclusion | 195

Bibliography | 197
Author Index | 207
Subject Index | 211
Geographical Index | 215
Ancient Document Index | 219

List of Figures

Figure 1.1. Doorway Guardian Figures (*ugallu and Lulal?*), west jamb, Door o, Room XXXI, Southwest Palace, Nineveh. British Museum, BM 118932. | 4

Figure 1.2. Doorway Guardian Figures (*uridimmu and apkallu?*), drawing of slabs attributed to Door a, Room XIV, Southwest Palace, Nineveh. British Museum, WAA, Or.Dr., II, 43. | 5

Figure 1.3. Doorway Guardian Figure (*uridimmu*), Slab 1, Door a, Room I, North Palace of Ashurbanipal, Nineveh. British Museum, WAA, Or. Dr., VII, 10. | 6

Figure 1.4. Ashurnasirpal II's Throne Room (Room B, plate 18A), Northwest Palace, Nimrud. British Museum, BM 124536. | 16

Figure 1.5. Ashurnasirpal II's Throne Room (Room B, plate 18B), Northwest Palace, Nimrud. British Museum, BM 124537. | 16

Figure 1.6. Ashurnasirpal II's Throne Room (Room B, plate 19A), Northwest Palace, Nimrud. British Museum, BM 124534. | 17

Figure 1.7. Ashurnasirpal II's Throne Room (Room B, plate 19B), Northwest Palace, Nimrud. British Museum, BM 124535. | 17

Figure 1.8. The Bow of Ashurbanipal, North Palace of Ashurbanipal, Nineveh. British Museum, BM 124867. | 20

Figure 1.9. A Neo-Assyrian Royal Seal, Kouyunjik. British Museum, BM 2276. | 40

Figure 3.1. Ashurnasirpal II's Royal Lion Hunt, Throne Room (Room B, plate 19A), Northwest Palace, Nimrud. British Museum, BM 124534. | 63

Figure 3.2. Ashurnasirpal II's Royal Lion Hunt, Nimrud. British Museum, BM 124579. | 65

Figure 3.3. Ashurnasirpal II's Royal Lion Hunt Relief, Nimrud. Staatliche Museen zu Berlin-PK, Vorderasiatisches Museum. | 66

Figure 3.4. Palace Gates, Band BM ASH II L5. Hunting lions. British Museum, BM 124698. | 67

Figure 3.5. Palace Gates, BM ASH II R5. Hunting lions. British Museum, BM 124699. | 67

Figure 3.6. Ashurbanipal's Royal Lion Hunt, North Palace, Nineveh. British Museum, BM 124861/862/863. | 72

Figure 3.7. Enlarged Image of the Royal Lion Hunting Inscribed on the Aediculum. British Museum, BM 124862. | 73

Figure 3.8. Preparation for the Hunt: Servants with Horses, North Palace, Nineveh. British Museum, BM 124859/860/861. | 74

Figure 3.9. Preparation for the Hunt: Huntsman with Mastiff, North Palace, Nineveh. British Museum, BM 124863. | 75

Figure 3.10. A Wounded Lion, North Palace, Nineveh. British Museum, BM 124864. | 76

Figure 3.11. Ashurbanipal Shooting at Lions from His Chariot, North Palace, Nineveh. British Museum, BM 124866/867. | 76

Figure 3.12. Lions Killed by Ashurbanipal, North Palace, Nineveh. British Museum, BM 124867/868. | 77

Figure 3.13. Ashurbanipal's Royal Lion Hunt, North Palace, Nineveh. British Museum, BM 124869/870. | 78

Figure 3.14. Ashurbanipal Slaying a Lion with His Lance, North Palace, Nineveh. British Museum, BM 124853/854. | 79

Figure 3.15. Wounded and Dying Lions and Lioness with a Horseman of the King's Company, North Palace, Nineveh. British Museum BM 124855/856/857. | 79

Figure 3.16. A Lion in a Cage, North Palace, Nineveh. British Museum, BM 124883. | 80

Figure 3.17. Royal Attendants with Hounds and Nets for a Hunt, North Palace, Nineveh. British Museum, BM 124893/894. | 81

Figure 3.18. Royal Attendants Taking a Mule with a Net on Its Back, North Palace, Nineveh. British Museum, BM 124896/897. | 82

Figure 3.19. Royal Attendants and Guards Returning from the Hunt, North Palace, Nineveh. British Museum, BM 124888/889/890. | 82

Figure 3.20. Ashurbanipal's Royal Lion Hunt, North Palace, Nineveh. Slabs A-B. Original Drawings V3 (original lost) (drawn by William Boutcher). British Museum. | 84

Figure 3.21. Ashurbanipal's Royal Lion Hunt (Louvre AO 19903). Slab C. Original Drawings V4 (drawn by William Boutcher). British Museum. | 86

Figure 3.22. Ashurbanipal's Royal Lion Hunt, North Palace, Nineveh. British Museum, BM 124886/7. | 88

Figure 4.1. An Assyrian Siege-engine under Attack, North-West Palace, Nimrud. British Museum, BM 124554. | 105

Figure 4.2. An Assyrian Siege against a City Wall, South-West Palace, Nimrud. British Museum, BM 118906. | 106

Figure 4.3. A Military Siege against a City, North-West Palace, Nimrud. British Museum, BM 124536. | 107

Figure 4.4. Escape across a River. Throne Room, North-West Palace, Nimrud. British Museum, BM 124538. | 108

Figure 4.5. A Campaign against Bit-Adini. The Gates from the Palace of Ashurnasirpal II, Balawat. British Museum ASH II L2, BM 124686. | 109

Figure 4.6. A Campaign against Ḫatti. The Gates from the Palace of Ashurnasirpal II, Balawat. British Museum ASH II L3, BM 124695. | 110

Figure 4.7. A Campaign against Bit-Adini. The Gates from the Palace of Ashurnasirpal II, Balawat. British Museum ASH II L7, BM 124692. | 111

Figure 4.8. A Campaign against Bit-Adini. The Gates from the Palace of Ashurnasirpal II, Balawat. British Museum ASH II R2, BM 124691. | 112

Figure 4.9. A Campaign against Bit-Yakin. The Gates from the Palace of Ashurnasirpal II, Balawat. British Museum ASH II R3, BM124688. | 113

Figure 4.10. Texts regarding Tiglath-pileser III's Campaign against Sarduri. | 124

Figure 4.11. Prisoners and Cattle Leaving a Babylonian City, Central Palace, Nineveh. British Museum, BM 118882. | 126

Figure 4.12. Assyrian Officers Shooting at a City, Central Palace, Nineveh. British Museum, BM 118904. | 127

Figure 4.13. Assyrian Army Attacking a Babylonian City, Central Palace, Nineveh. British Museum, BM 118902. | 128

Figure 4.14. Siege against the City of U[pa?], Central Palace, Nimrud. British Museum, BM 115634+118903. | 129

Figure 4.15. Siege of Alammu(?), Drawing of Slabs 8-11. Room XIV, Southwest Palace, Nineveh. British Museum (Drawn by Sir Austen Henry Layard). | 141

Figure 4.16. Sennacherib's Campaign against Lachish. Room XXXVI, South Palace, Nineveh. British Museum, BM 124904 (Slab 1). | 142

Figure 4.17. Sennacherib's Campaign against Lachish. Room XXXVI, South Palace, Nineveh. British Museum, BM 124904 (Slab II). | 144

Figure 4.18. Sennacherib's Campaign against Lachish. Room XXXVI, South Palace, Nineveh. British Museum, BM 124906 (Slab III). | 145

Figure 4.19. Sennacherib's Campaign against Lachish. Room XXXVI, South Palace, Nineveh. British Museum, BM 124906 (Slab IV). | 146

Figure 4.20. Ashurbanipal and His Troops Attacking the Elamite Royal City of Hamanu. Room H, North Palace, Nineveh. British Museum, BM 124931. | 150

Figure 5.1. Comparative Sequences of Sennacherib's Third Campaign. | 171–174

Figure 5.2. Huntsmen Trapping Deer in Nets. Ashurbanipal's North Palace, Nineveh. British Museum, BM 124871. | 182

Figure 5.3. Esarhaddon Holding Two Royal Captives. Zinjirli. Staatliche Museen zu Berlin-PK, Vorderasiatisches Museum. | 185

Acknowledgments

THIS BOOK IS A slightly revised version of my doctoral thesis, which was submitted at Drew University in 2016. I would like to express my deepest gratitude to Dr. Kah-Jin Jeffrey Kuan for his teaching and guidance. Since I began working with him in 2009, he has been a teacher and mentor throughout my doctoral program, scholarship, and career.

I also want to thank Prof. Herbert Huffmon for his steadfast support and critical advice on my research. Along with Dr. Kuan, his role has been essential to the completion of my doctoral dissertation and my ongoing academic work. I am likewise grateful to Prof. Kenneth Ngwa for his insightful reflections on my work, his kind encouragement, and his teaching.

Special thanks to Professor Katherine Brown for her thoughtful reading and meticulous editing of my dissertation. She devoted many hours—over days and weeks—to revising and polishing the manuscript. Any remaining errors, inaccuracies, or omissions are, of course, my sole responsibility.

I am deeply thankful to Little Falls United Methodist Church in New Jersey, Hyde Park Korean United Methodist Church in Chicago, and the United Methodist Campus Ministry at the University of Chicago. Without their support and understanding, I could not have completed my doctoral program or continued my research.

I am also grateful to Matthew Wimer, Robin Parry, Zane Derven, and the editorial team at Wipf and Stock for giving me the opportunity to publish my dissertation eight years after its completion. I appreciate their work and commitment as I prepared the final manuscript.

Finally, I would like to express my deepest love and gratitude to my family—my parents, Se Jong Lee and Ki Jeong Shin; my wife, Sang Mee Lee; and our children, Rael, Hael, and Dael. Without their love, care, prayers, support, and encouragement, neither the completion of my doctoral dissertation nor its publication would have been possible.

Abbreviations

CAD	*The Assyrian Dictionary of the Oriental Institute of the University of Chicago*
Or.	*Orientalia*
RIMA 2	*Royal Inscriptions from Mesopotamia: Assyrian Periods*, vol. 2. Grayson, A. Kirk. *Assyrian Rulers of the Early First Millennium BC I (1114–859 BC)*. Toronto: University of Toronto Press, 1991.
RIMA 3	*Royal Inscriptions from Mesopotamia: Assyrian Periods*, vol. 3. Grayson, A. Kirk. *Assyrian Rulers of the Early First Millennium BC II (858–745 BC)*. Toronto: University of Toronto Press, 1996.
RINAP 1	*Royal Inscriptions of the Neo-Assyrian Period*, vol. 1. Tadmor, Hayim, and Shigeo Yamada, eds. *The Royal Inscriptions of Tiglath-Pileser III (744–727 BC) and Shalmaneser V (726–722 BC), Kings of Assyria*. Winona Lake, IN: Eisenbrauns, 2011.
RINAP 3/1	*Royal Inscriptions of the Neo-Assyrian Period*, vol. 3/1. Grayson, A. Kirk, and Jamie R Novotny, eds. *The Royal Inscriptions of Sennacherib, King of Assyria (704–681 BC)*. Winona Lake, IN: Eisenbrauns, 2012.
RINAP 3/2	*Royal Inscriptions of the Neo-Assyrian Period*, vol. 3/2. Grayson, A. Kirk, and Jamie R Novotny, eds. *The Royal Inscriptions of Sennacherib, King of Assyria (704–681 BC), Part 2*. Winona Lake, IN: Eisenbrauns, 2014.

RINAP 4	*Royal Inscriptions of the Neo-Assyrian Period*, vol. 4. Leichty, Erle. *The Royal Inscriptions of Esarhaddon, King of Assyria (680–669 BC)*. Winona Lake, IN: Eisenbrauns, 2011.
VAT	Tablets in the collection of the Vorderasiatische Museum, Berlin

Chapter 1

INTRODUCTION

A Critical Analysis of Relevant Sources with Further Questions

THE SIMILE IN THE phrase "shut up/enclosed like a caged bird / a bird in a cage" was used in Sennacherib's inscriptions regarding his military campaign against Hezekiah of Judah. According to the inscriptions, his campaign in the southern Levant in 701 BCE included the receipt of gifts and tribute from several kings, the replacement of the rebellious king of Ashkelon with a pro-Assyrian king, the reinstallation of Padî as the Assyrian vassal king of Ekron, and an important battle with Egyptian forces in southern Palestine. It also included the destruction of Lachish, the "second city of Judah," of many other Judaean sites, the siege of Jerusalem, and the receipt of a substantial tribute from Hezekiah of Jerusalem. His apparent goal was to restore Assyrian supremacy in the area which was the gateway to Egypt. Of special interest in this study is the final action of his campaign, which was the siege of the Judaean city of Jerusalem, where King Hezekiah was residing. Sennacherib's inscriptions describe the success of this siege, using the simile: "I shut up Hezekiah in Jerusalem, his royal city, like a caged bird / a bird in a cage (*kīma iṣṣur qu-up-pi qé-reb* ^alū^*Ur-sa-li-im-mu āl šarru-ti-šú e-sír-šú*)."[1]

1. *RINAP 3/1* No. 4, 52 (p. 64); No. 15, 18–19 (p. 96); No. 16, col. iv, 8–10 (p. 115); No. 17, col. iii, 52 (p. 133); No. 18, col. iii, 27b–29a (p. 151); No. 22 (the "Chicago" Prism), col. iii, 27b–29a (p. 176); No. 23, col. iii, 33, 24–25 (p. 194).

The simile is used in other siege inscriptions as well as in royal hunting inscriptions. The inscriptions of Tiglath-pileser III (744–727 BCE) state that Rezin, the king of Damascus, took refuge from the Assyrian forces by fleeing to Damascus and "I (Tiglath-pileser III) set up my camp [aro]und his city and shut him (Rezin of Damascus) up like a caged bird / a bird in a cage (*kīma iṣ-ṣur qu-up-pi e-sir-šú*)."[2] In the annals of Tiglath-pileser III and Sennacherib, the simile is used to describe a siege with a verb of confinement, "shut up/enclose (*esēru*)." The simile was also used in earlier texts of Ashurnasirpal II (885–860 BCE), describing his pursuit of lions in a hunting field or arena. Ashurnasirpal II states, "I killed 370 strong lions like caged birds with the spear (3 *mēʾātu* 70 *nēšī dannūti kīma iṣṣūrī qu-up-pi ina* ^{iṣu}*pu-aš-ḫi a-duk*)."[3]

Various other animal similes can be found in Assyrian royal inscriptions as well as in biblical texts.[4] Chikako Watanabe has stressed the interaction between the primary subject and the secondary subject in the simile.[5] The intention of the use of the simile is to relate some of the properties or features of the secondary subject to the primary subject.[6] In the case of the simile, "like a caged bird / a bird in a cage," in Sennacherib's inscriptions regarding his siege against Hezekiah, the primary subject is Hezekiah of Jerusalem and the secondary subject is a caged bird. Watanabe also notes that Akkadian similes are typically accompanied with *kīma* or *–iš*.[7] Based upon her argument, Hezekiah is related to a certain aspect of a caged bird.

David Marcus categorizes the animal similes used in the inscriptions with their accompanying verbs, patterns, and forms. According to him, the similes are used for various aims: "to relate events on and off the battlefield," "to portray actions and movements of the king, his army and foes," and "to describe enemy territory."[8]

For example, the inscriptions of Sargon II state, "I (Sargon) surrounded/enclosed him and slaughtered (the warriors) at his feet like

2. Tadmor, *Inscriptions of Tiglath-Pileser III*, Ann. 23 Plates XX-XXII, 11', pp. 78–79; *RINAP 1* No. 20, 10'–11' (p. 59).

3. *RIMA* 2 A.0.101.2, 42b (pp. 226–27).

4. Rimbach, "Animal Imagery in the Old Testament"; Strawn, *What Is Stronger than a Lion?*, 16–17.

5. Watanabe, *Animal Symbolism in Mesopotamia*, 19.

6. Watanabe, *Animal Symbolism in Mesopotamia*, 19.

7. Watanabe, *Animal Symbolism in Mesopotamia*, 21.

8. Marcus, "Animal Similes in Assyrian Royal Inscriptions," 86.

lambs (*al-me-šu-ma ki-*[*ma*]j *as-li i-na pa-an šepī-ti-šú ú-nap-pi-ṣa*)."[9] The simile is used to describe Sargon II's vulnerable opponents. Another example can be found in the inscriptions of Tigalth-pileser III: "In order to save his life, he (Rezin) fled alone and entered the gate of his city [like] a mongoose (*a-na šu-zu-ub napšāte-šu e-[de]-nu-uš-šú ip-par-ši-id-i [ki-ma] šikkê abul āli-šú ērub^ub*)."[10] The simile offers an interpretation of Rezin's seeking refuge in his fortified city, which he might have considered a protective cage. For Tiglath-pileser III, however, Rezin sought protection and ended up vulnerable like a bird in a cage.

Other examples can be found in Sennacherib's inscriptions. In one of his inscriptions, Sennacherib notes, "They (Sennacherib's opponents) flew away like bats (living) in crevices in inaccessible places (*ki-ma su-tin-ni. iṣṣūri ni-gi-iṣ-ṣi e-diš ip-par-šú a-šar la 'a-a-ri*)."[11] In the same inscriptions, he says, "He (Marduk-apla-iddina [II]) flew away like a bird to the city Nagīteraqqi, which is in the midst of the sea (*a-na* ^ālu*na-gi-te-raq-qí ša qabal tam-tim iṣ-ṣu-riš ip-pa-riš*)."[12] He also used a simile describing himself as a lion. In his battle against the Elamites and Šuzubu, a Babylonian king, at the city, Ḫalulê, Sennacherib comments, "I (Sennacherib) raged up like a lion (*la-ab-biš an-na-dir*)."[13]

Regarding lion images, one of the apparent innovations in Sennacherib's reliefs is that he added a new type of protective figure, showing "a lion-headed and eagle-footed man holding a mace and a dagger [Fig. 1.1]."[14] There is another guardian figure which, Russell assumed, had a "human head and the feet of a lion [Fig. 1.2; cf. Fig. 1.3 for a better-preserved Ashurbanipal example]."[15] These guardian figures with weapons in their hands seem to serve to protect the Assyrian king from any enemy.

9. Fuchs, *Inschriften Sargons II*, Ann. 344 (Lie, 410), 161; cf. 333–34, 302.

10. *RINAP 1* No. 22, 8'–9' (p. 59).

11. *RINAP 3/1* No. 22 (the "Chicago" prism), col. i, 18–19 (p. 176).

12. *RINAP 3/1* No. 22 (the "Chicago" prism), col. iii, 64–65 (p. 177).

13. *RINAP 3/1* No. 22 (the "Chicago" prism), col. v, 67b (p. 182).

14. Russell, *Sennacherib's Palace*, 180–81.

15. Russell, *Sennacherib's Palace*, 181–82.

Fig. 1.1. Doorway Guardian Figures (*ugallu* and *Lulal*?), west jamb, Door *o*, Room XXXI, Southwest Palace, Nineveh. British Museum, BM 118932. (Photo: © The Trustees of the British Museum); Russell, Fig. 95.[16]

16. Russell, *Sennacherib's Palace*, 181.

Fig. 1.2. Doorway Guardian Figures (*uridimmu* and *apkallu*?), drawing of slabs attributed to Door *a*, Room XIV, Southwest Palace, Nineveh. British Museum, WAA, Or.Dr., II, 43. (Photo: © The Trustees of the British Museum); Russell, Fig. 96.[17]

17. Russell, *Sennacherib's Palace*, 182 (fig. 96).

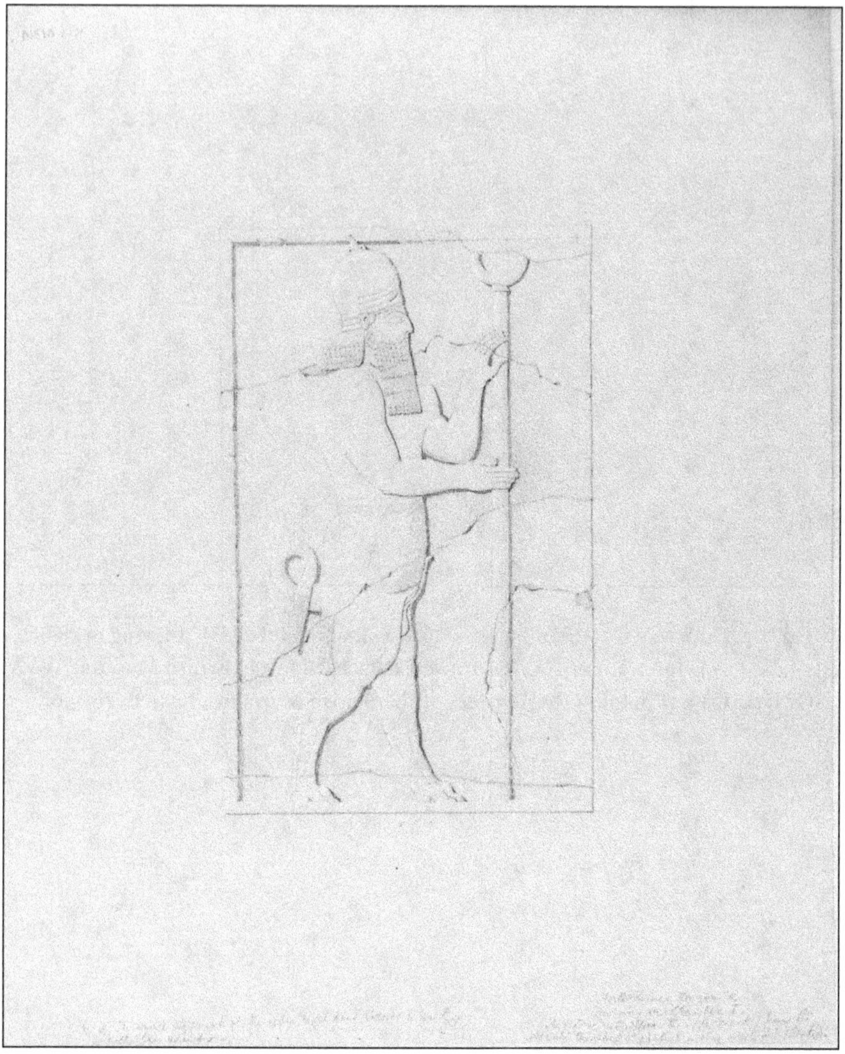

Fig. 1.3. Doorway Guardian Figure (*uridimmu*), Slab 1, Door *a*, Room I, North Palace of Ashurbanipal, Nineveh. British Museum, WAA, Or. Dr., VII, 10. (Photo: © The Trustees of the British Museum); Russell, Fig. 97.[18]

When used in similes without reference to being in a *quppu*, as in hunting and military contexts, *iṣṣūru/iṣṣūriš* seems to designate or imply quite opposite concepts, depending upon the contexts: "freedom of movement" or "cowardice/weakness." There are several examples of the

18. Russell, *Sennacherib's Palace*, 183 (fig. 97).

bird similes in which the context indicates freedom of movement. In the campaign inscriptions of Tiglath-pileser I (1114–1076 BCE), *iṣṣūru* is used in the simile without *quppu* to describe the withdrawal of the enemy. For example, in the campaign of Tiglath-pileser I against the city of Urraṭinaš, the enemy "flew like a bird to the tops of the high mountains (*a-na gi-sal-lat māti*ⁱ *ša-qu-ti ki-ma iṣṣūri ip-par-šu*),"[19] thus emphasizing the bird's ability or freedom to escape when not confined. When Tiglath-pileser I attacked the land of Adauš, the people of the land "flew like a bird to the tops of the high mountains (*a-na gi-sal-lat māti*ⁱ *ša-qu-ti ki-ma iṣṣūri ip-par-šu*)."[20] In the campaign of Sargon II, Sennacherib's father, against Urzana of the city of Muṣaṣir, the enemy "flew like a bird, climbing the steep mountain (*iṣ-ṣu-riš ip-par-riš-ma šadû mar-ṣu e-li*)."[21] In Sargon's account of his eighth campaign, Rusā, who transgressed against Šamaš and Marduk and dishonored the oath by Ashur, the king of the gods, was frightened by the noise of the weaponry of Sargon and "his heart palpitated like that of a rock partridge that flees from an eagle (*ki-ma iṣ-ṣur ḫur-re ša la-pa-an erî ip-par-šid-du it-ru-ku lìb-bu-šu*)."[22] In this same campaign, there is another example describing Sargon's opponents who abandoned their cities and "fled like birds into the midst of these fortresses (*a-na qé-reb bi-ra-a-ti šu-a-ti-na ki-ma iṣ-ṣu-re ip-par-šu*)."[23] Meanwhile, there is an example in which *iṣṣūru* is used in a simile without *quppu* to describe the massive attack of the Assyrian king or army, which designates freedom of movement. When Ashurnasirpal II attacked the land of Ḫabḫu, his army "flew like birds into the midst of them (the enemy) (*kīma iṣṣūrī muḫḫi-šu-nu iše-'u*),"[24] presumably emphasizing the freedom of movement that birds have in the difficult mountain areas and the capacity for predatory birds to swoop down and capture targets. Esarhaddon caught his enemies who felt safe in their mountains "like a bird in the midst of the mountains (*ki-ma iṣ-ṣu-ri ul-tu qé-reb māti*ⁱ *a-bar-šú-ma*)" and slayed them (literally, "bound his arms).[25] The concept of "the

19. *RIMA* 2 A.0.87.1, Col. ii, 41–42 (p. 15)

20. *RIMA* 2 Col. iii, 68–69 (p. 18).

21. Fuchs, *Inschriften Sargons II*, Ann.,153, 114.

22. Mayer, *Assyrien und Urartu*, col. ii, 148–149, pp. 110–11; Thureau-Dangin, *Relation de La Huitième Campagne de Sargon*, l. 148–49, pp. 24–27.

23. Mayer, *Assyrien und Urartu*, col. ii, 291, pp. 126–27.

24. *RIMA* 2 A.0.101.1, Col. i, 63 (p. 198).

25. *RINAP* 4 No. 1, col. v, 12–13 (p. 22); cf. iii, 30–31 (p. 17).

freedom of movement" of the Assyrian Empire, on the other hand, can be considered as "dreadfulness" to its enemies.[26]

Along with "the freedom of movement," some of the similes with *iṣṣūru* do not seem to be clear. For example, Esarhaddon besieged and caught Sanda-uarri, the king of the cities of Kundi and Sissû, "like a bird" from the midst of the mountains (*ni-i-tu al-me-šu-ma ki-ma iṣ-ṣu-ri ul-tu qé-reb šad-i a-bar-šu-ma*) and cut off his head.[27] In this example, the simile with *iṣṣūru* does not seem to provide any clear image or understanding.

As for the word, "cage (*quppu*)," its meaning includes "a wicker basket or wooden chest," "cage," and "a box for silver and precious objects."[28] The usage of *quppu* to refer to a "cage" is less frequent than "wooden chest," and "a box for silver and precious objects." Hunting and military inscriptions, however, use *quppu* only as a "cage" and its usage includes a metaphorical expression of a simile with *kīma*.

When *quppu* is used in the simile *kīma iṣṣūr quppi*, it expresses opposite viewpoints: "locking up in a deadlock situation" from the viewpoint of a captor and "being locked up in deadlock situations" from the viewpoint of a captive. The former can be found in the inscriptions of Ashurnasripal II, Tiglath-pileser III, and Sennacherib as cited above. Meanwhile, a prominent example for the latter can be found in the letters of Rib-Addi. The simile, "like a caged bird / a bird in a cage," was used by Rib-Addi, the king of Byblos, in his letters to the Egyptian Pharaoh during the Amarna Period.[29] In these letters, he describes himself "like birds, that lie in a net (*ki-ma iṣṣurāti* [> *iṣṣurī*, pl.][30] *ša i-na libbi*[bi] *ḫu-ḫa-ri ki-lu-bi*),"[31] and "like a bird, which lies in a net (*ki-ma iṣṣuri ša i-na libbi*[bi] [*ḫ*]*u-ḫa-ri ki-lu-bi*

26. Rimbach, "Animal Imagery in the Old Testament," 48.

27. *RINAP* 4 No. 1, col iii, 30–31 (p. 17).

28. "quppu," *CAD*, *Q*, 307.

29. Knudtzon et al., *El-Amarna-Tafeln*; Moran, *Amarna Letters*. No. 74.45–48 (Knudtzon, 1:376–77; Moran, 143); No. 78.13–16 (Knudtzon, 1:386–87; Moran, 148–49); No. 79.35–38 (Knudtzon, 1:390–91; Moran, 149); No. 81.34–36 (Knudtzon, 1:394–95; Moran, 151); No. 90.39–42 (Knudtzon, 1:426–27; Moran, 163); No. 105.8–10 (Knudtzon, 1:464–65; Moran, 178); No. 116.17–20 (Knudtzon, 1:502–3; Moran, 191).

30. Please note that there is a disagreement in transliteration and translation among *CAD*, Knudtzon, and Moran. *CAD* and Moran transliterates *MUŠEN* (*iṣṣur*) in a singular form and translate it "a bird," not "birds" ("iṣṣūru," *CAD*, *I/J*, 212; Moran, *Amarna Letters*, 143).

31. Knudtzon et al., *El-Amarna-Tafeln* 74.45–46 (1:376–77).

šá-ak-na-at)."[32] The simile in his letters represents a sense of being "locked up," unable to move about freely.[33] Rib-Addi, as a "captive," feels desperate in the situation. He is aware of his own lack of freedom of movement, his vulnerability or even his hopelessness.[34] In addition, the similes were used for the people of Byblos and the people of Ṣumur regarding their hopeless situations. In the war with ʿAbdi-Aširta, "like a bird, which lies in a [tr]ap/[ca]ge, so are they in [Gubl]a (*ki-ma iṣṣuri ša i-na li*[*bbi*^{bi}] [*ḫu*]-*ḫa-ri ki-lu-bi šá-ak*[*-na-at*] [*ki-*]*šu-ma šu-nu i-na libbi*^{bi} ^{ā}[^{lu}*gub-l*]*a*)."[35] The city of Ṣumur was under siege by the people of Arwada and "like a bird, which lies in a cage/trap, so is Ṣumur (*ki-ma iṣṣuri ša i-na libbi*^{bi} *ḫu*[*-ḫ*] *a-ri ki-lu-bi ša-ak-na-at ki-na-na i-ba-ša-at* ^{ālu}*ṣu-mu-ra*)."[36] In another letter regarding the siege of the city, Rib-Addi says to the Egyptian Pharaoh, "Moreover, give thought to Ṣumu[r]. It is like a bird, which lies in a t[rap]/c[age] (*ša-ni-tú mi-lik a-na at* ^{ālu}*ṣu-mu*[*-ra*] *ki-ma iṣṣuri ša i-na libbi*^{bi} *ḫu*[*-ḫa-ri*] *ki-lu*[*-bi*] [*š*]*a-ak-na-at*)."[37]

In particular, Mario Liverani argues that the king of Byblos portrays himself as a "righteous sufferer" in his letters, a view which was possibly influenced by Mesopotamian wisdom literature.[38] Being isolated and besieged by the enemies, he calls for help from the Pharaoh, his lord.[39] The king of Egypt is the only one who could save him from his deadlock situation.

However, William Moran questions Liverani's argument in that Rib-addi describes himself not as a "righteous sufferer" but as an "unrewarded loyal servant of Egypt."[40] The reason for the isolation of Rib-addi was not because of his righteousness but because of his political stance in favor of the Pharaoh.[41] Rib-addi wrote letters, "not as a Job but as a puzzled and unrewarded Caleb."[42]

32. Knudtzon et al., *El-Amarna-Tafeln* 79.35–36 (1:390–91).
33. See Rainey, *Canaanite in the Amarna Tablets*, 2:305; 3:143.
34. Moran, "Rib-Hadda," 173–81; Liverani, "Rib-Adda," 97–124.
35. Knudtzon et al., *El-Amarna-Tafeln* 81.34–36 (1:394–95).
36. Knudtzon et al., *El-Amarna-Tafeln* 105.8–10 (1:464–65).
37. Knudtzon et al., *El-Amarna-Tafeln* 116.17–20 (1:502–3).
38. Liverani, "Rib-Adda," 98–99.
39. Liverani, "Rib-Adda," 105–6.
40. Moran, "Rib-Hadda" 173–81.
41. Moran, "Rib-Hadda," 177–78.
42. Moran, "Rib-Hadda," 181.

The use of the simile, "like a caged bird / a bird in a cage," and the parallels cited from seemingly different kinds or even genres of the inscriptions—campaign reports and hunting inscriptions—as well as in the letters of Rib-Addi from Byblos, raises a question about a possible interrelationship in terms of their tactics and outcomes. It also raises a question as to an ideological or propagandistic aspect of the simile. Along with the verbal inscriptions, it is also necessary to probe the related nonverbal images presented in the reliefs which depict the military campaigns and the royal lion hunts, including hauling off lion cubs in cages and releasing captive lions from cages for the purpose of royal hunting sport.

Regarding these questions, this chapter first briefly surveys the most recent and the best sources for the inscriptions and the reliefs of the Neo-Assyrian kings regarding their campaigns and royal lion hunting inscriptions and reliefs, concentrating on the period from Ashurnasirpal II (885–860 BCE) to Ashurbanipal (668–631 BCE) for intervisual and intertextual studies. Its aim is to provide an overall understanding of the cultural and historical context within which the simile was used, with special emphasis on the inscriptions and the reliefs of Sennacherib, though Sennacherib does not specifically portray himself as a hunter.

This chapter then explores the scholarship on the historical and the ideological understandings of the Assyrian records and the biblical texts, with a focus on the descriptions of Sennacherib's military campaign that engaged Hezekiah. Finally, this survey will lead to further questions regarding the simile, "like a caged bird / a bird in a cage," in Sennacherib's description of Hezekiah's situation.

Textual Sources for the Interconnection Between the Military Campaigns and the Royal Lion Hunting Expeditions of the Neo-Assyrian Kings

The inscriptions of the Neo-Assyrian period are replete with the achievements of the kings, including their political and military achievements and, occasionally, their valor as hunters, with special reference to hunting lions. Fortunately, researchers now have easy access to comprehensive up-to-date editions of the royal inscriptions of most of the Neo-Assyrian kings that have been researched by Kirk Grayson, Jamie Novotny, Hayim Tadmor, Andreas Fuchs, Rykle Borger, Erle Leichty, and Shigeo

Yamada.[43] While at least some campaign records are preserved for most of the Neo-Assyrian kings, royal lion hunting records are known from fewer inscriptions and reliefs. The most important examples come from the inscriptions of Tiglath-pileser I (1114–1076 BCE) and Ashurnasirpal II (885–860 BCE).[44] After Ashurnasirpal II, records of the lion hunt appear again in the time of Ashurbanipal (668–627 BCE) when the hunt was even represented as a public spectacle.

Tiglath-pileser I (1114–1076 BCE)

The inscriptions of Tiglath-pileser I include his military campaigns and his lion hunting. Grayson provides the most recent and relevant resource for his inscriptions.[45] For Tiglath-pileser I, his hunting record follows his military campaigns.[46] According to the record, "I (Tiglath-pileser I) killed 120 lions on foot with my wildly outstanding assault by the command of the god Ninurta who loves me (2 *šu-ši nēšī i-na lìb-bi-ia ek-di i-na qit-ru-ub mi-it-lu-ti-ia i-na šēpī lu a-duk*)."[47] In addition, he felled another eight hundred lions from his light chariot (*ù* 8 *me'ati nēšī i-na narkabti-ia i-na pat-tu-te ú-šem-qít*).[48] It is notable that he says, "I brought down every kind of wild beast and winged bird of the heavens whenever I shot an arrow (*bu-ul* ᵈ*šákkan gi-mir-ta ù iṣṣūr šamê mut-tap-ri-ša e-em ni-sik qanīya lu-ú at-ta-di*)."[49]

Ashurnasirpal II (885–860 BCE)[50]

The inscriptions of Ashurnasirpal II describe his military campaigns and his lion hunting. It is notable that the number of the (preserved) inscriptions increased during his rule, compared to his predecessors. Amélie Kuhrt suggests that this increase in documentation during his reign reflects "the energetic campaigns and the huge effort involved in his extensive building

43. See *RIMA* 2; 3; *RINAP* 1; 3/1; 3/2; 4; Fuchs, *Inschriften Sargons II*; Borger, *Beiträge*.
44. Tadmor, "Propaganda, Literature, Historiography," 328.
45. *RIMA* 2, 2:5–84.
46. *RIMA* 2, A.0.87.1, col. i. 62-col. vi, 54 (p. 26).
47. *RIMA* 2, col. vi, 76–79 (p. 26).
48. *RIMA* 2, col. vi, 80–81 (p. 26).
49. *RIMA* 2, col. vi, 82–84 (p. 26).
50. Rogers, *History of Babylonia and Assyria*, 2:46.

at the city of Kalhu."[51] Based upon a number of preserved inscriptions, it becomes possible to trace back the military and political situation of his reign. Already in 1901, R. W. Rogers of Drew University described in detail the active military tactics employed by Ashurnasirpal II based on the then known inscriptions, showing that his campaigns enabled the empire to rise to become one of the major powers in the Near East.[52] In particular, he "killed 370 lions like birds in a cage with the spear (370 *nēšī kīma iṣṣūrī qu-up-pi ina* ⁱˢ*pu-aš-ḫi a-duk*)" in his royal lion hunt.[53]

Grayson has provided an up-to-date edition of the texts of Ashurnasirpal II in transliteration and translation, superseding earlier publications.[54] His comprehensive work greatly contributes to the understanding of the textual evidence for the military campaigns and the royal hunt of lions, ostriches, and wild oxen by Ashurnasirpal II.

Tiglath-pileser III (744–727 BCE)

After Ashurnasirpal II, the simile "like a caged bird / a bird in a cage" is not attested again until the reign of Tiglath-piileser III. Notably, it was used not in connection with royal lion hunting but in the annalistic description of his siege of Rezin in Damascus, ca. 732 BCE, following an engagement on the plain. His annals reveal that Tiglath-pileser III attacked the land of Rezin and besieged the city to which he had fled to save his life. In Tadmor's 1994 edition, it states that the Assyrian king "shut him up like a caged bird / a bird in a cage (*kīma iṣ-ṣur qu-up-pi e-sir-šú*)."[55]

In a footnote regarding the simile, Tadmor observes that the simile, used with *ēsiršu*, is first used here in connection with the siege of an opposing king, and that it is also found in Sennacherib's account of his siege against Hezekiah in Jerusalem in his 701 BCE campaign.[56]

51. Kuhrt, *Ancient Near East*, 2:483.

52. Rogers, *History of Babylonia and Assyria*, 2:46.

53. *RIMA* 2 A.0.101.2, 42b (pp. 226–27).

54. *RIMA* 2 2:189–393.

55. Tadmor, *Inscriptions of Tiglath-Pileser III*, Ann. 23, Plates XX–XXII, 11', pp. 78–79; *RINAP 1* No. 20, 11' (p. 59).

56. Tadmor, *Inscriptions of Tiglath-Pileser III*, 79.

Sennacherib (704–681 BCE)

The simile, "like a caged bird / a bird in a cage," occurs most famously in the inscriptions of Sennacherib regarding his military campaigns against Hezekiah of Judah in his fourth regnal year (701 BCE).[57] Eckart Frahm provides a thorough analysis of the inscriptions of Sennacherib.[58] Grayson and Novotny have also provided an excellent two-volume edition of the royal inscriptions of Sennacherib.[59] There is no reference to lion hunting by Sennacherib, however, or any other royal hunting by the king.

Esarhaddon (680–669 BCE)

For Esarhaddon, there is an abundance of preserved inscriptions regarding his military achievements and building activities. However, none of his military inscriptions uses the simile, "like a bird in cage," nor has any royal lion hunting relief or inscription from his reign been found. Borger provided a critical edition and an introduction to his reign,[60] and the *RINAP* volume for Esarhaddon, prepared by Leichty, provides the latest edition (2011) of the inscriptions of Esarhaddon.[61] In particular, Esarhaddon's campaigns seek to maintain the security of the boundaries that his predecessors established.[62] Among the campaigns was his successful siege of Memphis, south of present day Cairo, in 671. Esarhaddon became fatally ill in 669 while en route to another campaign against Egypt.

Ashurbanipal (668–631 BCE)

The inscriptions of Ashurbanipal include military campaign records and epigraphs accompanying his royal lion hunting reliefs. Those reliefs

57. *RINAP 3/1* No. 4, 52 (p. 64); No. 15, 18–19 (p. 96); No. 16, col. iv, 8–10 (p. 115); No. 17, col. iii, 52 (p. 133); No. 18, col. iii, 27b–29a (p. 151); No. 22 (the "Chicago" Prism), col. iii, 27b–29a (p. 176); No. 23, col. iii, 33, 24–25 (p. 194).

58. Frahm, *Einleitung in die Sanherib-Inschriften.*

59. *RINAP 3/1; 3/2.*

60. Borger, *Inschriften Asarhaddons.*

61. *RINAP 4.*

62. Kuhrt, *Ancient Near East*, 2:499. For the campaigns aginst Egypt, see *RINAP 4*, Nos. 15–16, 20, 34–39, 98 (with a relief of Esarhaddon and the Egyptian King) (pp. 1007, 1019).

powerfully present the Assyrian king as a mighty hunter of fierce wild animals. During the reign of Ashurbanipal, annalistic inscriptions were written with multiple editions in greater number, compared to the practice of his predecessors.[63] None of his known inscriptions, however, uses the simile, "like a caged bird / a bird in a cage."

The military and royal lion hunting inscriptions of Ashurbanipal were comprehensively studied by Maximilian Streck (1916), who included the meager inscriptions of Ashurbanipal's successors.[64] Streck's work remains invaluable, as is the comprehensive work by Borger that appeared in 1996.[65] Important editions of supplemental texts to those included in Streck were published by Theo Bauer (1933),[66] A. C. Piepkorn (1933; Editions E, B-5, D, and E),[67] J.-M. Aynard (1957; Louvre AO 19.939),[68] and J. Novotny (2014; Editions L3, L4, Prisms I and T, and related texts).[69] Regarding Ashurbanipal, Elnathan Weissert has provided a very important understanding of the relationship between the protection of the city, Nineveh, and the reliefs of a royal lion hunt. He argues that the number of the lions that the king killed during his royal hunting expedition (18) is related to the number of the city gates (18).[70] In other words, this lion hunt was a political symbol of the royal role as the protector of the city. Brent Strawn presented a careful study of the royal lion hunting reliefs and inscriptions, including Ashurbanipal's lion hunting record.[71]

Visual Sources for the Military Campaign and the Royal Lion Hunting Reliefs of the Neo-Assyrian Empire

In addition to the written language of the inscriptions, there is the non-written language of recovered reliefs that illustrate the military campaigns and the royal lion hunting scenes that have been studied in detail. As mentioned above, we begin with the military and hunting reliefs from the

63. Olmstead, *Assyrian Historiography*, 53–58.
64. Streck, *Assurbanipal und die letzten assyrischen Könige.*
65. Borger, *Beiträge.*
66. Bauer, *Inschriftenwerk Assurbanipals.*
67. Piepkorn, *Historical Prism Inscriptions of Ashurbanipal.*
68. Aynard, *Prisme du Louvre.*
69. Novotny, *Selected Royal Inscriptions of Assurbanipal.*
70. Weissert, "Royal Hunt and Royal Triumph," 355.
71. Strawn, *What Is Stronger than a Lion?*, 167–68.

times of Ashurnasirpal II, Tiglath-pileser III and Sennacherib, in whose inscriptions the simile, "like a caged bird / a bird in a cage," is attested. In addition to them, it is important to consider the lion hunting reliefs of Ashurbanipal, since they reinforce the importance of communication through the reliefs.[72] It is especially important to view the reliefs as originally grouped, not just as individually illustrated as if they were independent works of art. In his studies of the royal lion hunting reliefs, André Parrot argues that this activity was not only a sport but was also the best training for the battlefield.[73] Thus, hunting reliefs reflect a strong relationship between the hunting and the military campaigns.

Ashurnasirpal II (885–860 BCE)

R. D. Barnett of the British Museum was particularly active in publication and study of the military and the royal lion hunting reliefs of Ashurnasirpal II.[74] His work was also recently supplemented by the very important work on the Balawat Gates of Ashurnasirpal II, published by John Curtis and N. Tallis.[75] The reliefs of Ashuranisripal II include sieges as well as scenes of hunting lions and wild bulls.[76] Other volumes by Barnett include abundant illustrations of the reliefs of Ashurnasirpal II.[77] Also very useful is the reconstruction of the arrangement of the reliefs in Ashurnasirpal II's Northwest Palace in Kalḫu, studied by Janusz Meuszyński, which shows the juxtaposition of royal hunting scenes and siege scenes (Figs. 1.4–7).[78]

72. Weissert, "Royal Hunt and Royal Triumph," 339–58.

73. Parrot, *Arts of Assyria*, 54.

74. Barnett, *Assyrian Palace Reliefs*, 10–27.

75. Curtis and Tallis, *Balawat Gates of Ashurnasirpal II.*

76. Barnett, *Assyrian Palace Reliefs*, 10–27.

77. Barnett, *Assyrian Palace Reliefs*, plates 1–31; *Assyrian Sculpture*, plates 1–39.

78. Meuszyński et al., *Rekonstruktion der Reliefdarstellungen*, Tafel 1, B 20–B 18. See also Winter, "Royal Rhetoric," figs. 2–8; Porter, "Decorations, Political Posters," esp. 150–51, figs. 5–6.

Fig. 1.4. Ashurnasirpal II's Throne Room (Room B, plate 18A), Northwest Palace, Nimrud. British Museum, BM 124536. (Photo: © The Trustees of the British Museum.)

Fig. 1.5. Ashurnasirpal II's Throne Room (Room B, plate 18B), Northwest Palace, Nimrud. British Museum, BM 124537. (Photo: © The Trustees of the British Museum.)

Fig. 1.6. Ashurnasirpal II's Throne Room (Room B, plate 19A), Northwest Palace, Nimrud. British Museum, BM 124534. (Photo: © The Trustees of the British Museum.)

Fig. 1.7. Ashurnasirpal II's Throne Room (Room B, plate 19B), Northwest Palace, Nimrud. British Museum, BM 124535. (Photo: © The Trustees of the British Museum.)

Irene Winter sets her focus on the reliefs of the throne room of Ashurnasirpal II and argues for an ideological intention in the arrangement of the campaign and the hunting reliefs in the throne room.[79]

Parrot illustrates various hunting reliefs of Ashurnasirpal II in his magisterial work on Assyrian art.[80] In the reliefs, the Assyrian king is boldly hunting lions and bulls. Eva Strommenger also illustrates the hunting reliefs of Ashurnasirpal II but her pictures are basically individual

79. Winter, "Program of the Throneroom of Assurnasirpal II," 15–31.

80. Parrot, *Arts of Assyria*, 54–61.

scenes rather than comprehensive views.[81] Therefore, they do not show the interrelationship as provided by the Balawat gates and the inclusive scenes in the work of Parrot. She also presents pictures of the reliefs regarding his military campaigns.[82] Pierre Amiet also introduces some reliefs of Ashurnasirpal II from his palace at Nimrud.[83] J. E. Reade also includes a relief of the royal lion hunting by Ashurnasirpal II, with the reliefs of his military campaigns.[84]

Tiglath-pileser III (744–727 BCE)

Regarding Tiglath-pileser III, some military campaign reliefs have been published but no relief of a royal lion hunt has yet been found. R. D. Barnett and M. Falkner extensively survey the sculptures of Tiglath-pileser III (Plts. I–CVII), together with a few from Aššur-Naṣir-Apli II (883–859 BCE, Plts. CVIII–CXIII) and Esarhaddon (681–669 BCE, Plts. CXIV–CXXVII). The reliefs are from the Central and South-West Palaces at Nimrud and they include plates concerning military campaigns during the reign of the Assyrian king. They illustrate the first Babylonian campaign, the Arab campaign, the second Babylonian campaign, the Eastern campaign, the Anatolian campaign, the Urartian campaign and the Western Campaign.[85] Among the reliefs, some depict the battering rams that played an important role in siege warfare.[86] Barnett also introduces details of some reliefs from the Central Palace of Tiglath-pileser III at Nimrud.[87] Strommenger provides some reliefs which portray attacking archers of the Assyrian military camp, an attack on an enemy city, and booty being carried away from a conquered city, as well as the deported population.[88]

81. Strommenger, *5000 Years*, figs. 202, 203.
82. Strommenger, *5000 Years*, figs. 204, 205.
83. Amiet et al., *Art in the Ancient World*, figs. 103–6.
84. Curtis and Reade, *Art and Empire*, 44–49, 51.
85. Barnett and Falkner, *Sculptures of Tiglath-Pileser III*, xvi–xxv.
86. Barnett and Falkner, *Sculptures of Tiglath-Pileser III*, 51, 81, 83, 87, 88, 89, 112.
87. Barnett, *Assyrian Sculpture*, plates 50–57.
88. Strommenger, *5000 Years*, figs. 216–18.

Sennacherib (704–681 BCE)

Many military campaign reliefs from Sennacherib's reign have been found but no relief of royal lion hunting has been preserved. A possible exception has been noted by Parrot, who identified a crown prince as Sennacherib in a bird hunting relief.[89] This relief depicts a crown prince who has shot two birds with his arrows, while his servant is standing with a hawk in his right hand and a mace in his left hand. No explicit hunting relief of Sennacherib has been discovered.

John Malcolm Russell provides detailed images of Sennacherib's South-West Palace at Nineveh including campaign reliefs and associated inscriptions.[90] David Ussishkin has thoroughly explored the Lachish reliefs and their historical context regarding Sennacherib's conquest of Lachish in 701 BCE.[91] In particular, he argues for the importance of these reliefs in that they provide information regarding ancient warfare and art.[92] In other words, reliefs are an important source for the Assyrian siege ramps as well as the characteristic dress of the inhabitants.[93] Barnett provides Sennacherib's reliefs including the siege of Lachish.[94] Barnett, E. Bleibtreu, and G. Turner also include some details of Lachish,[95] with commentary.[96]

Ashurbanipal (668–631 BCE)

A great many reliefs of Ashurbanipal have been recovered. Among the prominent sources are Barnett's publications of reliefs from the time of Ashurbanipal. He has published the reliefs of the North Palace of Ashurbanipal at Nineveh, which include military campaign and hunting reliefs. In particular, he provided details of reliefs including lion hunts, the battle on the Ulai River, and the Arab war against Adiâ.[97] Weissert has provided an especially noteworthy analysis of one of the Ashurbanipal's royal lion

89. Parrot, *Arts of Assyria*, 62.
90. Russell, *Sennacherib's Palace*.
91. Ussishkin, *Conquest of Lachish*; *Biblical Lachish*.
92. Ussishkin, *Conquest of Lachish*, 11.
93. Ussishkin, *Conquest of Lachish*, 11.
94. Barnett, *Assyrian Sculpture*, plates 65–87.
95. Barnett et al., *Sculptures from the Southwest Palace*, 1:plates 322–52.
96. Barnett et al., *Sculptures from the Southwest Palace*, 2:101–5.
97. Barnett, *Assyrian Sculpture*, plates 88–179.

hunts.[98] At a time when the number of lions in the area around Nineveh had apparently increased, creating a threat to the people when they ventured outside the city walls, Ashurbanipal staged an impressive hunt, reinforcing his role as protector.[99] Paul Collins provides an interesting detail from one of the lion hunting reliefs, viz., that the king's bow is decorated with a lion's head (Fig. 1.8).[100]

Fig. 1.8. The Bow of Ashurbanipal, North Palace of Ashurbanipal, Nineveh. British Museum, BM 124867. (Photo: © The Trustees of the British Museum.)

98. Weissert, "Royal Hunt and Royal Triumph," 339–58.

99. Weissert, "Royal Hunt and Royal Triumph," 343.

100. Collins, *Assyrian Palace Sculptures*, 118–19.

The Assyrian king symbolically demonstrated his protection of the city by staging a public hunt in which he killed eighteen lions corresponding to the eighteen gates of the city, as noted by Weissert.[101] The only specific association of what the scene represents with the associated text that Weissert identifies—though not a perfect fit—in terms of piercing "the throats o[f] rag[ing] l[i]ons, each (lion) with a single arrow."[102] There is no preserved reference in the epigraph to the eighteen gates; it would have had to have come from the perception of an informed observer.[103] The scene speaks only to the informed viewer and the only direct evidence of this association is the larger relief scene itself.[104] Reade discusses another hunting scene in a full view, which shows the sequence from the hunting itself to the king's libation over the dead lion.[105] The lions involved in this hunting apparently had been previously captured or had been bred in captivity.[106]

Reade, who offers some color illustrations, also provides studies on the reliefs of the warfare against the Elamites.[107] In particular, a relief, which is related to the capture of an Elamite king, decribes a lioness creeping up on a wild goat.[108] He suggests that the hunt by the lioness is a symbolic "parallel with the Assyrians ineluctably stalking their prey."[109] This is an interesting feature of the reliefs in that such a symbolic combination is rare.

Biblical Passages Related to Sennacherib and Hezekiah

The biblical accounts of 2 Kgs 18–19, Isa 36–37, and 2 Chr 32 describe Sennacherib's attack on Judah, providing another perspective on Sennacherib's campaign. The biblical passages are not in agreement regarding their perspectives on Sennacherib's campaign, including the description of a

101. Weissert, "Royal Hunt and Royal Triumph," 355.

102. Weissert, "Royal Hunt and Royal Triumph," 354–55, 357.

103. Weissert, "Royal Hunt and Royal Triumph," 354–55, 357.

104. Weissert, "Royal Hunt and Royal Triumph," 354–55.

105. Curtis and Reade, *Art and Empire*, 86–87.

106. Weissert, "Royal Hunt and Royal Triumph," 354–55. The possibility of raising lion cubs can be found in the inscriptions of Ashurnasirpal II (*RIMA* 2 *A*.0.101.2, 33b–35a [p. 226]). According to the inscriptions, the king captured fifty lion-cubs in "cages" during his hunt.

107. Curtis and Reade, *Art and Empire*, 72–77.

108. Curtis and Reade, *Art and Empire*, 80.

109. Curtis and Reade, *Art and Empire*, 80.

divine intervention that led to the Assyrians lifting the siege and returning to Nineveh (2 Kgs 19:35–36; Isa 37:36–37). Second Kings 18:13 (Isa 36:1) describes that Sennacherib captured forty-six fortified cities of Judah. Second Kings 18:14–16 also cites Hezekiah's submission to Sennacherib and the payment of a significant tribute to the Assyrian king at his temporary headquarters at Lachish. Meanwhile, none of the biblical texts mentions Sennacherib's "bringing out" of Padî from Jerusalem, the Assyrian vassal king of Ekron who had been ousted in a rebellion and sent by the "rebels" to Hezekiah for imprisonment. Instead, the biblical tradition emphasizes the affirmation of YHWH's power triumphing over the imperial military power in favor of Hezekiah and his kingdom.

Numerous scholars have studied the Assyrian records and the biblical texts concerning Sennacherib and Hezekiah, attempting to reconstruct the history of that time. William Gallagher argues for the historical reliability of the related biblical texts, especially 2 Kgs 18–19, and Isa 36–37.[110] According to him, even though each text has its own theological stance, collectively they present a historical kernel of the military conflict between Sennacherib and Hezekiah along with fictional components such as the messenger/angel of YHWH.[111] Lester Grabbe, Bob Becking, Ehud Ben-Zvi, and Christoph Uehlinger provide various perspectives related to Sennacherib's invasion of Judah for the purpose of historical reconstruction.[112] In a more recent volume, Isaac Kalimi, Seth Richardson, Mordechai Cogan, Eckart Frahm, Frederick Mario Fales, and Peter Dubovský explore various subjects related to Sennacherib and Hezekiah including archaeological sources, Assyrian political and military history, and the interpretation of later literature about the military conflict between Sennacherib and Hezekiah.[113] Nazek Khaled Matty analyzes Sennacherib's campaign for a historical reconstruction.[114] Paul Evans argues that the biblical passages related to Sennacherib's campaign against Judah have historical reliability.[115] Furthermore, he even compared military conflict and the War of 1812 for the comparative historical value of both Assyrian and biblical narrative.[116]

110. Gallagher, *Sennacherib's Campaign to Judah*, 160–262.

111. Gallagher, *Sennacherib's Campaign to Judah*, 261–62.

112. Grabbe, *Like a Bird in a Cage*.

113. Kalimi and Richardson, *Sennacherib at the Gates of Jerusalem*.

114. Matty, *Sennacherib's Campaign*.

115. Evans, *Invasion of Sennacherib*.

116. Evans, *Sennacherib and the War of 1812*.

History and Ideology of the Neo-Assyrian Empire and Ancient Israel

Since the archaeological discovery of the Assyrian capitals in the nineteenth century and the decipherment of Akkadian, the field of Assyriology has enormously expanded our knowledge of ancient Assyria and the achievements of the Neo-Assyrian kings and of Assyrian culture.[117] There are rich sources in texts and artistic representations that have been part of a transformation in the understanding of the relations between Assyria and ancient Israel.[118] One of the important disciplinary interests has been the analysis of the ideology of the Assyrian Empire based on texts including annals and chronicles as well as images within its own culture and history.[119]

History, Ideology, and Propaganda in Ancient Near Eastern Studies

Johan Huizinga defines history as "the *intellectual form* in which *a civilization* renders *account* to itself of its *past*."[120] In his definition, he implies a relational concept of history: history is a means of connecting the past and the present. History has both particular and varied forms according to civilizations, but the relationship between past and present is a common feature.

Ancient Near Eastern studies have discussed the usage of the term "ideology," especially its applicability to the ideas or thought of ancient times such as the time of the Neo-Assyrian Empire. Even though the term was initially used in connection with a recent socio-political structure, its implications do not necessarily relate only to a recent context. Instead, the term tends to be generally used in relation to every socio-political structure and the power conflicts within the structure.

Based on the interrelationship between ideology and history in the ancient Near Eastern societies, K. Lawson Younger has studied ancient Near Eastern conquest accounts.[121] In his view, ancient Near Eastern history is artistically constructed and it does not follow a strict chronology in its format. Rather, it is a reconstructed past from the perspective of the

117. Foster, "Beginnings of Assyriology," 44–73; Frahm, "Images of Assyria," 74–94.

118. Liverani, *Israel's History and the History of Israel*, 143–64.

119. Mieroop, *Cuneiform Texts*, 39–85; Bahrani, *Graven Image*, 202–10.

120. Huizinga, "Definition of the Concept of History," 9.

121. Younger, *Ancient Conquest Accounts*, 25–58.

dominant ideology of the present society. He argues that a large part of the present discussion of ancient Near Eastern and biblical historical topics deals with the concept of ideology more than with other issues.[122] Along with a brief historical survey of its use from Karl Marx to Clifford Geertz, he presents the concept of ideology: "Ideology is a 'schematic image of social order,' 'a pattern of beliefs and concepts (both factual and normative) which purport to explain complex social phenomena' in which there may be simplification by means of symbolic figurative language, code shifting, and/or overcoding."[123]

Mario Liverani also argues for the applicability of the concept of ideology to the ancient Near Eastern world, with a focus on the Assyrian Empire.[124] In his view, the imperial structure usually includes opposition or conflict among entities. To resolve the conflict and, finally, to maintain the imperial structure, it is necessary for the ruling class to justify its own rule over the ruled class. There are two ways of resolution: a physical level and a non-physical level.[125] Both or either of them could be used for the maintenance of the ruling power. Liverani argues that the non-physical level is more efficient, and that ideology is a non-physical way to gain or maintain power in a social structure.[126]

Liverani's analysis of Neo-Assyrian imperial ideology is based on a structure of binary opposition.[127] In the situation of the opposition, the ruling class of the empire tried to justify their ruling over the ruled class and even the vassal states. The Assyrian inscriptions were used as a means of diffusion of a specific ideology to justify the ruling class of the empire, *but targeting multiple audiences, including the gods*. Considering the literacy level of the empire, the potential audience for the written records, unless they were read out as some potentially were, would be limited to scribes, high officials, and a few kings. It is notable that reliefs with written languages and/or visual images have been found in various places in the provinces, including Zinjirli and Nahr el-Kelb.

122. Younger, *Ancient Conquest Accounts*, 47.

123. Younger, *Ancient Conquest Accounts*, 51.

124. Liverani, "Ideology of the Assyrian Empire," 297–317; *Israel's History and the History of Israel*, 143–64.

125. Liverani, "Ideology of the Assyrian Empire," 298.

126. Liverani, "Ideology of the Assyrian Empire," 298.

127. Liverani, "Ideology of the Assyrian Empire," 305–14.

In his analysis of the ideology through the textual study of the inscriptions, Liverani mentions the term, "'cosmic' center,"[128] which needs further explanation. The ideology of the Assyrian Empire employs religious terms in many cases and such a "'cosmic' center" is the religious term referring to the expansive order of the Assyrian Empire from an earthly level to a universal level. In other words, it serves to describe the status of the Assyrian Empire as a center over other subject kingdoms as a universal or even divine order that justifies imperial rule. Accordingly, the expression of the concept of "'cosmic' center" in the inscriptions and reliefs was intended to contribute to the maintenance of the unbalanced power relations between the ruling class and the ruled class within the Assyrian Empire. In a land and a world marked by contrasts, there is "an opposition between a 'cosmic' center (that is, orderly and working according to norms) and a chaotic periphery."[129]

Hayim Tadmor analyzes the Assyrian royal inscriptions from Sargon to Ashurbanipal and he argues that there is a discrepancy between ideology and historical reality.[130] The reconstruction of historical events does not simply describe what happened in the past. Instead, it reconstructs the past according to the present socio-political ideology of the ruling class of the empire. Accordingly, the historical records of the Assyrian royal inscriptions reflect the discrepancy between ideology and historical reality. For example, Tadmor argues that the images of the king are pictured in two ways: a military hero or a pious builder of temples.[131] A military image of the Assyrian kings was pivotal in the diffusion of an ideology of the power of the Assyrian Empire over other subject kingdoms. In the process of the expansion of the empire, Assyrian kings employed military campaigns against other kingdoms. Therefore, the depiction of the king as a military hero makes himself a victor and his empire a powerfully ruled state. As a pious builder of temples,[132] the religious image of a king presents himself as a loyal agent of divine order.[133] Therefore, his rule is supported by the divine beings and his order is related to the divine or universal order.

128. Liverani, "Ideology of the Assyrian Empire," 306.

129. Liverani, "Ideology of the Assyrian Empire," 306.

130. Tadmor, "History and Ideology in the Assyrian Inscriptions," 26.

131. Tadmor, "History and Ideology in the Assyrian Inscriptions," 34.

132. Tadmor, "History and Ideology in the Assyrian Inscriptions," 34.

133. Meanwhile, the campaign texts and reliefs also invoke the power of Ashur.

Another notable feature of the royal inscriptions is flexibility in literary styles. The literary style of the inscriptions of the Assyrian kings is not uniform but varies according to the individual kings, i.e., the court scribes of these kings. The successive changes in the formulae and literary conventions, especially in terms of the styles and the content of the royal inscriptions within the relatively short period between Sargon and Ashurbanipal, reflect the changing views and styles of various influential royal scribes.[134]

This analysis of the inscriptions suggests that the historiography of the Assyrian royal inscriptions should be considered as manipulated reality rather than as objective or historical reality. Such a kind of historiography is easily found in the Bible as well. The Assyrian historiography is highly political and ideological in favor of the Assyrian kings, who head the ruling class. The royal inscriptions function as conveyors of the dominant royal ideology to the audience or to the reader(s) for the justification of the ruling power of the kings over their subjects, even though the identification of the audience is not particularly explicit.

In addition to the term "ideology," Tadmor also argues for the use of the term "propaganda," in the field of ancient Near Eastern studies, particularly with reference to the Assyrian royal inscriptions.[135] Propaganda may be defined as "a deliberative and systematic attempt to shape perceptions, manipulate conditions, and direct behavior to achieve a response that furthers the desired intent of the propagandist."[136] There has been some concern about the use of such terminology among scholars and it has been used less often in Near Eastern studies compared to other academic fields. In opposition to this attitude toward the use of the term "propaganda," Tadmor proposes to use the term in its traditional meaning in the studies on the Assyrian royal inscriptions.[137] The inscriptions have a political intention of manipulating the intended audience (including gods) in the desired direction of the ruling class including the Assyrian kings. Therefore, the study of propaganda is an important element in reviewing the inscriptions.

The applicability of the concept of ideology has also been discussed in the field of art. In relation to the cultural patterns of Mesopotamian art, Eva Strommenger argues that religious ideas stood at the center of all pictorial

134. Tadmor, "History and Ideology in the Assyrian Inscriptions," 45–46.

135. Tadmor, "Propaganda, Literature, Historiography," 332–33.

136. Jowett and O'Donnell, *Propaganda and Persuasion*, 16.

137. Tadmor, "Propaganda, Literature, Historiography," 332.

creations.[138] It is clear that many so-called historical scenes have a mythological and ideological meaning.[139] In other words, there is an interrelatedness among art, religion, and historical contexts. Based on Strommenger's perspective, art is not free from its own religious, socio-political, or historical context. Instead, it is deeply connected with its context, and it functions as a conveyor of a certain ideological perspective. Therefore, studies on Assyrian art should include the ideological aspect of art.

In her analysis of Assyrian military campaign and royal lion hunting reliefs, Zainab Bahrani argues that the royal images of the Assyrian kings should be understood as "political symbolic fiction."[140] The reliefs provide a propagandistic image of the king. She makes an important distinction, however, between the representation of the king in the lion hunt and the representation of him in the military campaign reliefs. In the hunting reliefs, the king, himself, is shown as having prowess and virility whereas in the military reliefs he is shown as expressing his power through his army.[141] Bahrani argues that the appearance of the kings in the military and hunting reliefs is not a simple record of the kings but an important means for expressing royal political power.

Barbara Porter, in her studies on the use of visual images in the Assyrian Empire, argues that the rulers understood visual images to be powerful and effective tools of public persuasion, i.e., propaganda.[142] In her view, the kings commissioned many of their reliefs and sculptures with a view toward shaping the political opinion of a diverse and not always cooperative population by means of publicly displayed, politically charged visual images.[143] Her study of Assyrian iconography is important in that she relates the iconography to its cultural and political context. Assyrian iconography is not simply artistic work; it is also political propaganda on behalf of the kings.

Julian Reade provides an important insight on the relationship between written inscriptions and non-written art, arguing that ideology and propaganda are inseparable in Assyrian art.[144] They both reflect the

138. Strommenger, *5000 Years*, 10.

139. Strommenger, *5000 Years*, 10.

140. Bahrani, *Graven Image*, 140.

141. Bahrani, *Rituals of War*, 213.

142. Porter, *Trees, Kings, and Politics*, 11.

143. Porter, *Trees, Kings, and Politics*, 11.

144. Reade, "Ideology and Propaganda in Assyrian Art," 329.

royal ideology and propaganda of the empire that justify Assyrian imperial dominance. In particular, he suggests that each of the Assyrian palaces was "a massive corpus of personal propaganda."[145]

Reade finds numerous examples of the ideology and propaganda of the Neo-Assyrian kings in their art.[146] The royal art not only aims at artistic beauty but also at the diffusion of political propaganda among the intended audiences. It seeks to lead the viewers to an adoption of a certain social view or thought through the recognition of the visual images. The recognition is immediate as they see it and the recognition leads to the conscious or unconscious adoption of the royal ideology. Ultimately, the images contribute to the naturalization of the justification of Assyrian rule among the audience and the maintenance of the power of the Assyrian Empire over its territory and its subject kingdoms.

Irene Winter argues that the royal image in reliefs and sculptures represents to viewers a dominant royal ideology of divine kingship with the aim of maintaining the power relations in the hierarchical society of the Assyrian Empire.[147] In the inscriptions and the reliefs, text and image are parallel, complementary, or even distinct.[148] Both of them, however, function in various ways as conveyors of royal ideology and propaganda to viewers, especially from the time of Ashurnasirpal II in the ninth century BCE to that of Ashurbanipal in the seventh century BCE.[149] The image of the Assyrian kings is balanced, compromised, or manipulated between "realism" and "idealism" to represent the ideology of divine kingship.[150] The image presents the king as an ideal human who serves as the manifestation of the gods on earth.[151] Therefore, the royal images, including reliefs and statues, are "sign-producing symbolic systems" used to construct the institution of kingship based on divinely sanctioned rule and the ideal qualities of the ruler.[152] Through the royal image, the ruling class, including the Assyrian kings, could diffuse the royal ideology to the intended audience or viewers. A good example is the program of the throne room of Ashurnasirpal

145. Reade, "Ideology and Propaganda in Assyrian Art," 331.

146. Reade, "Ideology and Propaganda in Assyrian Art," 329–43.

147. Irene Winter, "Art *in* Empire," 359–81.

148. Winter, "Art *in* Empire," 359.

149. Winter, "Art *in* Empire," 360–61.

150. Winter, "Art *in* Empire," 374.

151. Winter, "Art *in* Empire," 375.

152. Winter, "Art *in* Empire," 376.

II.[153] Winter points out that the hunting reliefs and the campaign reliefs are carefully programmed for the audience.[154] She argues that the visual juxtaposition of hunting and warfare in the throne room is a symbolic message about the Assyrian kingship to the intended audience.[155] The hunting is a much older motif, which goes back to ca. 3200 BCE.[156] The innovative aspects of the reliefs of the throne room are the specific arrangements of the hunting and warfare images and their articulation into a "unified sequential composition" for the political ideology of the kingship.[157]

In his studies on the use and function of leonine images and metaphors in the Hebrew Bible and the ancient Near East, Brent A. Strawn carefully examines the leonine images and metaphors of the Hebrew Bible in light of the ancient Near Eastern perception of lions.[158] In particular, he shows that the study of ancient images and metaphors is important for the understanding of both text and art, (though there is very little Israelite art that has been preserved), whether dealing with ancient Israel or the Neo-Assyrian world.[159] Regarding the use of the leonine images, he concurs with others that royal lion hunting represents the prowess of the king through his victory over the wild animal,[160] i.e., nature or the raw, or even chaos.[161]

Concerning the relationship between royal hunting and royal military triumph, Elnathan Weissert published an exceptionally insightful study in which he analyzed one of Ashurbanipal's well-illustrated lion hunts in connection with the urban plan of Nineveh at a time when there apparently was a threatening abundance of lions around the city. He associated this with an aspect of the *akītu* festival. He argues that the royal lion hunt is related to the royal military triumphs through the *akītu* festival, as found in a prism fragment of Ashurbanipal (82-5-22,2).[162] In this prism fragment, the topic moves on from the royal lion hunt to the festival in a rather sudden

153. Winter, "Program of the Throneroom," 15–31.

154. Winter, "Program of the Throneroom," figs. 4–7.

155. Winter, "Program of the Throneroom," 19, 27–28. Note Fig. 1.4 above.

156. Winter, "Royal Rhetoric," 10–11.

157. Winter, "Royal Rhetoric," 11.

158. Strawn, *What Is Stronger than a Lion?*

159. Foreman, "What Is Stronger than a Lion?," 136.

160. Strawn, *What Is Stronger than a Lion?*, 165.

161. Strawn, *What Is Stronger than a Lion?*, 170–71.

162. Weissert, "Royal Hunt and Royal Triumph," 349.

way.[163] Since the festival was sometimes associated with mundane military achievement, the victory over lions in the hunt can be related to a military victory over enemies as well as the divine triumph over cosmic enemies.[164] This association enables the identification of Ashurbanipal as an agent of Ashur and Ishtar in that the king imposes order over chaos, as represented by marauding lions (countered by the symbolic lion hunt) or human enemies (countered by campaigns), similar to the gods bringing order over against chaos caused by the divine enemies (countered in the *akītu* festival). Based on this affinity, the royal hunt is not only a royal sport but also a representation of the king's protection of Nineveh and the maintenance of divine order, demonstrated to the viewers of the hunt, and the participants in the *akītu* festival—viewers, auditors, and readers as well.

Weissert's argument for the connection between the royal lion hunt and the *akītu* festival in the cited prism fragment of Ashurbanipal is based on a concept of an opposite relationship between two entities: order and disorder (chaos), i.e., the Assyrian king/divine beings and the enemy. This type of opposition can be summed up as the opposition between culture and nature, which represent order and disorder (or even chaos), respectively. Ashurbanipal and divine beings such as Ashur and Ishtar embody the civilized rule, which reflects urban culture, over against the disordered plains or open fields.[165] Opposition between two entities is prevalent in the relations between the king and the lions, divine beings and their enemies, and the king and military enemies, as well as between culture and nature.

Furthermore, Weissert's analysis of the cited prism fragment of Ashurbanipal shows that the concept of opposite relationships is part of the political ideology of the empire. As the ruler of the empire, the king is described as a brave hunter. The *akītu* festival, itself, may be considered as visualizing and enacting the territorial control of the king over his world or even the universe,[166] just as the connection of the royal lion hunt with the *akītu* festival may be understood as reinforcing the political ideology of the divine kingship of Ashurbanipal: the king, who was ritually humiliated in the *akītu* festival, as a victor over lions and as an agent of divine beings, clearly illustrated by his victory over the ferocious animals, fits with the cosmic triumph of order over chaos. The inscriptions and

163. Weissert, "Royal Hunt and Royal Triumph," 346.

164. Weissert, "Royal Hunt and Royal Triumph," 347–48.

165. Weissert, "Royal Hunt and Royal Triumph," 349.

166. Pongratz-Leisten, "Interplay of Military Strategy and Cultic Practice," 252.

the reliefs convey this royal ideology and propaganda to the viewers and the readers. Ultimately, these representations and words serve to justify the rule of the Assyrian king over the empire and to maintain the ruling power in the hierarchical structure of the empire.

Regarding the general affinity between Assyrian warfare and royal hunting, Bustenay Oded argues that Assyrian warfare and hunting serve the same purpose: to demonstrate the heroism, valor, skill, and prowess of the kings involved.[167] They represent competitive "games" in which the kings demonstrate bravery and the necessary skills which enable them to triumph over their opponents.[168] In this oppositional relationship, the victories of the kings represent the establishment of order over disorder. In other words, the heroic aspect of the kings is a necessary component of order. Finally, this ideology of order contributes to the justification of the battles of the kings against human enemies or wild animals, especially, lions.

The Intended Audience

In the studies of the ideology of the inscriptions and the reliefs, one of the important issues is the identification of the intended audience. Based on the preserved Assyrian record, Russell suggests that the possible audience included two groups—those who work or live in the palace and visitors from outside.[169] From those two groups, he identifies and classifies the audience into twelve groups.[170] They are kings, the crown prince/royal family, courtiers, servants, foreign employees, foreign prisoners, future kings, gods, Assyrians, provincials, subject foreigners, and independent foreigners.[171] Similarly, Irene Winter suggests that the audience for the throne room of Ashurnasirpal II would include the gods, the king himself, various functionaries within the state, and visitors from outside the state.[172] Since the level of literacy varies according to the audience, the level of the understanding of the inscriptions and the reliefs would be quite varied.[173]

167. Oded, *War, Peace and Empire*, 140.

168. Oded, *War, Peace and Empire*, 141.

169. Russell, *Sennacherib's Palace*, 238.

170. Russell, *Sennacherib's Palace*, 238–40.

171. Russell, *Sennacherib's Palace*, 238–39.

172. Winter, "Program of the Throneroom," 27.

173. There were reliefs and inscriptions elsewhere that might have a larger audience, largely now unknown, but only the palaces had a real density of scenes such as those described here.

Meanwhile, it is notable that there is a difference among the audiences. In the case of the Assyrian inscriptions, the audience is limited by the low level of literacy. Only a limited audience such as scribes or high officials, and some kings could understand the written records, and they would require much more than a glance to register the texts. The gods were assumed to understand the inscriptions, as well as the reliefs. In contrast, the reliefs, with or without accompanying inscriptions, were accessible to a much wider audience. All who saw the reliefs could understand most, if not all, of the visual images, though some scenes, such as the killing of the eighteen lions discussed by Weissert, require a knowledge of the city's plan, with its eighteen gates, and the danger of marauding lions to comprehend the whole scene. Therefore, it is quite clear that the visual language of the reliefs communicates with the largest audience. For most, comprehension of the inscriptions would require a learned guide.

An Ideological Approach to the Simile, "Like a Caged Bird / a Bird in a Cage"

One of the possible ways to embed an ideology in ancient historical inscriptions is to take advantage of the communicative possibilities of language such as found in the use of similes. Tadmor argues that a new literary genre, viz. Royal Annals, came into being during the reign of Tiglath-pileser I (1114–1076 BCE).[174] This new genre blends the genre of the heroic epic and the genre of the chronicle. Examples of this newly emerged genre are written in prose but are "heavily loaded with poetic similes, hyperbolae, typological numbers and repetitions," featuring "characteristic of epic style," in their descriptions "of the first five years of Tiglath-pileser I."[175] In other words, literary expressions such as similes are used to create a certain image or to convey aspects of the king and other characters in these historical accounts. The image or thought would reflect the political ideology of the ruling class, on whose behalf the Royal Annals are generated.

A good example from the period of the Assyrian Empire would be the animal simile, "like a caged bird / a bird in a cage," which can be found in the inscriptions of Ashurnasirpal II, Tiglath-pileser III, and Sennacherib as well as in modified form in the Amarna letters from Byblos. In Sennacherib's account of his military campaigns to the west in 701 BCE, he besieged

174. Tadmor, "Propaganda, Literature, Historiography," 327.

175. Tadmor, "Propaganda, Literature, Historiography," 327.

Jerusalem of Judah, the capital city of Hezekiah's kingdom. According to the inscriptions, Sennacherib "shut him up like a caged bird / a bird in a cage in his royal city, Jerusalem[176] (*kīma iṣṣur qu-up-pi qé-reb* [alū]*Ur-sal-li-im-mu alī šarru-ti-šú e-sír-šú*)."[177]

The use of this particular simile is rare but not unique. It is, as mentioned, found in other Assyrian inscriptions. The earliest usage of the simile by an Assyrian ruler is found in the hunting accounts of Ashurnasirpal II, which describe the killing of lions by the king. He states, "I killed 370 strong lions like caged birds with a spear (3 *mēʾātu* 70 *nēšī dannūti kīma iṣṣūrī qu-up-pi ina* [iṣu]*pu-aš-ḫi a-duk*)."[178] Given the number of lions killed, the word, "bird," was written in the plural form (MUŠEN.MEŠ, i.e., *iṣṣūrī*). Another notable point is that the word, "cage (*qu-up-pi*)" could be taken as a plural as well (*quppī*). The hunting inscriptions state that the lions were killed by the Assyrian king with the ease of killing birds in cage(s), i.e., they were totally vulnerable to the king.[179] Subsequently, the simile was used in the military inscriptions of Tiglath-pileser III who waged warfare against Rezin of Damascus. Rezin, having been defeated in a battle outside the city walls, took refuge in his fortified city. Tigalth-pileser III states that "I shut him up like a caged bird / a bird in a cage (*kīma iṣṣūr quppi ēsiršu*)," and the simile is most famously used by Sennacherib regarding Hezekiah of Judah.[180]

The use of the simile in royal annals, both in reference to military activity and royal hunting, shows the affinity of warfare narratives and hunting narratives. Both contexts emphasize the decisive power of the Assyrian king over against an opponent. Furthermore, the scenes of the royal hunting reliefs contribute to the understanding of the literary expression of the simile in vivid fashion. For example, one particular royal hunting scene in the reliefs of Ashurbanipal has a sequence of three segments in which a lion, having been released from a cage, attacks the nearby king, who then deftly kills the lion (BM 124886/7).[181] The simile, "like a caged bird / a bird in a cage," is used by Ashurnasirpal II in reference

176. Regarding the phrase "*kīma iṣṣūrī quppi* (GIM MUŠEN *qu-up-pi*)," its translation could be "like a caged bird" or "like a bird in a cage." The simile itself does not contain any preposition such as *ina*, because the phrase is a construct chain.

177. *RINAP 3/1* No. 22, col iii, 27b-29a (p. 176).

178. *RIMA* 2 A.0.101.2, 42 (pp. 226–27).

179. *RIMA* 2 A.0.101.2, 42 (pp. 226–27).

180. Tadmor, *Inscriptions of Tiglath-Pileser III*, 78–79.

181. BM 124886–87. Barnett, *Assyrian Palace Reliefs*, 90–93; Curtis and Reade, *Art and Empire*, figs. 28–29.

to killing lions, which were apparently hunted in open areas, and easily killed by the great warrior/hunter king.[182] The hunting is mentioned and illustrated in the wall reliefs, and in the reliefs on the gates of Ashurnasirpal II from Balawat with accompanying epigraphs.[183] A caged bird is rather more vulnerable than a caged lion, let alone a loose lion—even if formerly caged. The simile demonstrates the bravery and the power of the king over the ferocious lion, at times in a direct confrontation, "hand to claw." This powerful aspect of the Assyrian king as a hunter supports the military prowess of the Assyrian king as a warrior.

As noted above, the simile also can be found in the letters of Rib-Addi, the king of Byblos, who sent to the Egyptian Pharaoh during the Amarna Period (mid-fourteenth century BCE).[184] Under the threat of Aziru, he described himself "like birds, that lie in a net (*ki-ma iṣṣurī* šá *i-na libbi*[*bi*] *ḫu-ḫa-ri ki-lu-bi*),"[185] and "like a bird, which lies in a net (*ki-ma iṣṣuri šá i-na libbi*[*bi*] [*ḫ*]*u-ḫa-ri ki-lu-bi* šá-*ak-na-at*)" in his letters.[186] It is notable that the simile was used as a self-description by the king of Byblos himself, faced by a very close and present danger, i.e., Aziru. He is aware of his own vulnerability or even hopelessness, as he describes himself as in a desperate situation, needing immediate Egyptian assistance.[187]

An Ideological Approach to the Biblical Sources Related to Sennacherib and Hezekiah

Along with the Assyrian inscriptions and reliefs, various biblical passages concerning Sennacherib and Hezekiah also should be considered in terms of ideology. Sennacherib's military campaign can be found in 2 Kgs 18–19, Isa 36–37, and 2 Chr 32. These passages describe the same event

182. *RIMA* 2, A.0.101.2, 42 (pp. 226–27).

183. Curtis and Tallis, *Balawat Gates of Ashurnasirpal II*, 116–17, 132–33.

184. Moran, *Amarna Letters*, xiii.

185. Knudtzon et al., *El-Amarna-Tafeln*; Moran, *Amarna Letters* 74.45–46 (Knudtzon, 1:376–77; Moran, 143).

186. Knudtzon et al., *El-Amarna-Tafeln*; Moran, *Amarna Letters* 79.35–36 (Knudtzon, 1:390–91; Moran, 149).

187. On Rib-Addi's situation, see Moran, "Rib-Hadda," 173–81; Liverani, "Rib-Adda," 97–124. Regarding the cuneiform text, see Rainey, *Canaanite in the Amarna Tablets*, 2:305; 3:143.

but from different perspectives related to their own theological and even political ideologies.

In the case of 2 Kgs 18–19, its perspective reflects the Deuteronomistic History (DH). Martin Noth argued that the books from Joshua to Kings comprise the Deuteronomistic work, known as the DH. There have been countless discussions about the theory of the DH regarding its structure, composition and date.[188] Noth argues that the DH is a work by a single "Deuteronomistic editor" or rather by "Deuteronomistic editors."[189] In his study of 1 and 2 Kings, Rad argued that the deuteronomist represents the fulfillment of YHWH's redemption in his work.[190] Hans W. Wolff suggested that the deuteronomist calls for the repentance of the exiles in keeping with the pattern of sin (disobedience), judgment, repentance and deliverance.[191] Regarding the authorship, Ernest Nicholson and Moshe Weinfeld suggested that the DH is the work of the Deuteronomistic circle.[192] Mordecai Cogan and Hayim Tadmor suggest that the author of Kings follows the thought of the Deuteronomistic school: the loyalty of the monarch to the God of Israel as worshiped in Jerusalem determines the course of history.[193]

Regarding the theological perspective of the Deuteronomistic school, it is notable that T. R. Hobbs suggests a relational concept of binary opposition in the books of Kings.[194] The Exile was a time of disorder for the compiler/author/editor. Confronting the disorder, the book shows an interest in order, conformity, and social solidarity.[195] Hobbs argues that these values are manifested throughout the book of 2 Kings.[196]

188. See McKenzie, *Trouble with Kings*; "Deuteronomistic History"; Person, *Deuteronomic School*; Campbell and O'Brien, *Unfolding the Deuteronomistic History*; Pury et al., *Israel Constructs Its History*; Römer, *Future of the Deuteronomistic History*; *So-Called Deuteronomistic History*; Knoppers and McConville, *Reconsidering Israel and Judah*; Raney, *History as Narrative in the Deuteronomistic History*; Peterson, *Authors of the Deuteronomistic History*.

189. Noth, *Deuteronomistic History*, 4.

190. Rad, *Problem of the Hexateuch*, 221.

191. Wolff, "Kerygma of the Deuteronomic Historical Work."

192. Nicholson, *Deuteronomy and Tradition*, 108–9; Weinfeld, *Deuteronomy and the Deuteronomic School*, 9.

193. Cogan and Tadmor, *II Kings*, 3.

194. Hobbs, *2 Kings*, xxxiv.

195. Hobbs, *2 Kings*, xxxiv.

196. Hobbs, *2 Kings*, xxxiv.

A brief account of the military campaign of Sennacherib can be found in 2 Kgs 18:13b—19:37, focusing on the potentially precarious situation of Jerusalem. Bernhard Stade suggests the presence of three sources in the narrative which was later revised by Brevard Childs.[197] Following their arguments, Cogan and Tadmor suggest that this account can be divided into two distinguished sources: 2 Kgs 18:13b–16 (A) and 2 Kgs 18:17—19:37 (B).[198] According to them, source A is a chronistic record, which is terse and factual.[199] They argue that this record "agrees in great measure with Sennacherib's own account of his Judean campaign."[200] In this account, Hezekiah sent his submission to Sennacherib at Lachish (2 Kgs 18:14a), followed by his assigned tribute (2 Kgs 18:14b–16).

Meanwhile, Cogan and Tadmor describe source B as a lengthy and discursive narrative.[201] Source B can be divided into two accounts of B1 (2 Kgs 18:17—19:9a, 36) and B2 (2 Kgs 19:9b–35).[202] In particular, they suggest that the account of 2 Kgs 19:9b–35 (B2) "bears the imprint of the Deuteronomic school."[203] In particular, Hezekiah's prayer (2 Kgs 19:15–19) reflects "language typical of the Deuteronomists."[204]

Simon Parker also analyzes the account of 2 Kgs 18:13—19:37.[205] According to him, the account can be divided into three segments: account A (2 Kgs 18:13–16), account B (2 Kgs 18:17—19:9a, 36–37), and account C (2 Kgs 19:9b–35).[206] While account A is a brief statement about "buying off the invader," two following narratives are constructed on the pattern of the divine deliverance through "a royal appeal to the deity."[207] In particular, he suggests that account B and account C show different plots, though both of them describe the salvation by YHWH from the military and political

197. Stade, "Miscellen," esp. 172–83; Childs, *Isaiah and the Assyrian Crisis*, 73–103.
198. Cogan and Tadmor, *II Kings*, 240.
199. Cogan and Tadmor, *II Kings*, 240–41.
200. Cogan and Tadmor, *II Kings*, 241.
201. Cogan and Tadmor, *II Kings*, 241.
202. Cogan and Tadmor, *II Kings*, 241–44.
203. Cogan and Tadmor, *II Kings*, 243.
204. Cogan and Tadmor, *II Kings*, 243.
205. Parker, "Stories of Miraculous Deliverance," 105–30.
206. Parker, "Stories of Miraculous Deliverance," 113.
207. Parker, "Stories of Miraculous Deliverance," 113.

threat by the Assyrian Empire.[208] As Parker notes, account B represents a confrontation between the god of Israel and the king of Assyria.[209]

In the case of Isa 36–37, even though the text is similar to 2 Kgs 18–19, the passage reflects its own religious thought or ideology, which is that of "the Zion traditions."[210] Throughout the book of Isaiah, the Zion theology is prevalent.[211] Isa 37:32, for example, says, "For from Jerusalem a remnant shall go out, and from Mount Zion a band of survivors. The zeal of the LORD of hosts will do this." In this verse, Jerusalem is identified as Mount Zion, which itself represents the cosmic mountain at the center of the world.[212] In particular, J. J. M. Roberts argues that Assyria played a role as YHWH's agent for the divine judgment and salvation of Jerusalem in the book of Isaiah.[213] Sennacherib's military campaign against Hezekiah of Judah, then, is considered to represent a part of the overarching plan of God for salvation. Isa 37:33–38 describes the divine intervention that led to the departure of Sennacherib from Jerusalem. Roberts further argues that the miraculous deliverance of Jerusalem contributed to the motif of YHWH's defeat of the enemy at the gates of Jerusalem.[214] Charles K. Telfer argues that the Hezekiah-Narrative of Isa 36–39 is a selective and historical source, which is independent of 2 Kgs 18–20.[215] In other words, Isa 36–37 should be considered as having its own thoughts or ideology, distinct from 2 Kgs 18–19, even though these accounts have similar content.

Second Chronicles 32 offers a different account of Sennacherib's military campaign against Hezekiah, who is himself described in a positive way.[216] Regarding the reason for the military attack, it states that Sennacherib invaded Judah in order to subdue its fortified cities (2 Chr 32:1). Hezekiah prepared for the military conflict and even encouraged the people (2 Chr 32:2–8). The account, like 2 Kgs and Isa, is silent about the Padî affair. Also, unlike 2 Kgs 18, the Chronicler does not mention Hezekiah's

208. Parker, "Stories of Miraculous Deliverance," 118.

209. Parker, "Stories of Miraculous Deliverance," 118.

210. For the details of the Zion traditions, see Levenson, "Zion Traditions"; Roberts, "Davidic Origin."

211. Levenson, "Zion Traditions," 1099.

212. Blenkinsopp, *Isaiah 1–39*, 191.

213. Roberts, "Isaiah in Old Testament Theology," 140.

214. Roberts, "Davidic Origin of the Zion Tradition," 344.

215. Telfer, "Toward a Historical Reconstruction," 7–17.

216. Klein, *2 Chronicles*, 470.

submission or tribute. Instead, though the text mentions the Assyrian headquarters set up at Lachish (v. 9), it makes no reference to any Assyrian conquest, implying that Sennacherib gained nothing from his campaign and returned to his land (2 Chr 32:21).[217]

Second Chronicles 32 reflects the theological thought of the Chronicler—the assumed author. The intent of the Chronicler was to provide a lesson for the people of his time and situation through the description of the past (history).[218] The author considers history as the concrete expression of the interrelationship between God and Israel.[219] Therefore, the Chronicler does not describe the past in any objective sense but interprets the past from his own viewpoint of divine intervention.[220] Therefore, Chronicles includes a religious evaluation of the kings throughout the history of Israel.[221] Ralph W. Klein argues that Hezekiah is considered by the Chronicler as a good king in that he cleansed the temple (2 Chr 29:12–36), celebrated a Passover (2 Chr 30) and supported the Levites (2 Chr 32:12–19).[222]

Further Questions and Issues

One of the questions yet to be addressed is the "linguistic" and artistic connection between the royal lion hunting scenes, and the campaign tactics of the Neo-Assyrian kings. To answer this question, it is necessary to explore both hunting and military tactics. Do they have any common features? If so, what would be those features? The parallel question is how such features might relate to the similes?

Regarding the simile, "(shut up) like a caged bird / a bird in a cage," used to describe Sennacherib's siege of Hezekiah in his city, an important issue to address is the reason why the scribes used this expression to describe a military achievement. Since the simile is also used—indeed, the first attested usage in the Assyrian royal inscriptions—in connection with Ashurnasirpal II's royal lion hunting,[223] it raises a question about the interrelationship

217. For more discussions, see Kuan, "Hezekiah"; Kalimi, "Sennacherib's Campaign to Judah."

218. Myers, *II Chronicles*, xx.

219. Japhet, *I & II Chronicles*, 44.

220. Japhet, *I & II Chronicles*, 44.

221. Japhet, *I & II Chronicles*, 48–49.

222. Klein, *1 Chronicles*, 45.

223. Regarding the early use of nets to confine opponents and animals/fish, see Osten-Sacken, "Netz. B."

between the military and lion hunting inscriptions. As surveyed above, there have been only a few intertextual studies of the simile. Presumably because Sennacherib, like Tigalth-pileser III, Sargon II, and Esarhaddon, is not associated with hunting lions in the preserved annals, there have been few comments that explicitly connect the "caged bird" to the Assyrian royal hunting practices as represented in texts and reliefs.

Along with the intertextual studies on the simile, the intervisual studies on royal lion hunting and the military reliefs should be considered. The visual language describes the success of the lion hunt and the military sieges in their own ways. Therefore, a close look into them, especially as to the arrangement of the scenes in the royal palaces as opposed to the fragmented representation of the scenes in museum collections or volumes of isolated illustrations, is needed to understand the interrelationship between the hunt and the siege in the Assyrian understanding. Indeed, such reliefs were sometimes located close to or even directly adjacent to each other in the Assyrian palaces and on Ashurnasirpal II's Balawat Gates.[224]

The lion hunting image—more specifically a lion-killing image—is also shown on a Neo-Assyrian stamp-seal (Fig. 1.9),[225] which is considered a royal seal.[226] The seal shows the king killing a lion in direct combat. Lions were prominent enemies which "threatened the security of the realm."[227] The image of the king as a hunter killing a lion is intended to illustrate the rule of the king, based on his prowess and power to overcome the ferocious animal in hand to claw battle.[228]

224. Curtis and Tallis, *Balawat Gates of Ashurnasirpal II.*

225. Reade, "Ideology and Propaganda in Assyrian Art," 332.

226. For more details about the seals or the Assyrian royal seals, see Collon, *Near Eastern Seals*; Curtis and Reade, *Art and Empire*, 179–89; Strawn, *What Is Stronger than a Lion?*, 101–20.

227. Reade, "Ideology and Propaganda in Assyrian Art," 332.

228. Aruz et al., *Assyria to Iberia*, 59.

Fig. 1.9. A Neo-Assyrian Royal Seal, Kouyunjik. British Museum, BM 2276. (Photo: © The Trustees of the British Museum.)

The image of the king as a protector is related to Ashurbanipal's hunting reliefs with similar scenes as discussed above. The empire employed an image of the cultural practice of royal lion killing to express the political ideology of the Assyrian king as a powerful, courageous, and effective ruler.

Another question about the simile is its ideological aspect. Only a few scholars have studied its use in terms of ideological implications. Oded observes that defeat of the enemy may be compared with the hunting scenes.[229] Regarding the hunting, he points out that the gods assigned the animals to the king for hunting.[230] The hunting and the military campaign resemble each other in that they both show the triumph and superiority of the Assyrian king.[231] Note the example of a simile from Sargon II's account of his eighth campaign:[232] "like (an animal) fleeing from the hunter, he (the enemy) hid in the recesses of his mountain (*ki-i mun-nab-ti ṣa-a-a-di e-mid-da ša-ḫa-at šadî-šú*)."[233] Tadmor comments on the use of the simile in the military inscriptions of Tiglath-pileser III, but he does not pursue any

229. Oded, *War, Peace and Empire*, 149–50.

230. Oded, *War, Peace and Empire*, 149.

231. Oded, *War, Peace and Empire*, 150.

232. Oded, *War, Peace and Empire*, 150.

233. Mayer, *Assyrien und Urartu*, col. ii, 150, pp. 110–11.

details regarding the inscriptions.[234] As for Sennacherib's military campaign to Judah, Gallagher points out that the simile, "like a caged bird / a bird in a cage," occurred earlier in the Assyrian royal hunting inscriptions.[235] He argues that the simile describes "the utter hopelessness of the enemy."[236] Regarding the Assyrian "siege" fortresses (*bīrāti*), Mayer suggests that they represented no actual siege of Jerusalem with the fortresses.[237] Gallagher rejects this suggestion and argues that the fortresses were built against Jerusalem for the starvation of its inhabitants into submission.[238] Andreas Fuchs recently published a detailed analysis of Assyrian siege tactics.[239] He endorses the argument that Sennacherib was forced to lift the siege of Jerusalem, due to the outbreak of an epidemic among his solders.[240] He also argues that Sennacherib left a detachment in place to force the defenders of Jerusalem to surrender.[241] However, his suggestion is not supported by any convincing evidence from Sennacherib's inscriptions.

This study evaluates the Assyrian sources and the relevant biblical passages which describe Sennacherib's campaign, his siege or confinement of Hezekiah in Jerusalem, and the outcome of that engagement. Assyria appeared to attain its goals; the biblical texts cite the divine destruction of the Assyrian army and the departure of the Assyrian remnant. Each major party makes claims in keeping with their own perspectives.

Finally, there are important questions about the goals and the outcome of Sennacherib's military "siege" against Hezekiah. Was it successful for the Assyrians by their standards? Was Hezekiah successful by his standards? Was it a lose/lose, win/win, draw, or a win/lose? The parties involved presumably had different goals to achieve and different criteria for evaluation; it was not a sports contest with a declared winner and only one gold medal to be won.

Regarding the purpose and the result, there is another factor to consider: Esarhaddon and Ashurbanipal's campaigns in Egypt. After Sennacherib, both of them undertook successful military campaigns against Egypt

234. Tadmor, *Inscriptions of Tiglath-Pileser III*, 79.

235. Gallagher, *Sennacherib's Campaign to Judah*, 133.

236. Gallagher, *Sennacherib's Campaign to Judah*, 133.

237. Mayer, *Politik und Kriegskunst der Assyrer*, 360–61.

238. Gallagher, *Sennacherib's Campaign to Judah*, 134–35.

239. Fuchs, "Über den Wert von Befestigungsanlagen."

240. Fuchs, "Assyria at War," 391.

241. Fuchs, "Über den Wert von Befestigungsanlagen," 57; "Assyria at War," 391.

to subdue Memphis and even Luxor. The territory of the kingdom of Judah was along their route and their military campaigns make no mention of any resistance or interference from Judah or any other regional powers in southern Syria-Palestine. This situation contributes to the understanding of the purpose and result of Sennacherib's campaign against Judah. It is also worthwhile to note that there is no reason to dispute the Assyrian report of the recovery of Padî, the Assyrian vassal who had been ruling in Ekron, from his captivity in Jerusalem. The Assyrian and biblical accounts concur regarding the substantial tribute given by Hezekiah to Assyria. The tribute suggests that there was a submission of Judah to the empire. Subsequently, Judah plays no role in the Assyrian campaigns that proceeded through southern Palestine, on the way to Egypt.

Primarily based on intertextual and intervisual studies of the simile in its Assyrian context with a comparative analysis of the related biblical passages, this book evaluates the outcome of Sennacherib's military campaign and the differing perceptions of his confinement of Hezekiah behind the walls of Jerusalem. It also employs a sociolinguistic analysis of the Assyrian records and the biblical traditions. Hopefully, this approach will contribute to a better understanding and assessment of the outcome of the military campaign and the contrasting ideologies and perceptions reflected in Assyrian and biblical sources.

Chapter 2

THEORY AND METHODOLOGY

A Relational Theory of Form Criticism and Critical Discourse Analysis in Ancient Texts

As noted in the previous chapter, the simile in the literary expression, "shut up/confined like a caged bird / a bird in a cage" in Sennacherib's inscriptions regarding Hezekiah of Jerusalem, raises critical questions. One question related to the relationship between the descriptions of the Assyrian lion (and ostrich) hunting and military inscriptions, both of which make use of the same simile. Another question concerns how the linguistic forms of the metaphor can be related to nonverbal and pictorial images. This second question needs to be considered in terms of the general patterns of the Assyrian lion hunting and military campaign records. Furthermore, a related question to consider is the comparison between Sennacherib's record and the related biblical passages as those two sources apparently offer contrasting ideological descriptions of the outcome of Sennacherib's siege of Jerusalem.

In order to respond to these questions, the present study employs Critical Discourse Analysis (CDA) to analyze the ancient texts and related (Assyrian) reliefs. CDA is one of the approaches that the discipline of sociolinguistics has developed for the analysis of the variation of the linguistic forms in certain social settings. Norman Fairclough has developed CDA with special reference to modern English society. In contrast to the theoretical sociological approach, CDA is more practical.[1] CDA sets its focus on language forms and analyzes the social processes of how language contains social thoughts or ideas, which is ideology.[2]

Since Critical Discourse Analysis has been mainly applied in reference to modern English society, one may question its application to the ancient Assyrian texts and biblical texts. In developing CDA, Fairclough includes oral language and pictorial language such as images and photos, as well as written language. However, he does not discuss its applicability to an ancient society. Instead, his focus is on modern society. Therefore, it is necessary to consider first its applicability to the ancient society that has limited amounts of written texts and pictorial images without any spoken language preserved.

The essential argument of CDA is that linguistic forms and social contexts are interrelated and this relationship is a general feature of human society at any time or place. Even though the theory has been proposed and developed in England during the late twentieth century, its theoretical aspect reflects the interrelationship between language and society in general. If a human society has a language, one can agree that mutual influence between language and society exists in that society. In other words, CDA can be applied even to an ancient language and society, albeit with some limitations.

In such an interrelationship, CDA sets its focus on two themes: the ideology embedded in the language and the power relations between the social groups (a dominant group and a dominated group). The application of CDA to the text would begin with an analysis on a certain linguistic form amidst its own historical and social setting. The analysis would explain what kind of social thought or ideology can be found embedded in the linguistic form.

In the case of an ancient text, such as the Assyrian inscriptions and reliefs, and biblical texts, it would provide a "thick description"[3] to an ideological aspect of certain linguistic forms in its cultural context. This would be one of the possible contributions of CDA to the study of ancient texts. As mentioned above, the oral speech of ancient language is not a well-known entity and is not accessible for CDA. Nevertheless, CDA

1. Fairclough, *Language and Power*, 12–13.

2. Fairclough, *Language and Power*, 1–5.

3. Geertz, *Interpretation of Cultures*, 3–30.

should be able to clarify the ideological concept of a linguistic form used in the ancient texts.

Before examining CDA in greater depth, this chapter explores the disciplines which deal with the interrelationship between language and society, based on a relational theory: form criticism in biblical studies and sociolinguistics. These disciplines have studied different subjects but maintained common theoretical interests regarding language and society. Therefore, interdisciplinary studies on them might provide a theoretical basis for the applicability of CDA to the ancient Near Eastern texts in their respective social contexts.

Relational Theory of Form Criticism

The interrelationship between language and society is not a recently developed topic in biblical studies. Form criticism has been interested in the interrelationship and it has developed a relational perspective which can also be found in other disciplines, including sociolinguistics.

Traditional Form Criticism

After the Documentary Hypothesis regarding the formation of the Pentateuch had been comprehensively summarized by Julius Wellhausen, Hermann Gunkel introduced the discipline of form criticism, which connects a literary form to its traditio-historical context (*Sitz im Leben*).[4] Gunkel was interested in the history of Hebrew literature along with the history of tradition and he argued that a literary type originally belonged to its own distinct "setting in the life."[5] His approach was called "type criticism" and later, "form criticism."[6] In his analysis of the literary type or form, genre was considered as a critical issue.

Form criticism, as developed by Gunkel, has two main tasks.[7] The first task is the isolation of the original individual literary units. Through such isolation, Gunkel tried to trace an earlier stage of the literary units. The second one is the reconstruction of the earlier stages in the history

4. Gunkel, *Genesis*, 3–7.

5. Gunkel, *Genesis*, 7.

6. Gunkel, *Genesis*, 7.

7. Gunkel, *Genesis*, 7.

and the growth of the literature itself, seeking to identify a life situation that would be suitable for such a literary form. In this way, form criticism aims at the elucidation of the interrelatedness between the literary form and its traditio-historical context.

Gunkel applied form criticism especially to Genesis and Psalms. He analyzed each collection and sought to isolate the original individual literary units for specific classified genres. Along with this classification, he reconstructed the traditio-historical context for the use of each literary genre.

In his analysis of the book of Genesis and the book of Psalms, his arguments need to be considered from a critical viewpoint. First, he differentiates legends from history, arguing that legends are based on oral traditions while historiography is based on objective observance.[8] In other words, objectivity would be a critical boundary between legends and historiography. Furthermore, his argument implies that oral traditions would not be objective compared to the written tradition.

However, the objectivity of historiography has been disputed even in the field of historical studies. Writing history reflects a specific viewpoint of a historian or the historian's paymaster. In other words, the subjectivity of the viewpoint influences the historiography, while the objectivity of the historiography cannot be taken for granted.

Second, Gunkel presupposes an evolutionary idea about the history of literary works and the history of religion, following Wellhausen and others. He argues that old accounts are thoroughly "crude."[9] In his argument, he seems to presuppose that the stages of the formation of the text reflect not only transformation or change but also development from being crude to being sophisticated. Considering his use of the term "crude," he also seems to assume that the literary quality or value of the ancient oral tradition is expected to be lesser than that of the recent written documents.

Regarding the history of the Psalms, Gunkel argues that the oldest genre was "simple" and "pure."[10] Here questions arise regarding his concept of linear development. Does genre always proceed from being simple and pure to being mixed? What is the concept of the "pure" and "simple?" Is it not possible to consider that old genres might have included a "mixture of genres"[11] such as, later genres have in his view?

8. Gunkel, *Genesis*, vii–viii.

9. Gunkel, *Genesis*, lxiii.

10. Gunkel, *Introduction to Psalms*, 19.

11. Gunkel, *Introduction to Psalms*, 19.

Third, Gunkel argues for the classification or delineation of genres with clear boundaries. Regarding the book of Genesis, he argues that the book consists of primal legends, which are about God, and patriarchal legends, which are about humans or Israel.[12] The legends of Genesis developed from earlier existing traditions and myths. The form of the accounts is described as rhythmic prose.[13] In his *Introduction to Psalms*, he argues for the necessity to classify genres for the individual literary units of psalms.[14] Together with genre identification, he also asserts that literary work is rooted in its own context.[15]

However, Gunkel's classification of the genres in their own contexts has been under scholarly dispute and reevaluation. Even though Gunkel argued for the development of genres from "simple" and "pure" to "mixed" form,[16] the classification and development has not yet been settled clearly in the field of literature.[17] Furthermore, there is another problem in that the contexts of the literary genres are hypothetical. They are reconstructed or guessed at, and they still need additional evidence for proof. Consequently, the reconstruction of the historical process or development of the genre based only on form is not convincing.

Regardless of these issues related to Gunkel's theory, his understanding of the interrelatedness between literary forms and their own traditio-historical or social contexts is an important insight for the historical study of the ancient texts. Although it is apparent that the world in a text is different from what the world outside the text really is, historical assessment of the ancient world would depend on written texts and archaeological artifacts. In this sense, Gunkel's form criticism can contribute to the historical study on the ancient Near East, including ancient Israel, through the analysis of the ancient texts.

Following in Gunkel's wake, scholars have reevaluated his form criticism. Rolf Knierim is one of the prominent later critics of Gunkel. He argues that traditional form criticism is not a determinative factor for the history of the Old Testament literature and language but a heuristic tool for insight

12. Gunkel, *Genesis*, 13–14.

13. Gunkel, *Genesis*, 24.

14. Gunkel, *Introduction to Psalms*, 5–6.

15. Gunkel, *Introduction to Psalms*, 19.

16. Gunkel, *Introduction to Psalms*, 19–20.

17. Dowd, "Genre Matters in Theory and Criticism," 11–27.

into the reconstructed historical or social context of the text.[18] According to him, it is necessary to reconsider or even reshape form criticism through a flexible concept of genre.[19] Traditional form criticism has exposed problems in its supposition that a given genre is somehow fixed and that it is a determinative proof for the history of the Old Testament literature and language. In opposition to this proposition, Knierim argues that genre is not fixed but is flexible.[20] Mixed genres can be found in a biblical text.[21] Therefore, form criticism needs to adopt a flexible concept of genre in its approach toward the text. With a flexible application, it would function as a heuristic tool for the history of biblical literature and language.

Knierim also criticizes the understanding of traditional form criticism that "the relationship between a genre's structure and its content, mood, function, intention, or concern solely depends on the historical context."[22] The relationship is not fixed but flexible so that it cannot function as a clear window to its historical background. In the reconsideration regarding this problem, he first argues that the written text should be distinguished from its theoretical oral base and that form criticism should focus on the written text.[23] Since the written text has its own literary features independent of its oral base, it is not necessary for form criticism to consider the oral base.[24] Second, he argues that form criticism should consider both the typicality and the individuality of the text.[25] The written text has both general and individual features within it. Therefore, it is necessary to consider both of those features in the reshaped form criticism.

Knierim's argument for the flexible application of traditional form criticism to biblical texts is remarkable in that it relates the theoretical relationship of this criticism to other social scientific theories such as sociolinguistics.[26] In form criticism, typicality of literary expression or structure contributes to the understanding of the interrelatedness between a text and its supposed historical social context. As a part of culture, a text would

18. Knierim, "Old Testament Form Criticism Reconsidered."
19. Knierim, "Old Testament Form Criticism Reconsidered," 467–68.
20. Knierim, "Old Testament Form Criticism Reconsidered," 436.
21. Knierim, "Old Testament Form Criticism Reconsidered," 440.
22. Knierim, "Old Testament Form Criticism Reconsidered," 449.
23. Knierim, "Old Testament Form Criticism Reconsidered," 456–58.
24. Cf. Niditch, "Oral Tradition and Biblical Scholarship," 43–44.
25. Knierim, "Old Testament Form Criticism Reconsidered," 458.
26. Knierim, "Old Testament Form Criticism Reconsidered," 435.

reflect its context and the reflection would include social thoughts or aspects. Knierim's biblical form criticism is still a theoretical model like that of Gunkel but the idea about the interrelationship between text and history or society provides a link to other disciplines.

Along with Knierim, Marvin Sweeney and Ehud Ben-Zvi also argue that form criticism has adopted the concept of fluidity throughout its own history of scholarship.[27] One of the notable features of the reshaped form criticism is its understanding of the inherent fluidity of genres. Based on the unpredictable or flexible feature of genre or form, various disciplines, including structural anthropology and a literary approach, have been considered as a part of the form critical methodology.

The concept of fluidity in form criticism extends its range of application not only to the biblical text but also to other texts. The traditional form criticism of Gunkel has a fixed concept of genre with a focus on the biblical text. However, the relationship between the language (literature) and culture (society) is a general theme for the academic disciplines which deal with language and culture. With the fluidity of genres and the flexible application of the formal approach, it would be possible to analyze the relationship between text and society or culture, without being limited by a certain time or place.

Relational Form Criticism

Among biblical form critical scholars, Martin Buss has adopted a relational perspective which addresses the fluidity of relations.[28] The relational theory has developed in the twentieth century in Europe and the United States and it has maintained a common pattern in various academic disciplines.[29] The overall theme of the relational theory is that everything is interrelated with each other and the relations constitute a structure, which, in other words, can be understood as a form. Greek philosophers first raised thoughts about the relations. Afterwards, a recent relational theory argues that the relations between entities are not rigid but flexible and variant. Therefore, the structure of the relations is also flexible. Relations consider both the general pattern of relations between entities and the particular features of relations according to a specific context.

27. Sweeney and Ben-Zvi, *Changing Face of Form Criticism*, 1–11.

28. Buss, *Changing Shape of Form Criticism*, 1–142.

29. Buss, *Changing Shape of Form Criticism*, 221.

Based on the relational theory, Buss proposes reshaping traditional biblical form criticism for its further contributions in biblical studies.[30] He criticizes traditional form criticism as represented by Gunkel for its rigid definition of genres and the restricted relationship between a genre of oral speech and a specific situation (*Sitz im Leben*).[31] According to him, the relations between content, linguistic form, and context are not fixed or independent.[32] Instead of relating a specific genre or form to a particular context, Buss tries to describe how the general pattern of relations is presented in a particular context.[33] Genres are not limited to a certain historical context but can be used in various situations throughout history. A more important matter to consider is how it is related to its context. In that sense, the relational form criticism of Buss is a reshaped or reevaluated form criticism with a concept of flexible and variable relations.

The concept of flexible relationship between language and its context in relational form criticism is applicable not only to biblical texts but also to other ancient texts, including Assyrian inscriptions. In such a reshaped form criticism, the main insight is the flexible interrelatedness between language and culture or society. The relations could vary according to time and place, both of which constitute a particular context of language. However, the relations exist between the individual persons engaging the text at any time and any place. In other words, the interrelationship between language and its context is a transcendental general feature in human language and its cultural context which includes society or community. This is a basic assumption of the relational theory, and it makes it necessary to find the interrelatedness between the language and the society of ancient times. As for the Assyrian texts such as annals, they were written, transmitted, and revised by royal scribes in their own contexts. Therefore, the concept of flexible relationship between language and its context can be considered even in the studies on the Assyrian texts.

It is notable that Buss also argues for the existence of a common theoretical framework in the social science disciplines including anthropology, sociology, and sociolinguistics.[34]

30. Buss, *Changing Shape of Form Criticism*, 97–113.

31. Buss, *Changing Shape of Form Criticism*, 101–3.

32. Buss, *Changing Shape of Form Criticism*, 104.

33. Buss, *Changing Shape of Form Criticism*, 104–7.

34. Buss, *Changing Shape of Form Criticism*, 221–77.

Relational Theory of Critical Discourse Analysis

Norman Fairclough, a British social linguist, argues that ideology is naturalized and embedded within language in its social context of power relations.[35] In his view, the dominant class tries to maintain their power over the dominated class through their dominant ideology in social struggles for power and unequal power relations in society. He argues that the ideology is most effective when its workings are least visible.[36] For this invisibility, ideology is usually connected to "common sense," which is a naturalized assumption implied in discourse.[37] With the connection to common sense, the ideology of the dominant class is naturalized within discourse. When people use discourse without any consciousness of the naturalized ideologies, their discourse contributes to the maintenance of power relations in the society.[38]

Critical Discourse Analysis (CDA)

The relational theory contributes to the understanding and application of the relational concept of Critical Discourse Analysis to ancient languages, societies, and cultures. According to the relational theory regarding language and society, language reflects its social context. CDA also presumes that a language reflects social thought, especially, dominant social thought, which represents dominant ideologies, in a specific social context. This interrelationship among language, society, power, and ideology can be found in any type of society. Therefore, CDA is applicable to even an ancient society.

What is CDA?

Fairclough defines Critical Discourse Analysis (CDA) in three dimensions: (1) "a transdisciplinary analysis of relations between discourse and other elements of the social process"; (2) "some form of systematic analysis of texts"; and (3) a "normative" analysis to address "social wrongs in their discursive

35. Fairclough, *Language and Power*, 77–108.
36. Fairclough, *Language and Power*, 85.
37. Fairclough, *Language and Power*, 84.
38. Fairclough, *Language and Power*, 84.

aspects and possible ways of righting or mitigating them."[39] In the analysis of discourse, the aim of CDA is to clarify the ideological role of language in maintaining and changing power relations, based on the relational theory of language and society. In other words, it intends "to incorporate social-theoretical insights into discourse analysis."[40] Jan Blommaert and Chris Bulcaen describe CDA as "a recent school of discourse analysis that concerns relations of power and inequality in language."[41]

The basic assumption of CDA is "the social commitment and interventionism of language,"[42] and it needs to be explicated in two dimensions. First, it assumes that society is based on power relations and a class system. Second, CDA presupposes that discourse should be considered as a social process.[43] Discourse can be defined as a form of social language practice.[44] The production and the reproduction of a text is a reflection of social power relations and social ideology. Social power relations are asymmetrical. They represent a distinction or differentiation between the dominating class and the dominated class based on the acquisition of power. Ideology, as a set of beliefs or a worldview, is necessary for the maintenance of power by the dominating class. Discourse is important for the distribution of ideology to maintain power relations.

Fairclough pays a particular attention to "common-sense" or naturalized assumptions in discourse.[45] According to him, the ideology of the dominant class is naturalized as "common-sense" within discourse. In other words, the ideology is hidden and not clearly visible in the discourse. When people use language in their society, they are affected by the ideology without having any clear consciousness of that process. They even accept the hidden ideology through their language use in the society. In this way, the ideology of the dominant bloc will be distributed, maintained, and even reinforced in society.

39. Fairclough, *Critical Discourse Analysis*, 10–11.
40. Blommaert and Bulcaen, "Critical Discourse Analysis," 447.
41. Blommaert and Bulcaen, "Critical Discourse Analysis," 447.
42. Blommaert and Bulcaen, "Critical Discourse Analysis," 447.
43. Fairclough, *Language and Power*, 22–27.
44. Fairclough, *Language and Power*, 29.
45. Fairclough, *Language and Power*, 77–108.

Applicability of CDA to Ancient Texts and Society

In the application of CDA for the explication of any hidden ideology and unequal power relations, its notable methodological feature is that it considers diverse modes of language: spoken language (speech), written language (text), and even pictorial language (image) within their own social contexts.[46] Even though there are some cautions against the consideration of visual images due to a more text-based analysis among scholars,[47] Fairclough suggests that CDA should include the visual language as well as spoken language and written language.[48] Like the two other types of language, visual language also functions as a conveyor of a certain ideology to its audience. One, two, or even all of them can be used in one discourse. When used together in one discourse, they tend to be complementary to each other "in a mutually reinforcing way."[49]

The main interest of CDA is ideology and unequal power relations in discourse and these can be found in human language and culture, in general. In its application, Fairclough sets his focus on the relations between the language and the power relations in the context of England in the late twentieth century. However, the relationship between language and society, or even culture, is not limited only to modern society. Rather, the relationship can also be found in ancient societies.

In particular, the issues regarding the ideology and the power relations can be easily found in texts or discourse in ancient Near Eastern societies such as the Neo-Assyrian Empire and ancient Israel. The animal similes in the Assyrian inscriptions would be good examples for the application of CDA. They were often used to describe the king, his army, or enemies in the Assyrian annals that describe the Assyrian military campaigns.[50] Similes used for Assyrian kings or the army represent powerful and overwhelming aspects while similes used for their enemies represent powerless and helpless aspects.[51] For example, Esarhaddon conquered the city Arzā and bound Asuḫīli, the king of the city, like a pig (*kīma šaḫī*

46. Blommaert and Bulcaen, "Critical Discourse Analysis," 450.
47. Blommaert and Bulcaen, "Critical Discourse Analysis," 450.
48. Fairclough, *Language and Power*, 27–28.
49. Fairclough, *Language and Power*, 28.
50. Marcus, "Animal Similes in Assyrian Royal Inscriptions," 86.
51. Marcus, "Animal Similes in Assyrian Royal Inscriptions," 86–106.

arkušu).[52] This simile with action of binding symbolizes the controlling power of the Assyrian king and the controlled and even shamed aspect of the enemy king. For another example, Esarhaddon marched over difficult (steep) mountains like a wild bull (*šadê marṣūti rēmāniš aštamdiḫ*) advancing against Kush and Egypt.[53] The simile symbolizes the might and the great strength of the king over against his enemies.[54]

In this study, the focus of the analysis is on the simile, "(shut up/enclosed) like a caged bird / a bird in a cage," used in Sennacherib's description of his "siege" of Hezekiah, king of Judah, during his campaign in 701 BCE. The inscriptions about this campaign and the associated reliefs, viz., the reliefs portraying the siege and capture of Lachish, were written, edited, or produced under the patronage of the dominant class of the Assyrian Empire. Therefore, the events were described from the viewpoint or ideology of the Assyrian ruling class, more specifically, the royal court. Therefore, the analysis of the inscriptions and the pictorial reliefs will explicate the imperial ideology regarding the power relations between the empire and the kingdom of Judah in the cultural, and socio-historical context of the Neo-Assyrian Empire ca. 701 BCE.

Along with the Assyrian sources, this study also explores related biblical texts which describe Sennacherib's campaign, including the "siege" of Jerusalem. Since these texts also describe divine acts or intervention by an angel in the event (2 Kgs 19:35; 2 Chr 32:21; Isa 37:36), a question can be raised about its status as a historical source. However, it seems that biblical sources still have some detailed—though not at all complete—historical comments which are compatible with the sources from the Neo-Assyrian Empire. First, both the Assyrian sources and the biblical sources concur regarding the successful siege and capture of Lachish and a "siege" of Jerusalem. Second, both describe that the kingdom of Judah paid a significant tribute to the Assyrian king.

It should be noted that the Assyrian sources and the biblical sources present contrasting viewpoints toward the character and effectiveness of the "siege," and that each side reports some significant success. The precise authorship of the biblical texts, which reflect more than one tradition, is not yet clear but the authors or editors doubtlessly held a high social rank as scribes in ancient Israel. As in the Assyrian records, the

52. *RINAP 4* No. 32, Rev. 1 (p. 78).

53. *RINAP 4*, No. 34, Obv. 11' (p. 87).

54. Marcus, "Animal Similes in Assyrian Royal Inscriptions," 87.

scribes of the biblical texts, including 2 Kings, 2 Chronicles, and Isaiah present their own theological and political perceptions in their accounts of Sennacherib's campaign.

However, there are also some limitations in applying CDA to ancient discourse. First, CDA particularly includes spoken language in the analysis, but the ancient discourse has only written and pictorial languages for analysis. In the case of the inscriptions and the reliefs of the Assyrian Empire, they provide a limited number of their speech forms. Related biblical discourse provides written language with a limited number of reports of spoken language.

Second, the ancient texts have a certain limitation for using CDA, due to the lack of evidence regarding the authorship and the date of composition. The Assyrian inscriptions and reliefs have more specific dates, close to the time of the events. Meanwhile, the biblical text presents difficulties, as mentioned, in that the traditions have been written, rewritten, edited, and collected by multiple authors, editors, or even groups. Consequently, it will be difficult for CDA to uncover any precise social context of the biblical text and impossible to fully describe how the unequal power relations of the Neo-Assyrian Empire were maintained and understood in the kingdom of Judah.

Third, there is a limited range of discourse available for CDA regarding the status of literacy, a crucial factor for the conveyance of the ideology and the maintenance of the power relations through written language. The literacy level of the ancient societies such as the Neo-Assyrian Empire and the kingdom of Judah was quite limited, but estimates differ as to just how limited literacy was. Reliefs are also limited in that access to the palaces where they were displayed was rather restricted. Nonetheless, CDA will be able to contribute to the understanding of political ideologies and unequal power relations between Sennacherib of the Neo-Assyrian Empire and Hezekiah of the kingdom of Judah.

Regardless of these limitations, CDA can contribute to the understanding of political ideologies and unequal power relations between Sennacherib of the Neo-Assyrian Empire and Hezekiah of the kingdom of Judah based upon both written and visual languages. Only a few scholars, such as William Schniedewind and Frank Polak, have engaged in the application of sociolinguistic approaches to the related ancient texts.[55] This study focuses on CDA to show that it is useful in the understanding and

55. Schniedewind, "Prolegomena for the Sociolinguistics"; Polak, "Sociolinguistics."

explication of ideologies of the unequal power relations based upon both written and visual languages.

Along with the ideologies of the Assyrian Empire and Judah, CDA also can reveal ideological aspects of the scholarship regarding the outcome of Sennacherib's siege against Hezekiah of Jerusalem. Since the "siege" did not include the conquest or destruction of the city, there have been various discussions about its successfulness. What would be a successful outcome of the military campaign? In other words, what would be the ultimate goal(s) of the Assyrian military campaigns? Was a conquest the only goal? Or, did the goal(s) include not only conquest but also control?

From a sociolinguistic perspective, these questions can also be related to a question of the ideological stances of the scholars who have interpreted the outcome(s) of Sennacherib's campaign against Hezekiah based upon the Assyrian or the biblical resources. In the studies on Sennacherib's campaign against Jerusalem, scholars have referred to various resources. They have also interpreted the outcome of the military campaign in various ways. Their interpretations are related to their perspectives on the resources about the campaign. A sociolinguistic approach or perspective related to their arguments can reveal their own ideological stances or assumptions in their perceptions of the result(s) of the military conflict.

Chapter 3

ASSYRIAN ROYAL LION HUNTING

The records of the Assyrian royal lion hunt are found in texts and reliefs of various kings throughout the period of the Assyrian Empire. According to the records, the kings confronted the ferocious beasts during their hunt in the fields or arenas. The records describe the kings as brave and powerful hunters who hunted down and killed the wild animals, sometimes in public.

This chapter focuses on the records of the Assyrian royal lion hunt to analyze the general patterns and concepts of the hunt. Lion hunting records are found mainly in texts and reliefs of Ashurnasirpal II (885–860 BCE) and Ashurbanipal (668–631 BCE). None of the related texts, epigraphs, or reliefs fully describes the whole process and all aspects of the strategy. Therefore, it is necessary to extensively explore related materials to gather the general features.

Based on the general patterns and concepts of the royal lion hunt, this chapter probes the political ideology embedded in the pertinent texts, epigraphs, and reliefs, using Critical Discourse Analysis (CDA). Lion hunting was considered a sport of kings and good training for the fields of battle.[1] It also seemed to include a ceremonial ritual to symbolically

1. Parrot, *Arts of Assyria*, 54.

present the royal prowess of the Assyrian kings to various audiences.[2] Watanabe emphasizes this ritual aspect of the royal lion hunt.[3] She argues that there is an association between the lion hunt and the myths and rites of Ninurta.[4] According to her, the lion hunt "establishes and reinforces the Assyrian kingship in the same manner as Ninurta achieves his divine kingship by slaying monsters."[5] In other words, the lion hunt can be understood as a form of political propaganda. A sociolinguistic approach of Critical Discourse Analysis explores a political aspect of the hunt in greater detail. Furthermore, this approach considers both written and visual languages as conveyors of ideology to the multiple audiences. Therefore, it can explicate that the records about the hunts tend to imply or even boldly represent the royal ideology of the Assyrian kings.

The Written and Visual Language of the Royal Lion Hunting Inscriptions and Reliefs

Assyrian royal lion hunting records are found in the inscriptions of various kings. The first example is from the inscriptions of Tiglath-pileser I (1114–1076 BCE).[6] His hunting record follows the account of his military campaigns.[7] According to the record, he successfully hunted 120 lions on foot by the command of the god, Ninurta, who loved him (*i-na si-qir* ^{d}*nin-urta ra-'i-mi-ia* 2 *šu-ši nēšī i-na lìb-bi-ia ek-di i-na qit-ru-ub mi-it-lu-ti-ia i-na šēpī lu a-duk*).[8] In addition, he killed another eight hundred lions from his light chariot (*ù* 8 *me'ati nēšī i-na narkabti-ia i-na pat-tu-te ú-šem-qít*).[9] It is notable that his hunting included every kind of "winged bird of the heavens (*iṣṣūr šamê mut-tap-ri-ša*)."[10]

In the inscriptions of Aššur-bēl-kala (1073–1056 BCE), his hunting record follows his military campaigns.[11] In the hunt, he hunted three

2. Reade, "Religious Ritual in Assyrian Sculpture," 22–25.
3. Watanabe, *Animal Symbolism in Mesopotamia*, 77–78.
4. Watanabe, *Animal Symbolism in Mesopotamia*, 79.
5. Watanabe, *Animal Symbolism in Mesopotamia*, 82.
6. *RIMA* 2, A.0.87.1, vi.76–84 (p. 26).
7. *RIMA* 2, i.62–vi.54 (pp. 14–25).
8. *RIMA* 2, vi.76–79 (p. 26).
9. *RIMA* 2, vi.80–81 (p. 26).
10. *RIMA* 2, vi.82–83 (p. 26).
11. *RIMA* 2, A.0.89.2, i.1'–iii.28' (p. 93).

hundred lions (iii.30') as well as the winged birds of the heavens (*iṣṣūrī šamê mut-tap-r[i-ša]*).[12] Another reference to the lion hunt[13] also accompanies his military campaign record.[14] According to the record, he killed 120 lions in his wild heart in his vigorous assault from his chariot and, on foot, with a spear (2 *šu-ši nēšī ina lì b-bi-šu ek-di ina qi-it-ru-ub me-eṭ-lu-ti-šu ina narkabti-šu pa-at-tu-te ina šepī-šu ina* ^iṣu^*pa-aš-ḫi i-duk*),[15] and an unknown number of lions with the mace (*nēšī ina* ^iṣu^*nàr-ʾa-am-te ú-šam-qit*).[16] In addition to his lion hunting record, this record describes his various hunting activities and his collection of animals.[17]

In the inscriptions of Aššur-dān II (934–912 BCE), the hunting record of the Assyrian king[18] follows his military campaign record.[19] According to the record, the gods Ninurta and Nergal commanded the Assyrian king to hunt ([*epēš bu-"u-r*]*i iq-bu-ni-ma*, 69a). He killed 120 lions from his chariot and on his swift feet (2 š*u-ši nēšī i-na qé-reb* [. . . *i*]*-na narkabti-ia pa-tu-te i-na šepī-ia la-sa-ma-t*[*e*] [*ina pašḫi*] *a-duk*).[20] He also hunted 1,200 wild bulls, captured 2 wild bulls, and killed 56 elephants.[21]

The hunting record of Adad-nārāri II (911–891 BCE)[22] follows his military campaign record[23] and one report of palace construction.[24] The gods, Ninurta and Nergal, commanded the Assyrian king to hunt (*e-peš ba-ʾa-ri iq-bu-ni*).[25] In the hunt, he killed 360 lions from a chariot with his valorous assault and on his swift feet with a spear (6 š*u-ši nēšī ina narkabti-ia pa-at-tu-te ina* [*qí*]*-it-ru-ub me-eṭ-lu-ti-ia ina šepī-ia* [*la*]*-as-ma-te ina* [*pa-aš* (?)]*-ḫi a-duk*).[26] The hunting included the killing of 240 wild bulls,

12. *RIMA* 2, iii.34 (p. 93).
13. *RIMA* 2, A.0.89.7, iv.9b–12a (p. 103).
14. *RIMA* 2, i.1–iii.32 (p. 103).
15. *RIMA* 2, iv.9b–11a (p. 103).
16. *RIMA* 2, iv.11b–12a (p. 103).
17. *RIMA* 2, iv.1–34a (pp. 103–4).
18. *RIMA* 2, A.0.98.1, 68–72 (p. 135).
19. *RIMA* 2, 1–67 (pp. 132–35).
20. *RIMA* 2, 69b–71a (p. 135).
21. *RIMA* 2, 71b–72 (p. 135).
22. *RIMA* 2, A.0.99.2, 122–127 (p. 154).
23. *RIMA* 2, 39–119 (pp. 149–54).
24. *RIMA* 2, 120–121 (p. 154).
25. *RIMA* 2, 122b (p. 154).
26. *RIMA* 2, 123–124a (p. 154).

the capture of nine strong wild virile bulls with horns, the killing of six elephants, and the capture of four elephants.[27] In particular, he "captured five (elephants) with a snare/trap (5 *ina kip-pi aṣ-bat*)."[28] The word *kippu* implies a sense of "circumference" or "enclosure," and it shows that one of the hunting strategies was to enclose the hunting objects.

Regarding the lion hunting inscriptions of Aššur-dān II and Adad-nārāri II, Watanabe relates the lion hunt to the rite of Ninurta.[29] She sets her focus on the word *lasmu/lasmātu* or *lassamātu*, "swift," which is used to explain *ina šēpī*, "on foot."[30] She points out that this expression is related to a rite of Ninurta.[31] This association connects the victorious image of Ninurta over monsters with the triumphant image of the kings over their hunted objects—lions.[32] Her comments on the relationship between the royal lion hunt and the rite of Ninurta emphasize the ritualistic and ideological aspect of the royal lion hunting.

In the case of the Tukulti-ninurta II (890–884 BCE), the hunting record[33] follows the record of military campaigns and the construction of palaces.[34] The gods Ninurta and Nergal commanded the Assyrian king to hunt (*e-peš ba-'u-ri*[35] *iq-bu-ni*).[36] In the hunt, "I (He) killed sixty (?) strong [lions] from my chariot with my wildly vigorous assault with the spear" (60[?] x x *dan-nu-ti ina narkabti-ia pa-at-tu-ti ina libbi-a ek-di ina qìt-ru-ub me-eṭ-lu-ti-ia ina* ^iṣu^*pa-áš-ḫi* [*a(d)dāk*^ak^]).[37]

The inscriptions of Shalmaneser III (858–824 BCE) also describe the king's royal hunt.[38] According to the record, the gods Ninurta and Nergal commanded the Assyrian king to hunt (*e-peš ba-'u-ri iq-bu-ni*).[39] Shalmaneser III killed the wild beasts including 373 wild bulls and 399 lions from his

27. *RIMA* 2, 124b–126a (p. 154).
28. *RIMA* 2, 126b (p. 154).
29. Watanabe, *Animal Symbolism in Mesopotamia*, 78.
30. Watanabe, *Animal Symbolism in Mesopotamia*, 80.
31. Watanabe, *Animal Symbolism in Mesopotamia*, 81.
32. Watanabe, *Animal Symbolism in Mesopotamia*, 81–82.
33. *RIMA* 2, A.0.100.5, 134–35 (p. 178).
34. *RIMA* 2, 9–133 (pp. 171–78).
35. *Bâru* means "to catch or trap (with a net), to hunt."
36. *RIMA* 2, 134 (p. 178).
37. *RIMA* 2, 134b–35 (p. 178).
38. *RIMA* 3, A.0.102.6, iv.40–44a (p. 41).
39. *RIMA* 3, iv.41–42a (p. 41).

. . . chariot with his valorous assault during the hunt (3 *me'āt* 73 *rīmī* 3 *me'āt* 99 *nēšī ina narkabtī-ia pa-tu-te ina qi-it-ru-ub meṭ-lu-ti-ia a-duk*).[40]

Strawn comments that these hunting inscriptions show a high degree of similarity.[41] This similarity shows that they have certain formulae to follow.[42] One of the notable formulae is the connection between the gods (Ninurta and Nergal) and the hunt.

In the case of the lion hunting records of Ashurnasirpal II and Ashurbanipal, they include visual records of hunting. There are no associated reliefs that show lion hunting by the kings other than Ashurnasirpal II and Ashurbanipal. Meanwhile, there are relatively abundant resources, including textual and visual records, for lion hunting by Ashurnasirpal II (883–859 BCE) and Ashurbanipal (668–631 BCE).

Ashurnasirpal II (885–860 BCE)

Inscriptions

The royal lion hunting by Ashurnasirpal II is recorded in the inscriptions inscribed on numerous colossal bulls and lions from Calah. This text mainly describes the king's military expedition to the Mediterranean coast.[43] Beginning with lengthy royal titles, it records the king's successful military campaigns and the tribute received.[44] After the report of the tribute from the campaigns, the text records his hunting expedition.[45] In his hunt, "With my outstretched hand and my fierce heart, I captured 15 strong lions from the mountains and forests (*ina ti-ri-ṣi qāti-ia ú šu-uš-mur libbi-ia 15 nēšī dannūti ištu šadê ù qišāti ina qāte^te aṣbat^bat*)."[46] During the course of this hunt, the king captured fifty lion-cubs and brought them into Calah and the palaces of his land, having put them "into cages (literally, 'into place of confinement [*ina bīt e-sir*]')," (50 *mu-ra-ni nēšī lu aš-šá-a ina ^ālukal-ḫi ù ēkallāt māti-ia ina bīt e-sir lu ad-di-šú-nu*).[47] The lion

40. *RIMA* 3, iv.42b–44a (p. 41).
41. Strawn, *What Is Stronger Than a Lion?*, 164.
42. Strawn, *What Is Stronger Than a Lion?*, 164.
43. *RIMA* 2, p. 223.
44. *RIMA* 2, A.0.101.2, 1–33a (pp. 224–26).
45. *RIMA* 2, 33b–38a (p. 226).
46. *RIMA* 2, 32b–33a (p. 226).
47. *RIMA* 2, 33b–35a (p. 226).

cubs, which could be potentially threatening animals, were now under control (or, literally, "enclosed or confined [*esēru*] in cages"). He also seized various kinds of wild animals such as fully grown lions, wild oxen, elephants, wild asses and gazelles.[48] He brought them to Calah and let "all the people of the land" behold the wild animals that he seized alive.[49] He gave a warning to future princes and other people that they should not despise (*la ta-ṭa-píl*) (these animals) before Aššur.[50]

Ashurnasirpal II's hunting includes not only catching the animals alive to bring them to Calah but also the actual killing of them in the field. The text continues by describing the king's hunting and killing of wild animals including elephants, wild oxen, and lions.[51] His strategies and weapons include the ambush of the elephants, chariots for chasing wild oxen, and the use of javelins when hunting lions. In the hunt, he "killed 370 lions like caged birds with the spear (370 *nēšī kīma iṣṣūrī qu-up-pi ina* ^iṣu^*pu-aš-ḫi a-duk*)."[52] This literary expression, "like caged birds," can be related to any "enclosed," or "confined" situation of the hunting objects during or after the hunt.

Hunting expedition by Ashurnasirpal II is also mentioned in the inscriptions engraved on a large stone slab at the Northwest Palace at Calah.[53] The hunting record comes after the record of the erection of the palace and various temples at Calah,[54] and the reconstruction of the land.[55] According to the hunting record, the hunt started at the command of Ninurta and Nergal.[56] In the hunt, the Assyrian king killed 450 lions (4 *me'āt 50 nēšī danānī a-duk*).[57] He also killed two hundred ostriches "like caged birds (2 *me'āt lurmī ki-ma iṣṣūrī qu-up-pi ú-na-pi-iṣ*)."[58] As noted above, this expression can be related to an "enclosed," or "confined" situation of hunting

48. *RIMA* 2, 35b–37a (p. 226).
49. *RIMA* 2, 37b–38a (p. 226).
50. *RIMA* 2, 38b–39 (p. 226).
51. *RIMA* 2, 40–42a (pp. 226–27).
52. *RIMA* 2, 42b (p. 227).
53. *RIMA* 2, 288.
54. *RIMA* 2, A.0.101.30, 20–77 (pp. 289–91).
55. *RIMA* 2, 78–84a (p. 291).
56. *RIMA* 2, 84b–86a (p. 291).
57. *RIMA* 2, 86b (p. 291).
58. *RIMA* 2, 89–90a (p. 291).

objects. In addition to the killing of the wild animals, he captured alive twenty strong lions, fifty wild bulls, and 140 ostriches.[59]

There is a brief record of a lion hunt by Ashurnasirpal II in the "Kurkh Monolith," which describes that the king killed five lions with his fierce bow before the city of (Mal)ḫina, in the land of Ḫatti (5 *nēšī ina muḫḫi* ālu [*mal*(?)]-*ḫi-na ina* māt*ḫat-te ina qašti-a ez-ze-te ú-šam-qit*).[60] This lion hunting is also closely connected to the military campaign record in that the hunt occurred during his second military campaign to the land of Nairi.[61]

Reliefs

Three royal lion hunting reliefs of Ashurnasirpal II have been found at his Northwest Palace at Nimrud.[62] All of them depict the confrontation between the Assyrian king and various lions (or lionesses). Their depictions seem to be very similar, with only minor variations.

BM 124534

Fig. 3.1. Ashurnasirpal II's Royal Lion Hunt, Throne Room (Room B, plate 19A), Northwest Palace, Nimrud. British Museum, BM 124534. (Photo: © The Trustees of the British Museum.)

59. *RIMA* 2, 91–94 (pp. 291–92).
60. *RIMA* 2, A.0.101.19, 33–34 (p. 258).
61. *RIMA* 2, 27.
62. Albenda, "Ashurnasirpal II Lion Hunt Relief BM124534," 167.

Regarding the relief, BM 124534 (Fig. 3.1), Pauline Albenda suggests that it belongs to the series of wall reliefs of the palace of Ashurnasripal II.[63] Its exceptional design suggests that it was made by a master artist who used an innovative and unprecedented style of composition.[64] In other words, creative work by an artist was represented on the wall reliefs.

In the relief, Ashurnasirpal II stands with an attendant in a chariot harnessed to three horses. He wears a royal cap on his head and a band around his waist. He also has a sword sheath around his waist. He turns and looks behind himself to shoot his bow at the lion that is attacking the chariot at the back. The lion seems to be driven by soldiers on foot with shields and daggers. Under the three chariot horses, another lion has fallen to the ground with an arrow in his body. This relief shows a dynamic aspect of the royal hunt, with an emphasis on the king as a brave figure who hunts down ferocious beasts.

It is notable that the royal lion hunting reliefs and military campaigns such as sieges of enemy citadels are located together in the throne room of Ashurnasirpal II.[65] Winter argues that the arrangement of those seemingly different activities, hunting and warfare, is not arbitrary but, rather, is "programmed."[66] In the program, the arrangement of the inscriptions is carefully planned to represent royal activities as an aspect of the ideology of the Assyrian imperial power.[67]

BM 124579

Another relief of Ashurnasirpal II, BM 124578 (Fig. 3.2), was found on the pavement in a chamber of the palace at Nimrud.[68]

63. Albenda, "Ashurnasirpal II Lion Hunt Relief BM124534," 167.
64. Albenda, "Ashurnasirpal II Lion Hunt Relief BM124534," 167–68.
65. Winter, "Program of the Throneroom" Fig. 2, p. 17.
66. Winter, "Program of the Throneroom," 27.
67. Winter, "Program of the Throneroom," 27–28.
68. Albenda, "Ashurnasirpal II Lion Hunt Relief BM124534," 167.

Fig. 3.2. Ashurnasirpal II's Royal Lion Hunt, Nimrud. British Museum, BM 124579. (Photo: © The Trustees of the British Museum.)

In this relief, the archer, who is shooting a bow, is wearing a royal diadem. He could be Ashurnasirpal II or his son and heir, Shalmaneser III.[69] He has two dagger sheathes in his waist belt. He also has a sword sheath on his left side. Two quivers each with an axe are hanging down on the front side of the chariot. A royal attendant next to the king is driving the three-horse chariot. Reade suggests that the hunter's bowstring is not fully represented perhaps because it would run over the face of the king.[70] Under the running horses, a lion is falling down with three arrows shot in his head and body. A depiction of "a fallen enemy or victim beneath the horses drawing the victor's chariot" is conventional in Assyrian art.[71]

A Relief from the Staatliche Museum in Berlin

This royal lion hunting relief (Fig. 3.3) is similar to the relief of Fig. 3.2 in its overall composition.

69. Reade, "Royal Lion Hunt," 51.
70. Curtis and Reade, *Art and Empire*, 51.
71. Curtis and Reade, *Art and Empire*, 51.

Fig. 3.3. Ashurnasirpal II's Royal Lion Hunt Relief, Nimrud. Staatliche Museen zu Berlin-PK, Vorderasiatisches Museum. (Photo: © Staatliche Museen zu Berlin-PK, Vorderasiatisches Museum, Foto: Olaf M. Teßmer).

In the relief, Ashurnasirpal II is wearing a royal diadem and is shooting a bow at the lioness in front of him. An attendant next to the king is driving the three-horse chariot. The bowstring is again not fully represented, parallel to the relief of Fig. 3.2. One recognizable difference is that there is a lioness, instead of a lion, in the relief of Fig. 3.3. She has not fallen down yet. Rather she is still standing and looks back toward the chariot with two arrows shot in her head and body. This hunting relief seems to depict more tension between the hunter and the hunted prey than the relief of Fig. 3.2.

Reliefs with Epigraphs: The Balawat Gates of Ashurnasirpal II

Royal lion reliefs with epigraphs are found on the Balawat Gates of Ashurnasirpal II.

Fig. 3.4. Palace Gates, Band BM ASH II L5. Hunting lions. British Museum, BM 124698. (Photo: © The Trustees of the British Museum.)

Inscription: *nēšī ina muḫḫi nāri ba-li-ḫi a-duk*[72]

Translation: I killed lions at the River Balih.

From the left side of the bronze band (Fig. 3.4), Assyrian archers on a chariot are running over a fallen lion and shooting at another lion which rears up in front of them. Three archers on foot are following the chariot. In the center, an Assyrian archer is aiming at a lion cub which is sitting among some rushes. On the right side, the Assyrian king, standing in a chariot, is shooting at a lion which has reared up. An Assyrian spearman is approaching against the lion with a round shied in his left hand. Another lion has fallen under the king's chariot. Behind the king, another Assyrian chariot is running over a fallen lion and advancing against another lion which rears up. An Assyrian archer on the chariot is aiming at the lion.

Fig. 3.5. Palace Gates, BM ASH II R5. Hunting lions. British Museum, BM 124699. (Photo: © The Trustees of the British Museum.)

Inscription: *ēkal Aššurnasirpal šar*$_4$ *kiššati šar*$_4$ $^{[\text{māt}]}$*Aššur mār Tukulti-Ninurta* [*šar*$_4$ ^{māt}*Aššur*] *mār Adad-Nirari šar*$_4$ ^{māt}*Aššur*-ma *nēšī ina muḫḫi nāri ba-li-ḫa a-duk*[73]

72. Curtis and Tallis, *Balawat Gates of Ashurnasirpal II*, 34; *RIMA* 2, 2:350.

73. Curtis and Tallis, *Balawat Gates of Ashurnasirpal II*, 42.

Translation: The palace of Ashurnasirpal, king of the world, king of Assyria, son of Tukulti-ninurta, king of Assyria, son of Adad-nirari, king of Assyria: I killed lions at the River Balih.

In this band (Fig. 3.5), two chariots are advancing from the left. The first chariot is running over a lion which has fallen to the ground. Even though the band is broken in the middle, a lion seems to rise up on its rear legs to intimidate the advancing chariots. Two Assyrian soldiers with daggers and shields are surrounding and attacking another lion which rises up on its rear legs. Another Assyrian archer is shooting down at a lion which is sitting between the tree and the bush. On the right side of the band, an Assyrian archer is aiming at a lion which has reared up. An Assyrian bowman is carrying a mace and a bow behind the advancing chariot.

Ashurbanipal (668–631 BCE)

Inscriptions

Prism Fragment (82-5-22,2)[74]

The text from this Prism fragment provides a record of a lion hunt. According to the text, Ashurbanipal went out hunting for pleasure.[75] The text also states that "hug[e lions, a fier]ce [mountain breed, attacked] (there) the cattle-p[ens] ([*el-la-m*]*u-ú-a šur-bu-t*[*e la-ab-bi i-lit-ti hur-šá-a-ni*] [*ez-z*]*u-ú-te tar-*[*ba-ṣu iš-hi-ṭu*])."[76] The Assyrian king went with his team to hunt the ferocious lions ([*ina* 1-*et*] *ú-re-ia ṣi-mit-ti ru-kub b*[*ēl-ti-ia*]).[77] Within forty minutes of daybreak, he pierced the throats of raging lions, each (lion) with a single arrow ([10 *u*]*š* u_4-*mu ina a-la-*[*ki*] [*ša*] [*nē*]*šī na-ad-ru-*[*ti*] *ina* 1$^{\text{ta.àm giš}}$*šil-ta-hi nap-šá-te-šú-nu ap-*[*ru*]-[*u'*]).[78]

Describing what the king did, the record also seems to play the role of political propaganda: a representation of the image of Ashurbanipal as a brave and swift lion hunter. First, it provides "the image of the brave and impatient warrior."[79] He responded to the damage of the cattle-pens due

74. Bauer, *Inschriftenwerk Assurbanipals*, 1:30, plate 59f.
75. Borger, *Beiträge*, 198–99; Weissert, "Royal Hunt and Royal Triumph," 3' (p. 357).
76. Weissert, "Royal Hunt and Royal Triumph," 5'-6' (p. 357).
77. Weissert, "Royal Hunt and Royal Triumph," 7' (p. 357).
78. Weissert, "Royal Hunt and Royal Triumph," 8'-10' (p. 357).
79. Weissert, "Royal Hunt and Royal Triumph," 343.

to the lions in the field. He went out with a team of his royal attendants to hunt down the dangerous beasts. Second, it provides the image of "the swiftness of the action."[80] He hunted the lions down within forty minutes after daybreak. These images contribute to the establishment of the image of the king as a courageous and skillful hunter.

One of the remarkable features of the text is that this hunting account is followed by the reference to the *akītu* festival. The topic of the record turns from the lion hunt to the festival in the month of Addar (*ik-šu-dam-ma addaru warḫu i-sin-ni bīt-á-ki-i*[*t*]).[81] Weissert argues that the *akītu* festival was sometimes related to military triumphs.[82] In particular, the return of Ishtar from the *akītu* temple in Milqiya to the temple of Egashankalamma was combined with the presentation of captives and booty to the cheering public.[83]

Ashurbanipal's prism inscription connects three seemingly distinguished topics: a lion hunt by chariot for the establishment of order over disorder and the *akītu* festival, which is related to a military triumph.[84] The lion hunt and the *akītu* festival have an affinity in that they describe the establishment of order over chaos. A difference would be whether the place is a plain field (the royal lion hunt) or universe (the *akītu* festival). This affinity makes it possible that the lion hunt would be related to a military triumph in that the latter is also about the establishment of order over chaos. Therefore, the lion hunt, the *akītu* festival, and the military triumph can be interrelated to each other with their common theme about order over disorder.

The Great Hunting Text (K 2867+)[85]

This text describes a royal lion hunt by Ashurbanipal. In the text, Ashurbanipal hunted lions for pleasure ([*ki-i mu*]*l-ta-'u-u-ti al-li-ka*

80. Weissert, "Royal Hunt and Royal Triumph," 346.

81. Weissert, "Royal Hunt and Royal Triumph," 11' (p. 357).

82. Weissert, "Royal Hunt and Royal Triumph," 347.

83. Pongratz-Leisten, *Ina Šulmi Īrub*, 79–83; Weissert, "Royal Hunt and Royal Triumph," 348.

84. Weissert, "Royal Hunt and Royal Triumph," 348.

85. Bauer, *Inschriftenwerk Assurbanipals*, 1:87–89, plate 31f; cf. Borger, *Beiträge*, 330–31.

ṣēr-uš-šú-un).[86] As in the Prism Fragment 82-5-22,2, the hunt has another reason: a complaint by shepherds and herdsmen that lions were attacking the cattle-pen(s) and sheep-fold(s) (*i-bak-ku-ú* [lú]*rē'û lúna-qí-di šá la-ab-bi -/- ik-k*[*a-lu ina tar-ba-ṣi u*] *su-pu-ru*).[87] Finally, the king went out to hunt down the lions and his hunting was successful: "During my campaign, I inflicted upon them a defeat, (and) scattered their prides. (*ina me-ti-iq gir-ri-ia . . . dabdâ-šú-*[*nu*] *áš-kun qin-na-a-ti-šú-nu ú-par-ri-ir*)."[88] In other words, the king, as a brave hunter, succeeded in establishing order over the disorder that the lions had caused in the field.

The Hunt in the Nineveh Arena (K 6085)[89]

In this text, Ashurbanipal hunted lions in an arena in the city of Nineveh, instead of outside in the field. He hunted the lions with a single team, forty minutes after daybreak.[90] The hunt concluded with the killing of eighteen lions by the king. The text says that "I [quelled] the tumult of eighteen raging lions (*ša* 18 *nēšī na-ad-ru-ti uz-za-šú-nu* ⌜*ú*⌝-[*šap-ši-iḫ*])."[91] In particular, the restored word, *ušapšiḫ*, represents the pacification which can be related to achieving the status of order against disorder. The Assyrian king brings order in place of the disorder that the symbolic eighteen lions represented.

A notable feature of the text is its intimate relationship to the royal lion hunt reliefs from Room C of the North Palace at Nineveh. Weissert suggests that a lion hunt within a city can be found not only in the text, K 6085, but also in the reliefs in Room C of the North Palace.[92] Another basic similarity between them is that both of them describe the hunting and killing of the eighteen lions by the king.

Based on this similarity, Weissert further notes that the number of the hunted lions represent the number of the gates in the walls of greater Nineveh.[93] The royal lion hunt within the city walls was not only a sport for pleasure, but it implies political and military propaganda of the Assyrian

86. Weissert, "Royal Hunt and Royal Triumph," K 2867+, i.33b (p. 344).
87. Weissert, "Royal Hunt and Royal Triumph," i.31; ii, 27–32 (p. 344).
88. Weissert, "Royal Hunt and Royal Triumph," ii.34-35 (p. 345).
89. Bauer, *Inschriftenwerk Assurbanipals*, 1:89, plate 43.
90. Weissert, "Royal Hunt and Royal Triumph," K 6085, 5'–6' (p. 345).
91. Weissert, "Royal Hunt and Royal Triumph," 6'b (p. 345).
92. Weissert, "Royal Hunt and Royal Triumph," 351.
93. Weissert, "Royal Hunt and Royal Triumph," 355.

royal ideology. By hunting eighteen lions, which represent the total number of the gates of the city walls, in public within the extended walls of the city, the king effectively shows the spectators his image as a hunter and as a ruler who brings order out of the disorder that the lions or enemies represent. Finally, "in the eyes of the ancient spectators, the public image of a triumphant king and the public image of the lion hunter merged into a single figure—that of Ashurbanipal."[94]

Reliefs

One of the remarkable features of the lion hunt reliefs of Ashurbanipal is their artistic mastery. Parrot argues that the reliefs of Ashurbanipal show an innovative change and a mastery of art, compared to the reliefs of earlier kings.[95] The sculptors of Ashurbanipal seem to have had "a better grasp of animal anatomy" and caused "a drastic change" in "the whole handling of forms."[96] Shortcomings which can be found in the reliefs of other kings, do not appear in the reliefs of Ashurbanipal.[97]

Room C

Reliefs

The royal lion hunt reliefs of Ashurbanipal have been recovered from room C of the North Palace of Ashurbanipal at Nineveh.[98] The reliefs of room C show the stages and various methods of a lion hunt, identified as "the Great Lion Hunt."[99] In these hunting scenes, the king is shown in his fast hunting chariot, which is specially designed for open country.[100] The British Museum holds almost the whole series and exhibits the reliefs in sequence, as described below.[101]

94. Weissert, "Royal Hunt and Royal Triumph," 350.
95. Parrot, *Arts of Assyria*, 60.
96. Parrot, *Arts of Assyria*, 60.
97. Parrot, *Arts of Assyria*, 60.
98. Weissert, "Royal Hunt and Royal Triumph," 354–55.
99. Strommenger, *5000 Years*, 453.
100. Strommenger, *5000 Years*, 453.
101. Strommenger, *5000 Years*, 453.

The slabs of Figs. 3.6 and 3.7 were found in room C of the North Palace at Nineveh.[102] An aediculum stands on the top of the hill and there is a stele in the aediculum. The stele shows an image of a lion hunt: a king shooting a lion from a one-horse chariot, with a driver. It could be a monument marking the hunting area. This image seems to be related to the events of the larger composition.[103]

Fig. 3.6. Ashurbanipal's Royal Lion Hunt, North Palace, Nineveh. British Museum, BM 124861/862/863. (Photo: © The Trustees of the British Museum.)

102. Strommenger, *5000 Years*, 453.

103. Strommenger, *5000 Years*, 453.

Fig. 3.7. Enlarged Image of the Royal Lion Hunting Inscribed on the Aediculum. British Museum, BM 124862. (Photo: © The Trustees of the British Museum.)

The whole sequence of reliefs in the room C reveals a notable feature of the hunt: a line of soldiers standing around the lion hunt on each side. It seems that the king is hunting lions with his attendants inside a barrier of armed soldiers. Behind the array of the guards and the royal attendants are the spectators for the royal lion hunt. They are moving about on a wooded hill so as to watch the royal hunt and some of them are even climbing up trees for a better view of the hunt. Indeed, the royal lion hunt was impressive to observers, seeing the power and valor of the king. It was important for him to have spectators for the hunt, as shown in the reliefs, to display his protecting power.

Fig. 3.8. Preparation for the Hunt: Servants with Horses, North Palace, Nineveh. British Museum, BM 124859/860/861. (Photo: © The Trustees of the British Museum.)

Fig. 3.9. Preparation for the Hunt: Huntsman with Mastiff, North Palace, Nineveh. British Museum, BM 124863. (Photo: © The Trustees of the British Museum.)

The reliefs of Figs. 3.8 and 3.9 depict some of the preparation for the hunt. The hunt began at daybreak.[104] The king's attendants bring horses for the chariot(s) of the king (Fig. 3.8). They also prepare a mastiff for the hunt (Fig. 3.9). The lions are restless, having been detained in cages.[105]

When the preparations are complete, the lion hunt begins. During the hunt, the king's tactics for the fray seem to be unerring as in a battle.[106] The climax of the hunt is the killing of the eighteen lions by the king, as depicted in the following reliefs from room C (Figs. 3.10–13).[107]

104. Parrot, *Arts of Assyria*, 64.

105. Parrot, *Arts of Assyria*, 64.

106. Parrot, *Arts of Assyria*, 64.

107. Strommenger, *5000 Years*, 453.

Fig. 3.10. A Wounded Lion, North Palace, Nineveh. British Museum, BM 124864. (Photo: © The Trustees of the British Museum.)

Fig. 3.11. Ashurbanipal Shooting at Lions from His Chariot, North Palace, Nineveh. British Museum, BM 124866/867. (Photo: © The Trustees of the British Museum.)

Fig. 3.12. Lions Killed by Ashurbanipal,
North Palace, Nineveh. British Museum, BM 124867/868.
(Photo: © The Trustees of the British Museum.)

Fig. 3.13. Ashurbanipal's Royal Lion Hunt, North Palace, Nineveh. British Museum, BM 124869/870. (Photo: © The Trustees of the British Museum.)

The reliefs of Fig. 3.13 come from room C at the North Palace of Ashurbanipal at Nineveh. In the reliefs, a lion is being released from a cage. A notable point in the reliefs is the line of attendants and solders who seem to surround the whole hunting field on the right. They are holding shields toward the field to keep the lions inside the hunting field. Once the lion is released from the cage, it cannot escape from the hunter.

This series of reliefs shows a very successful hunt by the courageous king. After spectators have arrived to watch the hunt and the royal attendants have finished their preparation for the hunt, the royal lion hunt begins within the enclosing line of armed soldiers. Then, the hunting culminates with the slaying of the lions by the king.

There is a second series of the royal lion hunting reliefs in room C.[108] Like the first set of reliefs, this set of reliefs provides a concluding scene of the lion hunt by the king, as shown below (Figs. 3.14–16).

108. Barnett, *Sculptures from the North Palace*, plates X–XIII.

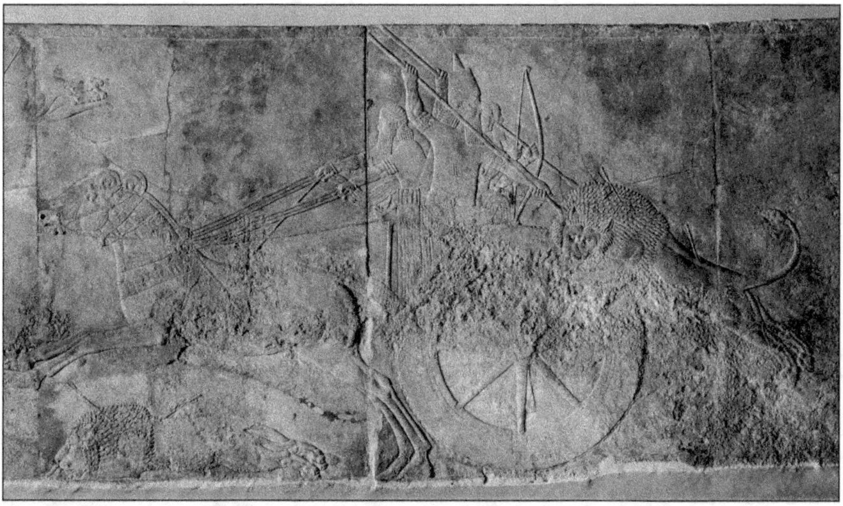

Fig. 3.14. Ashurbanipal Slaying a Lion with His Lance, North Palace, Nineveh. British Museum, BM 124853/854. (Photo: © The Trustees of the British Museum.)

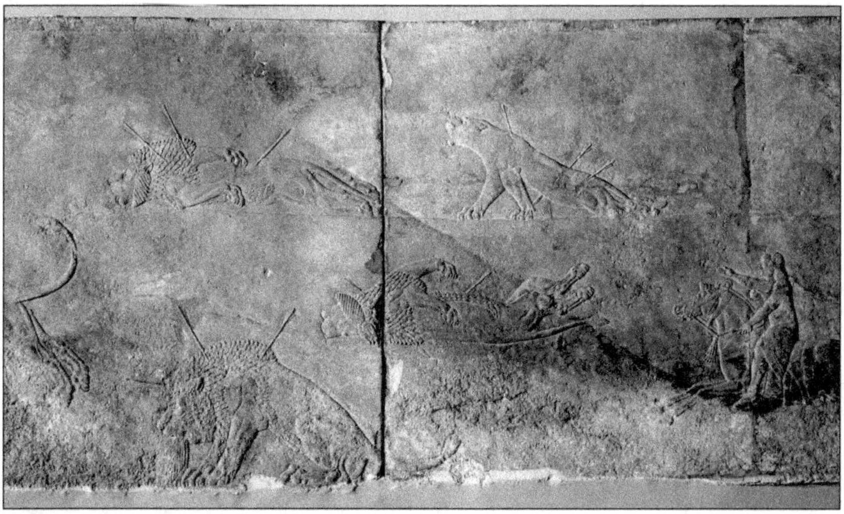

Fig. 3.15. Wounded and Dying Lions and Lioness with a Horseman of the King's Company, North Palace, Nineveh. British Museum BM 124855/856/857. (Photo: © The Trustees of the British Museum.)

Fig. 3.16. A Lion in a Cage, North Palace, Nineveh. British Museum, BM 124883. (Photo: © The Trustees of the British Museum.)

According to this second series of reliefs, the lion hunt is completed successfully with the king's victory over the lions (Fig. 3.14). The arena is filled with dead or dying lions, that are left dead or dying behind the progress of the hunt. Parrot comments that the reliefs of the "dying lioness" and the "lions and lioness" are "incomparable masterpieces of animal sculpture."[109]

The reliefs of Fig. 3.15 illustrate a part of the royal lion hunt.[110] In the reliefs, the royal attendants are riding horses to assist Ashurbanipal during his lion hunt. There is also a lion which is not yet released from a cage behind the royal attendants (Fig. 3.16). Even though the relief does not show the result for the lion, its fate would be same as the other lions: hunted and killed by the king.

109. Parrot, *Arts of Assyria*, 61.

110. Strommenger, *5000 Years*, 453. In the case of the lion hunt described on the reliefs of Room S, the hunt concludes with a libation pouring over dead lions (Fig. 3.22).

Room R

Reliefs

Hunting reliefs also have been found at Room R of Ashurbanipal's palace and they provide some additional details about the process of the hunt. They include the preparation for the hunt and the return from the hunt but not the hunting scenes proper. Nevertheless, their description contributes to the understanding of the hunt as a whole together with other reliefs from Rooms C and S.

Fig. 3.17. Royal Attendants with Hounds and Nets for a Hunt, North Palace, Nineveh. British Museum, BM 124893/894. (Photo: © The Trustees of the British Museum.)

Fig. 3.18. Royal Attendants Taking a Mule with a Net on Its Back, North Palace, Nineveh. British Museum, BM 124896/897. (Photo: © The Trustees of the British Museum.)

Fig. 3.19. Royal Attendants and Guards Returning from the Hunt, North Palace, Nineveh. British Museum, BM 124888/889/890. (Photo: © The Trustees of the British Museum.)

In the reliefs of the hunt from Room R, one of the interesting points is that the royal attendants are carrying nets for the hunt (Figs. 3.17, 18). Even though the reliefs do not show if nets were used in hunting lions or only for smaller animals,[111] it is quite clear that various types of nets were used in hunting. In Fig. 3.19, the royal attendants and the guards are returning from the hunt. Some of the royal attendants are carrying a dead lion while other attendants are holding birds and a rabbit which presumably have been hunted.

Room S

The hunting scenes in room S are displayed in three friezes.[112] Each of the friezes shows, independently, various episodes and forms of hunting.[113] In the reliefs, the king hunts lions, onagers, and other wild animals. While the reliefs of room C depict the king as hunting from his royal chariot, the reliefs of room S show the king hunting wild animals on foot, from a boat, or on horseback (for hunting onagers).[114] Another characteristic feature of the hunting scenes of room S is that many of them show direct combat with animals.[115] Strommenger suggests that these scenes might be related to specific occasions which have not yet been clarified.[116]

Reliefs with Epigraphs

The royal lion hunting scenes of Ashurbanipal include some inscriptions associated with the reliefs.

111. See Osten-Sacken, "Netz. B.," 239–42.
112. Strommenger, *5000 Years*, 453.
113. Strommenger, *5000 Years*, 453.
114. Strommenger, *5000 Years*, 453.
115. Strommenger, *5000 Years*, 453.
116. Strommenger, *5000 Years*, 453.

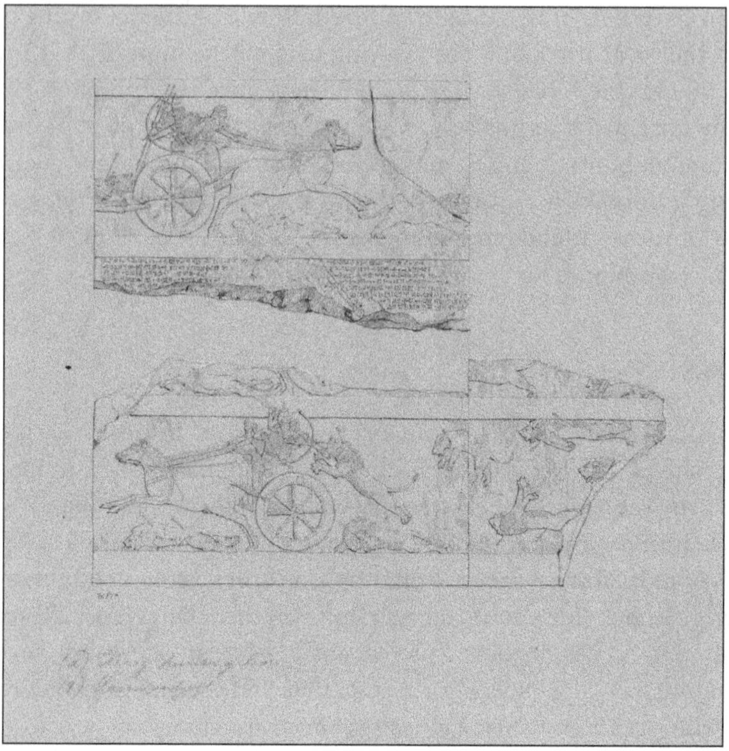

Fig. 3.20. Ashurbanipal's Royal Lion Hunt, North Palace, Nineveh. Slabs A-B. Original Drawings V3 (original lost) (drawn by William Boutcher). British Museum. (Photo: © The Trustees of the British Museum.)

These lion hunting reliefs of Ashurbanipal with associated epigraphs were found in room S of the North Palace in Nineveh. The hunting epigraph is written in the first person to present the viewpoint of the king himself.

The epigraphs and the images of the reliefs represent the prowess of the king as a whole. The epigraph states that Ashurbanipal hunted lions on the plain at the command of the gods and his hunt showed his heroic aspect.[117] According to the text, lions attacked the king and surrounded his royal chariot in a wide field (*ina ṣēri aš-ri rap-ši la-ab-bi na-ad-ru-[u]-ti i-lit-ti ḫur-ša-a-ni izzūti it-bu-[u-ni] il-mu-u* *^{iṣu}narkabtu ru-kub šarru-ti-ia*).[118] The word "surrounded (*il-mu-u*)" does not refer to "the king surrounding the lions"

117. Streck, *Assurbanipal*, 2:308–11; Russell, *Writing on the Wall*, 201–2.

118. Jagdinschrift ε), 3–4a (Streck, *Assurbanipal*, 2:308–11; Russell, *Writing on the Wall*, 201–2).

but rather, to "the lions surrounding the king." The text describes the critical moment of the hunt. The king finally overcame this crisis and hunted down the ferocious beasts, in accord with the command of Assur and Ishtar.[119] The text also states that a lion sprang upon Ummanapa, son of Urtaki, king of Elam, who was rescued by Ashurbanipal.[120] When the lion attacked him, he was afraid and implored the Assyrian king to help.[121]

The images of the reliefs visualize what the epigraph describes regarding the hunting scene. On the top part of the reliefs, the king is in his chariot with his armed attendants and the driver. The attendant is riding a horse to chase a lion which has arrows in its body. On the chariot, the king is turning backward and shooting an arrow at the lion. Most of the middle register is missing but there seems to be a dead lioness under the chariot and other lions (or lionesses) are behind the chariot. In the bottom part of the reliefs, the king is with his attendants in the chariot. One of his attendants is driving the chariot which is about to run over—or past—a dead lioness. The king is turning backward and shooting an arrow at a lion which is jumping at the chariot with one arrow shot in his head. The royal attendants behind the king are thrusting spears against the lion. There are three lions and one lioness lying down on the ground behind the chariot. The right side of the bottom part of the reliefs seems to partially show a lion, which is being released from a cage.

119. Jagdinschrift ε), 4b–6a? (Streck, *Assurbanipal*, 2:310–11).

120. Jagdinschrift ε), 6b–7? (Streck, *Assurbanipal*, 2:310–11).

121. Jagdinschrift ε), 8 (Streck, *Assurbanipal*, 2:310–11).

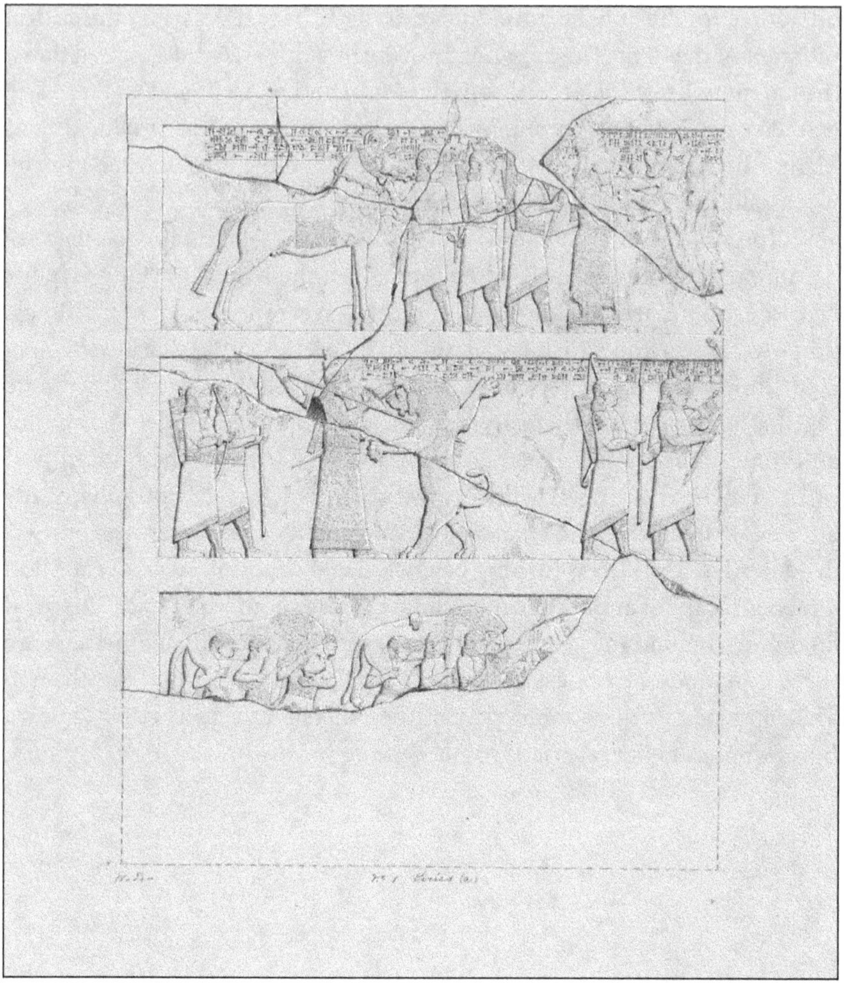

Fig. 3.21. Ashurbanipal's Royal Lion Hunt (Louvre AO 19903). Slab C. Original Drawings V4 (drawn by William Boutcher). British Museum. (Photo: © The Trustees of the British Museum.)

This relief (Fig. 3.21) is slab C from room S of the North Palace of Ashurbanipal in Nineveh. This relief has two epigraphs, and both of them are written in the first person. Like slabs A-B, the epigraphs and the images of the relief of slab C represent the prowess of the king in his lion hunting on foot and its ensuing result.[122] The epigraphs describe how the king, himself, killed lions on the plain at the command of gods.

122. Streck, *Assurbanipal*, 2:306–9; Russell, *Writing on the Wall*, 201.

In particular, the text in the top register describes that the king hunted a lion which was released from a cage. According the text, they (the royal attendants) brought an enraged lion to the hunting field for the king's great sport (or game) (*ina me-lul-*[*ti rubû-ti-ia*]).[123] In the hunt, they released the furious lion of the plain from a cage ([*nêšu*] *iz-zu ša ṣēri-šu ištu libbi iṣuna-bar-ti ú-še-ṣu-nim-ma*).[124] Then, "I (Ashurbanipal) did not kill the lion on foot and his(?) . . . According to the command of Nergal, king of the world, granted power and virility to me (Ashurbanipal). Afterwards, in a release of iron of my (sword) belt, I (Ashurbanipal) pierced it (the lion) and it died. (*ina šēpī-ia ina* [iṣu]*Kakt*[i]*–šu*[?] *as-?-ut*[?] [*na*]*-piš-ta-šu úl* [ú]-*q*[át]*-ti ina qí-bit* [ilu]*nèrgal šar ṣēri šá dun-nu zik-ru-*[*t*]ú *ú-šat-*[*li-ma*]*-an-ni arka ina paṭri parzilli šib-bi-ia as-ḫul-šú* [*n*]*a-piš-tam iš-kun*)."[125]

Based on this text, the lion has already been caught and detained in a cage prior to the hunt. It is possible that the lion was originally from the plain but the king did not catch it by himself in the field. Instead, the royal attendants had possibly seized the lion and put it into a cage. When the hunt started, the lion was released from the "enclosed place," only to be hunted and finally killed by the king.

The upper register of the slab depicts the king who is standing on the right side of the relief and killing the upright lion with his dagger. There are three royal attendants and a horse behind the king. In the middle register, the king is standing in the middle of the relief and piercing the lion with his spear. There are two armed attendants behind him and two other attendants behind the lion. In the bottom register, the preserved section shows two groups of three attendants, each group carrying a dead lion.

123. Jagdinschrift δ), 1a (Streck, *Assurbanipal*, 2:308–9; Russell, *Writing on the Wall*, 201).

124. Jagdinschrift δ), 1b–2a (Streck, *Assurbanipal*, 2:308–9).

125. Jagdinschrift δ), 2b–4 (Streck, *Assurbanipal*, 2:308–9).

Fig. 3.22. Ashurbanipal's Royal Lion Hunt, North Palace, Nineveh. British Museum, BM 124886/7. (Photo: © The Trustees of the British Museum.)

These reliefs (Fig. 3.22) are slabs D-E in room S of the North Palace of Ashurbanipal at Nineveh. These slabs have three registers. The middle and bottom registers contain epigraphs that are also written in the first person.[126] The epigraphs describe that the king smashed the lion with his mace, killing it, and made libation over the dead lions.

In the top register, the king is shooting an arrow at a lion that is jumping toward him. Barnett stated that there are another two lions behind the first one, the last one coming out of a cage the gate of which an attendant has opened.[127] However, Julian Reade indicates that this is a continuing scene featuring but one lion.[128] According to Reade, a lion runs toward the king after being released from a cage. Even though the lion already has an arrow in its body, it jumps toward the king, who is shooting another arrow at it. There is a royal attendant next to the king and there are three other attendants behind him.

In the middle register, the king is holding a lion by its tail. Another lion is lying on the ground and roaring at the king's attendant who is sitting

126. Jagdinschrift γ) (Streck, *Assurbanipal*, 2:306–7; Russell, *Writing on the Wall*, 202).

127. Barnett, *Assyrian Palace Reliefs*, 29–30.

128. Reade, *Assyrian Sculpture*, 57–58.

on a horse holding a whip. Behind the horse, other royal attendants are standing by on a chariot headed in the opposite direction.

In the bottom register, royal attendants approach an altar area from the left, carrying a dead lion as they follow behind two musicians. The king, facing the altar, is standing over three dead lions, pouring a libation over them with his right hand and holding a bow in his left hand. Behind him are several attendants and two horses.

Reliefs Without an Epigraph

Barnett introduces reliefs from room S of the North Palace of Ashurbanipal in Nineveh.[129] In the reliefs, Ashurbanipal is shooting at a lion from a boat, as the lion springs from the water toward the boat. Royal attendants have apparently driven the lion into the water, while other attendants stand with the king on the boat. Based on this scene, the royal lion hunt includes a rather different strategy. The king hunted lions not only from a chariot or by foot on land, but also from a boat.

Strategic Patterns of the Royal Lion Hunt

The texts, reliefs, and epigraphs of the lion hunts by the Assyrian kings provide formulaic patterns of strategy for lion hunting. Regarding the place of the lion hunt, it seems that the hunt occurred in various places—an open field, a watercourse, or an arena.[130] The king was actively involved in the hunt, and the hunt concluded with the killing of one or more lions by the king. A ritual could follow in which the king prepares an offering and makes a libation over dead lions.

As mentioned above, the records of royal lion hunting in the inscriptions of Tiglath-pileser I, Aššur-bēl-kala, Adad-nārāri II, Tukulti-ninurta II, and Shalmaneser III provide a limited hunting strategy. In most of the records, the royal hunting strategy is not described in any detail. However, it seems that the hunt usually included both hunting on foot and from a chariot with weapons such as bows or spears. Meanwhile, no royal hunting reliefs related to those particular kings have been found to date.

129. Barnett, *Sculptures from the North Palace*, plate LIV.

130. Strommenger, *5000 Years*, 453.

The royal lion hunting inscriptions and reliefs of Ashurnasirpal II show hunting strategies comparable with those of other kings. His hunts were similar to the hunts by other kings, in that he hunted lions from his chariot. In the reliefs, he uses a bow to hunt the lions from his chariot. His hunting, however, shows a distinct feature in that he did not only kill lions and other animals, but also caught some of them alive. After catching them, he took them home and displayed them in his capital city.

While providing a more complete glimpse of the hunting process and strategies, Ashurbanipal's lion hunt reliefs from his North Palace at Nineveh provide some notable features. First, some lions that have been captured and caged are then released from the cages, as in Figs. 3.13, 16, 20, and 22. It is not clear who caught and caged them, but it seems to be clear that they were destined to be hunted and killed by the king. Second, the slabs BM 124861/862/863 (Fig. 3.6) and BM 124869/870 (Fig. 3.13) depict the human enclosure for the hunt. Third, the reliefs from Room S depict several ways of hunting other than hunting from a chariot: the king hunts on foot (Figs. 3.21, 22), on horseback (for hunting onagers), and even from a boat (Room S).

Based on these texts and reliefs, royal hunting has general strategic patterns with variations and differences in detail. First, the lion hunt is generally conducted under *controlled circumstances* with the deployment of royal attendants. The location of the hunt is usually an open field or arena. The main figure in the hunt is the king but there are armed attendants around him. Their roles are to help the king hunt and kill the lions successfully. It is essentially the king who does the killing of the wild beasts. In helping the king, the roles of the attendants are not passive but active: they prepare the lion hunt before it begins, open the cage of the lion, drive the royal chariot, even defend the king against lions from the chariot, chase the lions, and secure the open field or the arena while the king hunts down the lions. They also ceremoniously carry the dead lions at the end of the hunt. The whole situation of the hunt is under control for an ultimate aim: to make the king a victorious hunter over the lions.

As a part of the *controlled situation*, the royal lion hunt generally includes *the confinement of the prey*. Based on the reliefs of Ashurbanipal, a lion is encircled by armed royal attendants or even held in a cage. The "battle" between the king and the lion(s) is often conducted in an enclosed area, like a contest in a large stadium. In the enclosed area, there is no exit for the lion to be freed or released from the fight. It was a forced confrontation for the lion without any escape.

Finally, the general conclusion of the hunt is *the victory of the king over the lion*. In an enclosed area, the king triumphs over the valiant lion with the support of his attendants. The victory of the king means the defeat and death of the lion. The lion never wins. The king always triumphs over his prey.

Critical Discourse Analysis of the Royal Lion Hunt: The Ideology of Power Relations

An important contribution of Critical Discourse Analysis to the study of the royal lion hunting records is an integrative ideological analysis of the written and visual languages used in the records. According to Norman Fairclough, as described in a previous chapter, a language reflects a dominant ideology in the social context of power relations.[131] In this analysis, a language includes all possible types of language including written, visual, and even spoken languages.[132] Based on this premise, this sociolinguistic approach emphasizes the exhaustive analysis of ideology through all possible types of languages used in discourse.

Critical Discourse Analysis in relation to the royal lion hunt texts, including inscriptions, epigraphs, and reliefs reveals that they function together as effective media for Assyrian ideology through the power relations of the king to his subjects: lions. The types of language used in the discourse are written and visual languages. Therefore, it is necessary for CDA to consider both types of language for the understanding of the ideology embedded in the lion hunting record.

While used together in the lion hunting record, the texts and the reliefs are in complementary interrelationship when describing the general patterns of the hunt. Both of them record and describe the royal lion hunts by the Assyrian kings, but their contents are not identical. For example, the texts usually set their focus on the king without any description of the royal attendants or their roles in the royal lion hunt while the reliefs display the involvement of the royal attendants in the hunt as well as the king. While the texts provide information on time and place, the reliefs visualize

131. Fairclough, *Language and Power*, 1–5.

132. Fairclough, *Language and Power*, 22–28.

specific hunting scenes including the kings, their hunting strategies, instruments, chariots, and royal attendants.

Through the general patterns that are reconstructed based on the lion hunting texts and reliefs, a sociolinguistic analysis of the hunt records clearly reveals Assyrian ideology regarding the power of the king and the related divine order over chaos, which is represented by the lions. The general patterns of the hunt vividly demonstrate the valor and prowess of the Assyrian king. Even though the Mesopotamian lion was smaller than the African lion, it was still a threatening enemy.[133] In the hunting record, the lion represented the wild forces of nature, causing chaos.[134] The king's duty was to quell the chaos and bring order as represented by the killing of the lions. According to Cornelius, "the killing of lions by the king was not only for the sake of a sport but was a religious act and became a symbol of royalty, the motif of the power of the king over the powers of chaos."[135] Reade further suggests that the lion hunt became "reserved for royalty alone" at some point.[136]

The aspect of the Assyrian kingship about protection of order against disorder in the lion hunting record can be related to the ideology of Assyrian political and military power. The image of "the Assyrian king as a hunter of wild animals" is also connected to the image of "the king as a reliable shepherd who protects his flock against wild animals."[137] The image of the king as a shepherd is related to the king as a protector of his people from any harmful enemy.[138] Finally, the images of hunter, shepherd, and protector are merged into one complete image of the Assyrian king.

One of the remarkable examples for the interrelationship between the images of the king would be Weissert's observation on the prism fragment of Ashurbanipal (82-5-22,2), as described above. He argues that the royal hunt and the royal triumph over lions are interrelated in the reliefs and the texts.[139] The royal hunt is not only a royal sport to show the prowess of the

133. Curtis and Reade, *Art and Empire*, 51.

134. Curtis and Reade, *Art and Empire*, 51.

135. Cornelius, "Lion in the Art of the Ancient Near East," 57.

136. Curtis and Reade, *Art and Empire*, 51.

137. Oded, *War, Peace and Empire*, 116.

138. Oded, *War, Peace and Empire*, 116.

139. Weissert, "Royal Hunt and Royal Triumph," 349–50.

king as a brave hunter but also as a representation of the military power of the king to the audience and to the readers.[140]

The ideological interrelationship between hunting and military conquest is not limited to the Assyrian Empire: it can be also found in ancient Egypt. Baines argues for the ideological connection between hunting and military campaigns through his analysis of ancient Egyptian texts and reliefs.[141] Egyptian hunting is a symbolic activity and it was carefully planned in advance.[142] Egyptians manipulated the environment of the hunt; for example, they enclosed areas for a hunt, just like "the line of soldiers providing an arena for Ashurbanipal's royal lion hunt."[143] Baines suggests that this royal sport is "interwoven with conceptions of military conquest and of the defense of order."[144] Like the military campaigns, the hunt also represents conquest and domination.[145] Therefore, the hunting, including lions, was a symbolic political activity for the Egyptian kingship along with their military campaigns.

The ideological and symbolic manipulation of the royal lion hunt served to convey political propaganda to the audience. The Assyrian royal lion hunt was carried out and recorded with a carefully planned scheme. The ultimate goal for the hunt would not be simply a royal sport for pleasure. It also had a political intention: the communication of the political and military ideology of the dominant Assyrian kingship to the audience. While amazed at the scenes and the records of the lion hunts, the audience would recognize and acknowledge the undeniable power of the Assyrian king who himself represents the entire Assyrian Empire. This power is certainly related not only to his image as a hunter but also to his image as the political ruler of the empire.

The audience for royal lion hunting could include a variety of types, based on the discussion by Russell.[146] In the case of the written inscriptions such as the annalistic texts which need a high level of literacy, a possible

140. The interrelationship between the hunt and the miltiary conquest can be also found in Egyptian inscriptions; cf. Baines, *High Culture and Experience*, 187–234.

141. Baines, *High Culture and Experience*, 187–234.

142. Baines, *High Culture and Experience*, 190–91.

143. Baines, *High Culture and Experience*, 191.

144. Baines, *High Culture and Experience*, 229.

145. Baines, *High Culture and Experience*, 229.

146. Russell, *Sennacherib's Palace*, 223–40.

audience or readers would be the scribes.[147] Even though the texts were not accessible to a large audience, they still functioned as a medium to convey political propaganda through the description of the royal lion hunt. In the case of the reliefs, together with their epigraphs, however, they are more accessible than the inscriptions.[148] Due to the visual language of the reliefs, their audience would have been much broader than that of the written inscriptions. The epigraphs are usually brief, and they are basically identical in content with the accompanying images. It would have been easier for the wider audience to understand them.[149] Based upon the categories that Russell suggests, the audience of the royal lion hunting reliefs and epigraphs would have included kings, crown princes (royal family), courtiers, servants, foreign employees, foreign prisoners, future kings, gods, Assyrian provincials, subject foreigners, and independent foreigners.

Different levels of literacy among the audience can be understood as an aspect of unequal social relations among them. Fairclough suggests that *literacy* is related to social power.[150] In other words, access to discourse would be a marker of a social class. Even though the social classification of modern English society, as presented in his own work, is hardly applicable to the ancient society of the Assyrian Empire, it is still valid to suggest that literacy was limited to certain segments of the population, including royal courtiers and scribes from across the empire. They had access to the written inscriptions. They also could read and understand those records. On the contrary, foreign kings and other foreign subjects had limited access to them.

Finally, Critical Discourse Analysis of the royal lion hunt reveals that the formulaic patterns and concepts of royal lion hunting were intended to maintain the dominant power and ideology of the Assyrian Empire over its subjects. Fairclough suggests that discourse reflects social power relations for the maintenance of that power.[151] The hunting record in written and visual languages is a discourse that reflects the power relations of the Assyrian Empire. More exactly, it reflects the dominant power of the Assyrian kings. The records show carefully designed patterns and concepts in favor of the Assyrian kingship: *the intimidating controlling power of the Assyrian*

147. Russell, *Sennacherib's Palace*, 239–40.

148. Russell, *Sennacherib's Palace*, 240.

149. Russell, *Sennacherib's Palace*, 240.

150. Fairclough, *Language and Power*, 62–65.

151. Fairclough, *Language and Power*, 73–74.

king as he encloses and conquers (or, even kills) the ferocious wild beasts, which could be considered an enemy, a representative of chaos/disorder. It is not simply a descriptive record of a royal sporting event. Rather, it is carefully manipulated political propaganda. It transmits the Assyrian political ideology in regard to the power of the kingship to the audiences and indirectly persuades them to acknowledge the unequal political power relations between the Assyrian kings and their subjects or enemies.

Chapter 4

ASSYRIAN MILITARY CAMPAIGN STRATEGIES AND SIEGES

ASSYRIAN MILITARY CAMPAIGNS, ESPECIALLY sieges of well-fortified cities, are recorded in the royal texts and reliefs commissioned by the Neo-Assyrian kings. The sieges typically began with a blockade (enclosure or confinement), which did not necessarily involve an actual assault on the city walls, but rather served as an initial stage. An actual assault is another stage that the Assyrian army could employ, depending on the military situation. In addition to reports of submission to Assyrian power, various texts and reliefs highlight the occasions and tactics of sieges carried out against resistant cities.

This chapter explores the annalistic texts describing sieges as well as the reliefs and their associated epigraphs to reconstruct the conception and pattern of siege warfare. In particular, the focus is on the records of the Neo-Assyrian Empire. However, it is also necessary to examine related materials more broadly to identify general features.

Based on the general patterns and concepts of Assyrian military sieges, this chapter examines political ideology in texts, epigraphs, and reliefs from a sociolinguistic perspective, which considers both written and visual language as discourses through which ideology is expressed. A successful military campaign as a whole is usually presented in the record as a major achievement of the king under the aegis of the god Ashur.[1] A good example would be Sargon II's report of his eighth campaign in the form of a letter to Ashur.[2] Considering that military sieges were often a part of the campaign with submission and tribute, one can expect that the reports of the sieges imply or even boldly represent specific royal ideologies to multiple audiences.[3]

The Written and Visual Language of the Military Campaign Inscriptions and Reliefs

There are extensive records of the military expeditions of the Assyrian kings in annalistic inscriptions, as well as in the palace and gateway reliefs of the Neo-Assyrian Empire. Earlier reports of sieges can be found in the inscriptions of Tiglath-pileser I (1114–1076 BCE). In these inscriptions, the Assyrian king confined the troops of Qumānu to one city, Arinu, at the foot of Mount Aisa (*a-na išten*^{en} *āli* ^{ālu}*a-ri-ni ša šēp šad a-i-sa lu-ú e-si-ir-šu-nu-ti*).[4] During the confinement, the enemy submitted to the Assyrian king and he spared the city (*šēpī-ia iṣ-ba-tu āla šu-a-tu e-ṭí-ir*).[5] After this submission, he took hostages, and imposed tribute and tax upon the city (*li-i-ṭí-i bilta ù ma-da-at-ta muḫḫi-šu-nu ú-kín*).[6] In the case of the city of Kipšuna, he surrounded the city (^{ālu}*kip-šu-na āla bēlū-ti-šu-nu lu al-mi*).[7] The king of the land of Qumānu submitted to the king because of his fear of the strong and aggressive attack of the Assyrian army and Tiglath-pileser I spared that city (*šar* ^{māt}*qu-ma-né-e ti-ib tāḫāz-ia dan-na e-du-ur-ma šēpī-ia iṣ-bat āla šu-a-tu e-ṭí-ir*).[8] The Assyrian king ordered the defeated king to destroy the city wall.[9] He also imposed more tribute and tax upon him (*bilta ù ma-da-ta muḫḫi ša pa-na ut-ter i-na muḫ-ḫi-šu aš-kun*).[10]

1. Holloway, *Aššur Is King!*, 72–76.
2. Hill et al., *Experiencing Power, Generating Authority*, 303–4.
3. For a detailed discussion about the audiences, please see chapter 1 (pp. X-REF).
4. *RIMA* 2, A.0.87.1, v.77–78a (p. 23).
5. *RIMA* 2, v.78–79 (p. 23).
6. *RIMA* 2, v.80–81 (p. 23).
7. *RIMA* 2, vi.23–24a (p. 24).
8. *RIMA* 2, vi.24b–26 (pp. 24–25).
9. *RIMA* 2, vi.27–29 (p. 25).
10. *RIMA* 2, vi.34–36 (p. 25).

In contrast to his engagements with the cities of Arinu and Qumānu, Tiglath-pileser I conquered the city of Ḫunusu and left it in ruins.[11] He used a siege-engine (*né-⸢pe⸣-še*) for the conquest of the city of Ḫunusu.[12] This military conquest of the city shows a different treatment by the Assyrian army during their military campaigns.

A military siege as a blockade can be found in the records of many kings including Adad-nirari II, Ashurnasirpal II, Shalmaneser III, Tigalth-pileser III, Sennacherib, and Ashurbanipal during the Neo-Assyrian Period. Even though almost all the Neo-Assyrian kings engaged in military campaigns, not all of them mention the use of blockades or the assault tactics for their campaigns, in terms of the preserved inscriptions. Meanwhile, sieges were not mentioned in the inscriptions of Tukulti-nirurta II (890–884 BCE) and Shalmaneser V (726–722 BCE). Therefore, this chapter will exclusively focus on the texts, the epigraphs, and the reliefs that describe the military siege strategies as one of several potential stages of the Assyrian military warfare.

Adad-nirari II (911–891 BCE)

Texts (A.0.99.2)

The annals of Adad-nirari II indicate that he launched military campaigns almost every year during his twenty-one years of his rule.[13] In his annals, his siege tactics are cited in the account of his expeditions to the land of Ḫanigalbat. In his third campaign to the land, Adad-nirari II captured the city of Ḫuzirina (^{ālu}*ḫu-zi-ri-na aṣ-ba-at*).[14] In the process, he completely surrounded the wall of the city (*dūra a-na na-al-ban lu al-bi-šu*).[15] In his sixth campaign to the land, he confined Nūr-Adad, the Temmanu, in the city of Naṣibina and established seven forts around it (^{m}*Nur-Adad* ^{māt}*te-man-na-a-ia ina* ^{ālu}*na-ṣi-bi-na* [*lu*] *e-si-ir-šu 7 ālā-ni bat-tu-bat-te-šu* [*lu*] *ad-di*).[16] Nūr-Adad had dug a ditch (*ḫi-ri-ṣa*) around the city to

11. *RIMA* 2, v.99–21 (p. 24).
12. *RIMA* 2, A.0.87.2, 34 (p. 34).
13. *RIMA* 2, p. 142.
14. *RIMA* 2, A.0.99.2, 45 (p. 149).
15. *RIMA* 2, 46 (p. 149).
16. *RIMA* 2, 63–65 (p. 151).

counterattack,[17] but this tactic did not succeed. The army of the Assyrian king "surrounded the moat with his warriors like a flame and they (the enemy) screamed like children about it (*qarrādi-ia ki-ma nab-li ḫi-ri-ṣa-šu ú-šal-bi i-ša-su-ú muḫḫi-šu ri-ig-mu śèr-ri*)."[18] The Assyrian king laid traps (*giš-pár-ri*), and deprived the city of grain.[19] A notable point is the conclusion of the process. After Adad-nirari II had taken booty from his palace,[20] . . . [(PN not preserved)] restored his throne.[21] He, possibly Nur-Adad, made a holy sacrifice and acknowledged the rule of the Assyrian king before his nobles.[22] Even though the military siege was a life-threatening attack to the enemy city, Adad-nirari II did not destroy the city or kill its king. Instead, he may have allowed Nūr-Adad to retain his throne, through only after he had taken an impressive booty from his palace. The enemy king—if so—finally acknowledged the rule of the Assyrian king over the city and Nur-Adad was taken to Assyria.[23]

In that same year, Adad-nirari II undertook a military campaign to the cities Sikkur and Sappānu. He surrounded (*al-mi*) those cities and fought with them and defeated them (ᾱˡᵘ*si-kur* ᾱˡᵘ*sa-pa-a-nu lu al-mi it-ti-šu-nu am-da-ḫi-ṣi di-ik-ta-šú-nu*).[24] He brought booty from them back to Ashur, and those who had fled from the Assyrian forces came and submitted to Adad-nirari II and pledged tribute to him.[25] The Assyrian king then took booty from these cities and imposed taxes and dues upon them.[26]

Ashurnasirpal II (885–860 BCE)

Texts

The inscriptions of Ashurnasirpal II report numerous military campaigns, many of which refer to sieges involving blockades. These reports include

17. *RIMA* 2, 64b–65 (p. 151).
18. *RIMA* 2, 66b–67a (p. 151).
19. *RIMA* 2, 67b–68a (p. 151).
20. *RIMA* 2, 68b–72 (p. 151).
21. *RIMA* 2, 73 (p. 151).
22. *RIMA* 2, 74–79 (p. 151).
23. *RIMA* 2, 78, 80 (p. 151).
24. *RIMA* 2, 86–87 (p. 152).
25. *RIMA* 2, 89–90a (p. 152).
26. *RIMA* 2, 90b (p. 152).

details about the areas, cities or kingdoms encountered, as well as the process and the result of the campaign.

A.0.101.1

An initial example of siege warfare can be found in the inscriptions concerning Ashurnasirpal II's campaign against the rebellious city, Sūru of Ḫalupe.[27] In this campaign, the Assyrian king approached the city. The "awe of the radiance of Ashur, my lord, overwhelmed them" and the city leaders came out to submit to Ashurnasirpal II.[28] However, the king besieged the city "with my staunch heart and fierce weapons" (*ina gi-piš lìb-bi-ia u šu-uš-mur kakkī-a āla a-si-bi*).[29] After the successful assault of the city, the city leaders surrendered and the soldiers, guilty of rebellion, were handed over to Ashurnasirpal II. The text reports that the king seized all the guilty soldiers and sent his nobles into the palace and the temples of the city[30] to gather extensive booty.[31] Later, he appointed Azi-ili as the new governor of the city.[32] In this military campaign, he did not destroy the city but he changed the administrative, took a large booty, and cruelly punished the rebellious leader, soldiers and officials.[33]

Another example involving a siege occurs in Ashurnasripal II's account of his expedition to the city of Kinabu, which belonged to Ḫullāiia.[34] In this campaign, the king . . . besieged and conquered the city Kinabu (*ina gi-piš ummānāti-a taḫazi-a šit-mu-ri āla a-si-bi aktašad*[ad]), killing eight hundred of the enemy troops, burning three thousand captives, not leaving one of them alive as a hostage.[35] In this military campaign, Ashurnasirpal II does not even mention taking any booty from the city. Instead, he destroyed and burnt the whole rebellious city, flayed the city ruler, and draped his skin over the wall of the (royal) city of Damdammusa.[36]

27. *RIMA* 2, A.0.101.1, i.75–95 (pp. 198–200).
28. *RIMA* 2, i.80–81 (p. 199).
29. *RIMA* 2, i.82 (p. 199).
30. *RIMA* 2, i.82–83a (p. 199).
31. *RIMA* 2, i.83b–89a (p. 199).
32. *RIMA* 2, i.89b (p. 199).
33. *RIMA* 2, i.89–93 (pp. 199–200).
34. *RIMA* 2, i.106–107a (p. 201).
35. *RIMA* 2, i.107b–108 (p. 201).
36. *RIMA* 2, i.110 (p. 201).

Following the destruction of Kinabu, Ashurnasirpal II moved on against the fortified city, Tēla, where many inhabitants of the area had taken refuge.[37] The people trusted in their well-defended city.[38] They did not submit to the king, and, in strife and conflict, he besieged and conquered the city (*šēpī-a la-a iṣ-bu-tú i-na mit-ḫu-ṣi u ti-du-ku āla a-si-bi aktašad*[ad]).[39] As in the case of the city of Kinabu, he killed many of his enemies (3,000) and took booty from the city.[40] Regarding the punishment that he imposed upon the captives, the case of the city of Tēla was much heavier than the case of Kinabu: he burnt many captives and cut off the body parts of others.[41] The campaign concludes with the destruction and burning of the city walls.[42]

When the people of the land of Nirbu in the area of Mount Kašiiari rebelled and took refuge in their fortified city, Išpilipria, and on a mountain, Ashurnasirpal II besieged and conquered the mountain peaks (*ú-ba-na-at šadî-e a-si-bi aktašad*[ad]).[43] The punishment of the rebels was harsh: killing, beheading, burning, and carrying off of captives and booty.[44] The Assyrian king did not demolish the city, but he built a tower of soldiers' heads in front of the city to signify his power.[45]

In his military campaign against Ammali, the fortified city which was ruled by Araštua, but which had offended the god, Ashur, by withholding tribute and corvée,[46] Ashurnasirpal II besieged and conquered the city (*āla a-si-bi aktašad*[ad]).[47] In the conquest, the Assyrian king killed eight hundred soldiers of Araštua and carried off many others.[48] He also razed, destroyed, (and) burnt the city.[49] The inscriptions do not mention any booty from Ammali, though booty is mentioned from other cities in

37. *RIMA* 2, i.112–113 (p. 201).
38. *RIMA* 2, i.114 (p. 201).
39. *RIMA* 2, i.115a (p. 201).
40. *RIMA* 2, i.115b–116a (p. 201).
41. *RIMA* 2, i.116b–118 (p. 201).
42. *RIMA* 2, ii.1–2a (p. 202).
43. *RIMA* 2, ii.16–17a (p. 203).
44. *RIMA* 2, ii.17–18a (p. 203).
45. *RIMA* 2, ii.18b–19a (p. 203).
46. *RIMA* 2, ii.50 (p. 205).
47. *RIMA* 2, ii.55a (p. 206).
48. *RIMA* 2, ii.55b (p. 206).
49. *RIMA* 2, ii.57 (p. 206).

the immediate area, such as Hudun,[50] associated with Araštua's coalition, which were destroyed.

When Ashurnasirpal II approached the city of Madara, the well-fortified city of Labṭuru, the son of Ṭupusu, he besieged the city (*āla a-si-bi*).[51] The people of the city were afraid of the Assyrian king and he received from them property, possessions, (and) sons as hostages.[52] He imposed upon them tribute, taxes, (and) labourers.[53] He also razed and destroyed the city.[54]

Moving on in his military expedition, Ashurnasirpal II besieged the city of Sūru, the fortified city of Kudurru, governor of the land of Suḫu, (*āl su-ú-ru āl dan-nu-ti-šú šá Kudurru šakin* [māt]*su-ḫi a-si-bi*).[55] He besieged the city, and on the second day, he fought his way inside (*āla a-si-bi ina* 2 *u_4-me mit-ḫu-ṣú ina lìb-be aš-kun*).[56] When Kudurru drew back from the city to the Euphrates, the Assyrian king conquered the city.[57] In the battle, he killed many enemies and took captives and booty from the city.[58] Then, he razed and destroyed the city.[59]

In his military campaign against Ḫemti-ili of the land Laqû, Ashurnasirpal II shut him up in his city ([m]*ḫe-em-ti-ili* [māt]*la-qa-a-a ina āli-šú e-sir-šu*).[60] With the support of Ashur, the rebellious king was then frightened by the mighty weapons, the fierce battle, (and) the perfect power of the Assyrian king,[61] who took the property of the palace, silver, gold, tin, bronze, bronze casseroles, and garments with multi-colored trim as booty.[62] He also imposed more tax than ever before upon the city.[63] It is

50. *RIMA* 2, ii.56–57 (p. 206).
51. *RIMA* 2, ii.99 (p. 209).
52. *RIMA* 2, ii. 99 (p. 209).
53. *RIMA* 2, ii.100a (pp. 209–10).
54. *RIMA* 2, ii.100a (pp. 209–10).
55. *RIMA* 2, iii.16b–17a (p. 213).
56. *RIMA* 2, iii.17b–18a (p. 213).
57. *RIMA* 2, iii.18b–19a (p. 213).
58. *RIMA* 2, iii.19b–22 (p. 213).
59. *RIMA* 2, iii. 23 (p. 213).
60. *RIMA* 2, iii.46 (p. 215).
61. *RIMA* 2, iii.46b (p. 215).
62. *RIMA* 2, iii.46b–47 (p. 215).
63. *RIMA* 2, iii.48a (p. 215).

notable that this report of the military campaign is followed by his hunt of wild bulls and ostriches.[64]

Ashurnasirpal II's annals then report an attack on the city of Kaprabu in the land of Bīt-adini, a well-fortified city that "hovered like a cloud in the sky (*kīma urpati ina šamê-e šu-qa-lu-la*),"[65] and whose inhabitants trusted in their own defenses and did not submit to Ashurnasirpal.[66] He besieged and conquered the city, using "tunnels or breaches," "battering-rams," and "siege-towers" (*āla a-si-bi ina píl-še na-pi-li ṣa-a-bi-te āli aktašad*[*ad*]),[67] offering a description of the siege techniques. In the campaign, he killed eight hundred of their soldiers, carried off captives and booty from the city, and resettled twenty-five hundreds of their troops in Calah.[68] He also "razed, destroyed, burnt, (and) consumed the city," thereby imposing "awe of the radiance of Ashur, my lord, upon Bīt-Adini."[69]

Following many other military successes, in his military campaign against Damdammusa, the fortified city of Ilānu, Ashurnasirpal II besieged the city (*āla a-si-bi*).[70] The inscription adds that "My warriors flew like bird(s) against them (*qu-ra-di-ia ki-ma iṣṣūri muḫḫī-šú-nu i-še-'i*)."[71] In the conflict, he killed six hundred of the enemy soldiers and cut off their heads.[72] He also captured four hundred of their soldiers alive[73] and brought out three thousand captives from the city.[74] Afterwards, he brought the heads and the live soldiers to the city of Amedu, the royal city of Ilānu.[75] He built a pile of heads there before the gate of the enemy, and impaled the live soldiers on stakes around the city.[76] He advanced through

64. *RIMA* 2, iii.48b–49 (pp. 215–16).
65. *RIMA* 2, iii.51 (p. 216).
66. *RIMA* 2, iii.52a (p. 216).
67. *RIMA* 2, iii.52b–53a (p. 216).
68. *RIMA* 2, iii.53b–54a (p. 216).
69. *RIMA* 2, iii.54b (p. 216).
70. *RIMA* 2, iii.105b (p. 220).
71. *RIMA* 2, iii.105b (p. 220).
72. *RIMA* 2, iii.106a (p. 220).
73. *RIMA* 2, iii.106b (p. 220).
74. *RIMA* 2, iii.107a (p. 220).
75. *RIMA* 2, iii.107b (p. 220).
76. *RIMA* 2, iii.107b–108 (p. 220).

the gate, and also cut down the city's orchards.[77] The end result of the attack on the city of Amedu, however, is not described.

After the siege and the conquest of Amedu, Ashurnasirpal II continued with a military expedition to the city Udu which was a fortified city of Labṭuru, son of Ṭupusu.[78] In the military campaign, he besieged (*a-si-bi*) and conquered the city with "tunnels or breaches (*píl-ši*)," "siege-towers (*ṣa-pi-te*)," and "(siege) machines (*ne-pe-še*)" (*āla a-si-bi ina píl-ši* ^{iṣu}*ṣa-pi-te ù* né-*pe-še āla akšud*^{ud}).[79] He killed fourteen hundred of his enemies and captured 780 soldiers alive.[80] He impaled the live soldiers on stakes around the city, gouged out the eyes of some, and brought some other captives to Assyria.[81] The inscription concludes that the Assyrian king took the city in hand.[82]

A.0.101.21 (VAT 9752, 9782)

Regarding the texts VAT 9752 and VAT 9782, Grayson argues that these texts belong to Ashurnasirpal II.[83] According to him, the geographic name, "the River Ḫarmiš,"[84] occurs only in the annals of Ashurnasirpal II.[85] Also, the restored phrase, [*īnēšunu ú-na-ap*]*-pil*,[86] is only attested for Ashurnasirpal II.[87] In these texts, the Assyrian king surrounded (*e-si-ir-šú*) Irbibu.[88] When Irbibu dug a moat (*ḫirīṣu*), the Assyrian king surrounded ([*ú*]*-šal-bi*) the city with six forts (6 *ālā-ni*).[89] Then, he took booty, including flocks from the city.[90]

77. *RIMA* 2, iii.109 (p. 220).
78. *RIMA* 2, iii.110 (p. 220).
79. *RIMA* 2, iii.111a (p. 220).
80. *RIMA* 2, iii.111b (p. 220).
81. *RIMA* 2, iii.112–113 (p. 220).
82. *RIMA* 2, iii.113 (p. 220).
83. *RIMA* 2, 265.
84. *RIMA* 2, A.0.101.21, 10' (p. 266).
85. *RIMA* 2, 265.
86. *RIMA* 2, A.0.101.21, 14'a (p. 266).
87. *RIMA* 2, 265.
88. *RIMA* 2, 9'a (p. 266).
89. *RIMA* 2, 9'b-10'a (p. 266).
90. *RIMA* 2, 10'b–11' (p. 266).

Reliefs

Together with the record of military sieges in the annals, Ashurnasirpal II also commissioned numerous reliefs depicting these sieges as carried out against his enemies. Some of them seem to match with the annals or, at least, they seem to show a part of what is written in the annals. Meanwhile, the images of the reliefs often show what is not explained or expressed in the written annals.

Fig. 4.1. An Assyrian Siege-engine under Attack, North-West Palace, Nimrud. British Museum, BM 124554. (Photo: © The Trustees of the British Museum.)

This relief of a siege (Fig. 4.1) was discovered in the throne room of Ahsurnasirpal II at Nimrud and its date is considered as about 865 BCE.[91] In the middle of this relief, the enemy lowers a chain from above, attempting to catch the battering ram. Meanwhile, Assyrian soldiers hold it down in position with hooks. An Assyrian siege-engine against the city wall of the enemy is supporting the battering ram. Blazing torches are being thrown from the wall to hamper the progression of the siege-engine, but two jets of water from the engine are used to control the flame.

This relief illustrates how the Assyrian army attacked a city wall. As noted in some of the texts, the Assyrian siege includes a battering ram attached to a siege-engine. In particular, the relief shows the intensity of the military siege.

91. Reade, *Assyrian Sculpture*, 30.

Fig. 4.2. An Assyrian Siege against a City Wall, South-West Palace, Nimrud. British Museum, BM 118906. (Photo: © The Trustees of the British Museum.)

This slab (Fig. 4.2) is a part of a series of wall-panels which illustrate an Assyrian siege against an enemy wall.[92] Its date is considered as about 875–860 BCE.[93] This relief provides some details about the strategies of the military siege. In the relief, the enemy fortress stands on a mound. The enemy archers are shooting arrows against the Assyrian army. Inside the walls, there is a pulley with ropes. Outside of the walls, an Assyrian soldier on the right side is holding a rope from which a bucket is hanging, and he

92. Curtis and Reade, *Art and Empire*, 47.

93. Curtis and Reade, *Art and Empire*, 47.

is trying to cut it with a knife. Reade suggests that the Assyrian soldier is cutting the rope with which the enemy inside the city walls is trying to get water from a source outside the walls.[94] Reade suggests that this solider is the same as the one on the left side of the panel, who holds a bucket on his left hand and lifts his right hand as a triumphant gesture towards someone.[95] The Assyrian soldier in the middle seems to hold a shield upward to protect his comrades from the attack of the enemy. The exact location and the date of this military siege is not clear, but Reade suggests that it would be somewhere in Syria about the ninth century BCE.[96] There are traces of the standard inscription at the top of the relief.[97]

Fig. 4.3. A Military Siege against a City, North-West Palace, Nimrud. British Museum, BM 124536. (Photo: © The Trustees of the British Museum.)

In the relief of Fig. 4.3, Ashurnasirpal II himself is participating in a military siege against an enemy city.[98] The Assyrian army is attacking the city from the left side, and enemy archers are shooting back from the city wall. A siege-engine is breaching the wall with a battering ram. The engine has six wheels and is covered by a protective body. An Assyrian

94. Curtis and Reade, *Art and Empire*, 47.
95. Curtis and Reade, *Art and Empire*, 47.
96. Curtis and Reade, *Art and Empire*, 47.
97. Curtis and Reade, *Art and Empire*, 47.
98. Porada, "5000 Years," 441.

archer is shooting at the enemies and another solder is holding a shield to protect the archer and himself on the turret of the siege-engine. Behind the machine, Ashurnasirpal II is shooting an arrow. Two royal attendants near him are holding round shields high in their left hands to protect him and carrying arrows or a spear in their right hands. Another attendant behind them is carrying a bow and an arrow.

Fig. 4.4. Escape across a River. Throne Room, North-West Palace, Nimrud. British Museum, BM 124538. (Photo: © The Trustees of the British Museum.)

This relief (Fig. 4.4) seems to be related to a situation described in Ashurnasirpal's annals: the withdrawal of Kudurru into the Euphrates after the siege of Sūru, his fortified city.[99] Its date is about 875–860 BCE.[100] It does not depict the siege of an enemy city, but rather its aftermath of a siege: the enemy's withdrawal to save their lives from the Assyrian army. On the left side of the relief, two Assyrian archers are shooting at the enemy. They are dressed and armed as typical Assyrian soldiers: pointed helmets, short kilts, swords, bows and quivers.[101] Next to them there are trees, one of which seems to be a date-palm.[102] In the middle part of the relief, three enemies are swimming toward a fortified city, which is located on the right side of the relief. They are wearing long robes, which indicate that all three are of high status.[103] One of them, swimming, has been hit by arrows and two others are using animal-skins for buoyancy in the water. The one without

99. Curtis and Reade, *Art and Empire*, 48–49.
100. Curtis and Reade, *Art and Empire*, 49.
101. Curtis and Reade, *Art and Empire*, 48.
102. Curtis and Reade, *Art and Empire*, 48.
103. Curtis and Reade, *Art and Empire*, 48.

a beard is presumably a eunuch.[104] The foundations of the enemy fortress seem to be of stone and the walls of mudbrick.[105] There are traces of the standard inscription at the bottom of the panel.[106]

Reliefs with Epigraphs

The Balawat Gates of Ashurnasirpal II provide scenes of military campaigns including scenes of sieges along with epigraphs. First, the palace gates describe the military campaigns of Ashurnasirpal II against enemy cities.

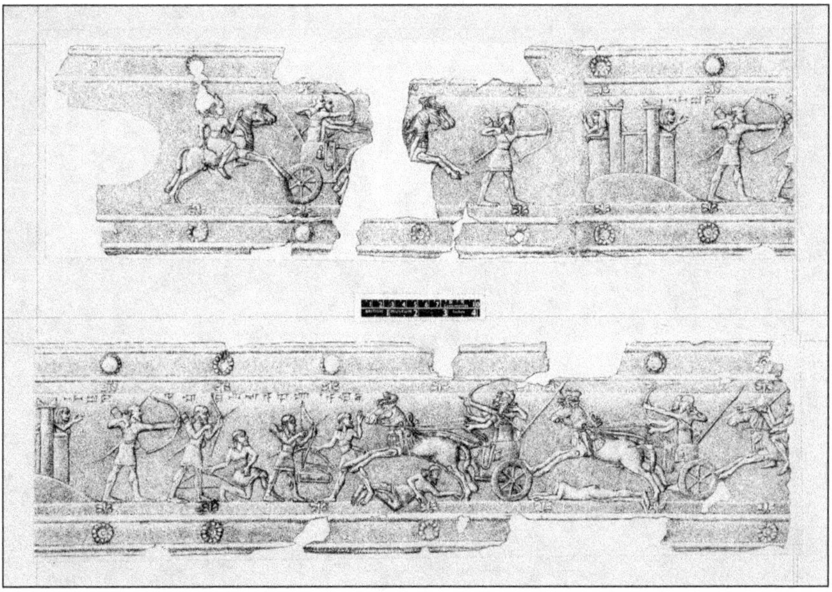

Fig. 4.5. A Campaign against Bit-Adini. The Gates from the Palace of Ashurnasirpal II, Balawat. British Museum ASH II L2, BM 124686. (Drawn by Marjorie Howard). (Photo: © The Trustees of the British Museum.)[107]

Inscription: *ti-du-ku* šá ^{ālu}*ma-ri-na-a šá bīt-*^{m}*a-di-ni*[108]

Translation: battle against the city Marinâ of Bit-Adini

104. Curtis and Reade, *Art and Empire*, 49.
105. Curtis and Reade, *Art and Empire*, 49.
106. Curtis and Reade, *Art and Empire*, 49.
107. Curtis and Tallis, *Balawat Gates of Ashurnasirpal II*, 111.
108. Curtis and Tallis, *Balawat Gates of Ashurnasirpal II*, 31.

This band (Fig. 4.5) depicts an Assyrian attack against the city of Marinâ in Bit-Adini. A pair of horses is coming from the left and the rider wears a conical helmet and carries a whip. There is a chariot in front of the horses, with a bowman aiming at the enemy city on the right. Another bowman in front of the chariot is also shooting at the enemy city. Two women of the battlements of the city raise their hands as a gesture of submission or supplication.[109] On the right side of the enemy cities, there are five enemy archers. The king's chariot is advancing against them, followed by another chariot and a pair of horses with a spearman. Two enemies have fallen down under the chariots, one already decapitated.

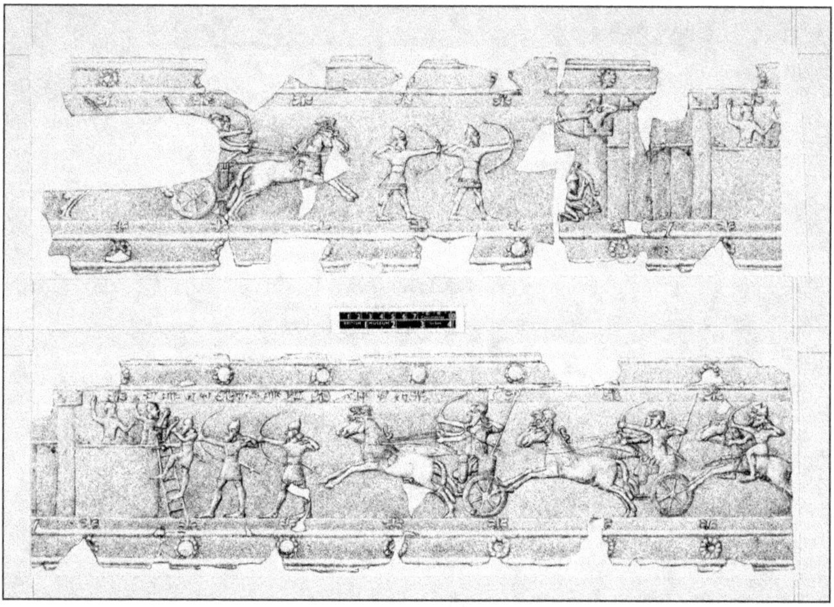

Fig. 4.6. A Campaign against Ḫatti. The Gates from the Palace of Ashurnasirpal II, Balawat. British Museum ASH II L3, BM 124695. (Drawn by Marjorie Howard). (Photo: © The Trustees of the British Museum.)[110]

Inscription: ^{ālu}*ú-[l]u-ba šá* ^{m}*sa-ga-ra* [*šar*$_4$ ^{m}]^{āt}*ḫa-te akšud*^{ud}[111]

Translation: The city Ulluba of Sagara, [king of] the land Ḫatti, I conquered

109. Curtis and Tallis, *Balawat Gates of Ashurnasirpal II*, 31.

110. Curtis and Tallis, *Balawat Gates of Ashurnasirpal II*, 113.

111. Curtis and Tallis, *Balawat Gates of Ashurnasirpal II*, 32.

This band (Fig. 4.6) describes the conquest of Ulluba of Sagara, king of Ḫatti. From the left side, a chariot is advancing against the enemy city and the archer in the chariot is shooting against the city. In front of the chariot, two archers are aiming at the fortified city. An Assyrian soldier crouches and tries to undermine the wall with his sword, while holding a round shield for protection. An enemy archer is shooting from the city wall. On the right side of the city wall, two enemy soldiers are hurling stones with their right hands.[112] An Assyrian soldier with a sword is climbing up a scaling ladder, while two archers behind him are shooting at the defenders on the city wall. The king's chariot is advancing with another chariot. A spearman and an archer on horses are following the chariots.

Fig. 4.7. A Campaign against Bit-Adini. The Gates from the Palace of Ashurnasirpal II, Balawat. British Museum ASH II L7, BM 124692. (Photo: © The Trustees of the British Museum.)

Inscription: ^{ālu}*i*[*a*(?)-*l*]*i-gu* [šá *bīt*]-*a-di-ni akšud*^{ud}[113]

Translation: The city I[all]igu of [Bit]-Adini, I conquered

In this band (Fig. 4.7), two mounted riders advance over a fallen enemy toward the enemy city wall from the left side. Two enemy archers are moving toward the city as if in retreat yet, while raising their right hands in a gesture of surrender.[114] On the battlements of the cities, two women are laying their hands on their foreheads. This gesture might represent horror or grief.[115] On the right side of the enemy city, an enemy chariot is coming to the city, followed by enemy archers, two of whom are raising their left hands. The king's chariot is following together with another chariot, with fallen enemies on the ground underneath the two chariots.

112. Curtis and Tallis, *Balawat Gates of Ashurnasirpal II*, 32.
113. Curtis and Tallis, *Balawat Gates of Ashurnasirpal II*, 36.
114. Curtis and Tallis, *Balawat Gates of Ashurnasirpal II*, 36.
115. Curtis and Tallis, *Balawat Gates of Ashurnasirpal II*, 36.

Fig. 4.8. A Campaign against Bit-Adini. The Gates from the Palace of Ashurnasirpal II, Balawat. British Museum ASH II R2, BM 124691. (Photo: © The Trustees of the British Museum.)

Inscription: *ēkal* [^{m}*aššurnasirpal*] šar$_4$ *kiš*[*šati šar*$_4$ *aššur mār tukulti-ninurta šar*$_4$ *aššur*] *mār adad-nirari šar*$_4$ *aššur-ma* $^{\bar{a}lu}$ [*r*]*u?-gu-lu-tú šá bīt-*^{m}*a-di-ni akšud*^{ud}[116]

Translation: palace of Ashurnasirpal, king of the world, king of Assyria, son of Tukulti-ninurta, king of Assyria, son of Adad-nirari, (who was) also king of Assyria: the town of Rugulutu of Bit-Adini I conquered

In this band (Fig. 4.8), the Assyrian army is attacking the town of Rugulutu in Bit-Adini. On the left side, two Assyrian chariots are advancing against enemy bowmen. Two Assyrian soldiers fight with the bowmen. One seizes his enemy by the hair and stabs him in the throat with a dagger. The other approaches a kneeling archer who is aiming at him. There are two women on the battlements of the enemy city. Each of them is holding one hand pressed down on to her head while putting the other hand to her ear. On the right side of the city, an enemy bowman is aiming at an Assyrian chariot which is running over a fallen enemy. Two other enemy archers raise their left hands in a gesture of submission.[117]

116. Curtis and Tallis, *Balawat Gates of Ashurnasirpal II*, 39.

117. Curtis and Tallis, *Balawat Gates of Ashurnasirpal II*, 39.

Fig. 4.9. A Campaign against Bit-Yakin. The Gates from the Palace of Ashurnasirpal II, Balawat. British Museum ASH II R3, BM124688. (Photo: © The Trustees of the British Museum.)

Inscription: *āla* [*x-x*]*-x-su šá bīt-*^{m}*ia-ḫi-ri akšud*^{ud}[118]

Translation: the city [. . .]su of Bit-Yahiri I conquered

In this band (Fig. 4.9), the Assyrian army is attacking a town in Bit-Yahiri. On the left side of the city, an enemy archer is shooting at the Assyrian king in a three-man chariot which is running over a fallen enemy.[119] Three enemy bowmen between them are fleeing toward the enemy city. Another chariot is following the king's chariot. Each of the women on the battlements of the city wall is putting one hand to her ear and the other hand upwards. On the right side of the city, an enemy archer is shooting at an Assyrian chariot. Two enemy archers are between them and a third has fallen to the ground.

Along with the palace gates, the gates of Ashurnasirpal II from the Temple of Mamu also have some scenes of the military campaigns of Ashurnasirpal II against enemy cities. A band from the gates of Ashurnasirpal II from the Temple of Mamu ("Campaign against Bit-Adini," BM ASH II R2) shows the conquest of the city of Marinâ of Bit-Adini.[120] From the left side, the king's chariot is advancing against the enemy city. Two other chariots and a pair of horses are following it. In front of the row of the chariots, Assyrian archers are shooting at the enemy city while one archer is climbing up a scaling ladder. Under the ladder, an Assyrian soldier is undermining the foot of the city wall. An enemy archer is shooting at the Assyrian army from the wall and there is a woman with an entreating gesture. On the right side of the city wall, Assyrian archers are shooting at the enemy city followed by Assyrian chariots.

118. Curtis and Tallis, *Balawat Gates of Ashurnasirpal II*, 40.
119. Curtis and Tallis, *Balawat Gates of Ashurnasirpal II*, 40.
120. Curtis and Tallis, *Balawat Gates of Ashurnasirpal II*, 177.

The band contains inscriptions as written below:

Inscription: [ālu]*ma-ri-n*[*a*]-[*a*] *šá bīt-a-di-ni*[121]

Translation: city of Marinâ of Bit-Adini

Another band from the temple gates ("Campaign against Bit-Adini," BM ASH II R7) shows the conquest of the city of Hilqian in Bit-Adini.[122] From the left side, two pairs of horsemen follow the king's chariot, advancing against the city wall. In front of them, Assyrian archers are shooting at the city while another Assyrian soldier is undermining the foot of the wall with his sword. Defending archers are shooting at the Assyrians, while some of them are falling off the wall with arrows shot in their heads. On the right side of the city wall, Assyrian archers are shooting at the enemy city. Behind them, Assyrian horsemen and a chariot are advancing toward the city.

The band contains inscriptions as written below:

Inscription: [ālu]*ḫi-il-qi-an šá bīt-a-di-ni*[123]

Translation: city of Hilqian of Bit-Adini

Shalmaneser III (858–824 BCE)

Texts

Aḫunu

Military campaigns against Aḫunu, the man of Bīt-Adini, occurred throughout the reign of Shalmaneser III.[124] In particular, A.0.102.1 and A.0.102.2 overlap with each other, and it is useful to group all the related texts together.

121. Curtis and Tallis, *Balawat Gates of Ashurnasirpal II*, 63.

122. Curtis and Tallis, *Balawat Gates of Ashurnasirpal II*, 187.

123. Curtis and Tallis, *Balawat Gates of Ashurnasirpal II*, 68.

124. Aḫunu is also cited by Ashurnasirpal II (*RIMA* 2, A.0.101.1, iii.55, 61, 63 [pp. 216–17]).

A.0.102.1 AND A.0.102.2

These two texts include the earliest version of the annals (A.0.102.1) and the more comprehensive but briefer "Kurkh Monolith" text (A.0.102.2), and they are intertwined in reporting about the first several years.[125] According to the "Kurkh Monolith" text, Shalmaneser III advanced to the city of Tīl-Barsip, a fortified city of Aḫunu, the man of Bīt-Adini.[126] In the process, apparently following a battle in the open field in which Shalmaneser prevailed, he shut up Aḫunu in his city (*i-na āli-šú e-sir-šú*),[127] but there is no official mention of a conquest of that city or of receiving booty from that city. Rather, Shalmaneser III moved on from that city and besieged and captured (*āla a-si-bi ak-ta-šad*) another city of Aḫunu, the city of Burmar'ina.[128] In this campaign, he killed three hundred of the enemy warriors and erected a tower of heads in front of the city.[129]

Based on the Fort Shalmaneser text, A.0.102.1, Shalmaneser III advanced to the city of Dabigu, another fortified city of Aḫunu, later in his first regnal year.[130] He besieged and captured the city (*a-si-bi ak-ta-šad*).[131] After the capture, he killed the people, took booty from the city and destroyed the city.[132] According to the "Kurkh Monolith" text, Shalmaneser III marched against Til-Barsip. Aḫunu himself engaged in battle, but Shalmaneser III prevailed and confined him to his city, Til-Barsip (*ina* [*ālīšu*] *e-sir-šú*).[133] The Assyrian king moved on and captured another six cities of Aḫunu, including the city of Dabigu.[134]

After his conquest of the city of Šilaia, Shalmaneser III yet again advanced against Aḫunu and his fortified city, Tīl-Barsip. With a full description, the text reports that, as for the fortified city, "I (Shalmaneser III) besieged the city Tīl-Barsip, his fortified city. I surrounded him with

125. *RIMA* 3, 7, 11–12.

126. *RIMA* 3, A.0.102.2, i.31b–32a (p. 15).

127. *RIMA* 3, i.32–33 (p. 15).

128. *RIMA* 3, i.34a (p. 15).

129. *RIMA* 3, i.34b–35a (p. 15).

130. *RIMA* 3, A.0.102.1, 90'–91'a (p. 11).

131. *RIMA* 3, 91'a (p. 11).

132. *RIMA* 3, 91'b-92'a (p. 11).

133. *RIMA* 3, A.0.102.2, ii.13–16a (pp. 17–18).

134. *RIMA* 3, ii.16b-18a (p. 18). However, there is no preserved reference to a siege of these cities in A.0.102.2, unlike the reference regarding Dabigu in A.0.102.1 (*RIMA* 3, 90'-91' [p. 11]).

my warriors, and did battle against him (ālu*tīl-bur-si-ip āla dan-nu-ti-šú a-si-bi qu-ra-di-ya* ⌜*ú-šá*⌝*-al-me-šu mit-ḫu-ṣu ina lìb-bi-šú áš-kun*)."[135] The Assyrian king proceeded to cut down the gardens of the city and to press the attack.[136] Aḫunu, however, fully intimidated, succeeded in escaping and went up into the mountains.[137] The text does not report a conquest of the city or the receipt of booty; the focus is on Aḫunu himself. What follows immediately is the report that in a subsequent campaign, Shalmaneser again went after Aḫunu and finally captured him.[138] Grayson dates this activity to 855 BCE.[139]

A.0.102.5

Based on the texts on the Balawat Gates, which involve one long text (A.0.102.5) and numerous short epigraphs (A.0.102.63–86),[140] somewhat carelessly inscribed, in 855 BCE (his fourth regnal year), Shalmaneser III advanced to the mountain city of Šītamrat to which Aḫunu, who had previously been confined to his city (*ina āli-šú e-sir-šú*),[141] had escaped for refuge. Shalmaneser III pursued him there in a subsequent campaign. He besieged the mountain peak (*ubānat šadê-e a-si-bi*),[142] routed 17,500 soldiers, and took them, Aḫunu and a substantial booty to his city, Ashur.[143]

Others

A.0.102.1 and A.0.102.2

A.0.102.1, a stone slab at Fort Shalmaneser is known as the earliest version of the annals of Shalmaneser III.[144] According to this text, he besieged and captured the city of Sugunia, the fortified city of Aramu the Urarṭian (*āla*

135. *RIMA* 3, A.0.102.2, ii.67b (p. 21).
136. *RIMA* 3, ii.68a (p. 21).
137. *RIMA* 3, ii.68b–69a (p. 21).
138. *RIMA* 3, ii.69–75a (pp. 21–22); see also A.0.102.8, 5'b–8'a (p. 45).
139. *RIMA* 3, 11 (p. 45).
140. A.0.102.68 accompanies a representation of Dabigu, a city of Aḫunu.
141. *RIMA* 3, A.0.102.5, iii.4 (p. 29).
142. *RIMA* 3, iii.5a (p. 29).
143. *RIMA* 3, iii.5b–6 (pp. 29–30).
144. *RIMA* 3, 7.

a-si-bi ak-ta-šad).[145] In this siege, he took the city, killed many people, and took some booty from it.[146] He even erected two towers of heads in front of the city and burned fourteen of the surrounding cities.[147]

Shalmaneser III employed a military siege in his campaign against the city of Aridu, the fortified city of Ninnu in the land of Simesi. In the campaign, he besieged and captured the city (*āla a-si-bi ak-ta-šad*).[148] He killed its people and took booty from it.[149] He even erected a tower of heads in front of the city and burned the boys and girls.[150]

According to A.0.102.1, Shalmaneser III also marched against the city Ali[ṣir] or Ali[muš], the fortified city of Sapalume, the Patinean, who had joined together with Aḫunu and many others.[151] In the campaign, Shalmaneser III besieged and took the enemy city (*āla a-si-*[*b*]*i ak-ta-*[*šad*]).[152] After the city was taken, he took booty from it and killed seven hundred of its warriors.[153]

The Kurkh Monolith reports that Shalmaneser III also advanced to the city of Sazabû, the fortified city of Sangara, the Carchemishite.[154] He besieged and captured the city (*āla a-si-bi ak-*[*ta-šad*]),[155] having killed many people of the city and taken booty from it.[156] He even destroyed and burned its surrounding cities.[157]

In a subsequent campaign, Shalmaneser III advanced to the city of Šilaia, a fortified city of Kāki who was king of the land of Ḫubuškia.[158] In this campaign, his strategy was the usual. He besieged and captured the city

145. *RIMA* 3, A.0.102.1, 29b–31a (pp. 8–9).
146. *RIMA* 3, 31b–32a (p. 9).
147. *RIMA* 3, 32.b–33a (p. 9).
148. *RIMA* 3, A.0.102.2, i.16a (p. 14).
149. *RIMA* 3, i.16b (p. 14).
150. *RIMA* 3, i.16b–17a (p. 14).
151. *RIMA* 3, A.0.102.1, 64'b–70'a (p. 10).
152. *RIMA* 3, 70'b (p. 10).
153. *RIMA* 3, 71'b (?)–72'a (p. 10). Cf. A.0.102.2, ii.3–4 (*RIMA* 3, 17).
154. *RIMA* 3, A.0.102.2, ii.18b-19a (p. 18).
155. *RIMA* 3, ii.19b (p. 18).
156. *RIMA* 3, ii.19b–20a (p. 18).
157. *RIMA* 3, ii.20b (p. 18).
158. *RIMA* 3, ii.63b–64a (p. 21).

(*āla a-si-bi ak-ta-šad*).[159] He killed many people of the city and took three thousand captives as well as extensive booty from it to Ashur.[160]

A.0.102.5

In 851–850 BCE, Marduk-bēl-usāte rebelled against Shalmaneser III's control, so the Assyrian king campaigned against his rebellious cities. In the first campaign, he approached the city of Mê-turnat.[161] He besieged and captured the city (*āla a-si-bi ak-ta-šad*),[162] and then plundered it. He moved on to the city Gannanate. Marduk-bēl-usāte came out to fight with him and was defeated, so Shalmaneser shut him up (*e-sir-šú*) in his city while despoiling his land.[163] In the following year, he approached the city of Laḫiru, which he besieged and captured the city (*āla a-si-bi ak-ta-šad*), killing many and plundering the city.[164] Marduk-bēl-usāte, who had taken refuge there, "escaped like a fox through a hole" and took refuge in Arman.[165] Shalmaneser III finally shut up Marduk-bēl-usāte in the city of Arman (*ina āli ar-man e-sir-šú*).[166] He besieged and captured the city (*āla a-si-bi ak-ta-šad*), and plundered it.[167] He finally killed the rebel and his *hupšu*-(low class) troops.[168]

In the same year, he approached the city of Baqānu, a fortress of Adinu, the man of Bīt-Dakkuri.[169] Shalmaneser III besieged and captured the city (*āla a-si-bi ak-ta-šad*).[170] He took booty from it, destroyed, and burned the city.[171]

159. *RIMA* 3, ii.64b (p. 21).
160. *RIMA* 3, ii.64b–65a (p. 21).
161. *RIMA* 3, A.0.102.5, iv.3a (p. 30).
162. *RIMA* 3, iv.3b (p. 30).
163. *RIMA* 3, iv.4–5a (p. 30).
164. *RIMA* 3, vi.6 (p. 30).
165. *RIMA* 3, v.1–2a (p. 30).
166. *RIMA* 3, v.2b (p. 30).
167. *RIMA* 3, v.2b–3a (p. 30).
168. *RIMA* 3, v.3a (p. 30).
169. *RIMA* 3, vi.6a (p. 31).
170. *RIMA* 3, vi.6a (p. 31).
171. *RIMA* 3, vi.6b (p. 31).

A.0.102.6

According to an edition of the annals that extend the reports to his sixteenth regnal year, Shalmaneser III advanced to the people of the land Paqaraḫubunu in his twelfth regnal year (847 BCE).[172] He besieged and captured the mountain peak (*ú-ba-na-at šadê-e a-si-bi ak-ta-šad*) where the people had taken refuge.[173] He killed the people and plundered the land.[174]

A.0.102.16

The most detailed account of Shalmaneser III's campaign in his twenty-first regnal year (838 BCE) and following is inscribed on a stone statue from Calah, reporting that the king marched against the cities of Hazael of Damascus.[175] He captured (*akšud*^{ud}) various fortified cities including Danabu and Malaḫu by means of "[breach(ing)] ([*pilše*])," "battering rams ([*na-p*]*í-li*)," and "siege towers (*ṣa-bi-te*)."[176] He finally razed, destroyed and burned the cities, a familiar trio.[177]

In his twenty-second regnal year (837 BCE), Shalmaneser III advanced to the Hatti land and moved on, going down "to the cities of Tuatti, the Tabalite. I (Shalmaneser III) razed, destroyed, (and) burned their cities. The fearful radiance of Ashur, my lord, overwhelmed Tuatti and he remained confined in his city (*ina āli-šu in-ni-sir*) to save his life."[178] The text continues, "I (Shalmaneser III) surrounded Artulu, his royal city (^{ālu}*ar-tu-lu āl šarru-ti-šú al-ti-me*). Kiki, his son, was afraid to fight and submitted to me. I received tribute from him."[179] The texts repeatedly use *esēru* and *lab*/*mû*.

In his twenty-sixth regnal year (833 BCE), Shalmaneser III surrounded Tanakun, the fortified city of Tullu (^{āl}[^{u}*tanakun*] [*āl dan*]-*nu-ti-šú šá* ^{m}*tu-ul-li al-*[*me*]).[180] Tullu submitted to the king without any other

172. *RIMA* 3, A.0.102.6, iii.16–17b (p. 38).
173. *RIMA* 3, iii.18–19a (p. 3).
174. *RIMA* 3, iii.19b–20 (pp. 38–39).
175. *RIMA* 3, A.0.102.16, 152'–162' (pp. 78–79).
176. *RIMA* 3, 158'a (p. 79).
177. *RIMA* 3, 158'b–159'a (p. 79).
178. *RIMA* 3, 165'–168' (p. 79).
179. *RIMA* 3, 168'–170' (p. 79).
180. *RIMA* 3, 217'b–218'a (p. 80).

military conflict between them.[181] The Assyrian king took hostages and tribute from him.[182] Then, he advanced to Mount Lamenaš and besieged and captured the mountain peak (*ú-ba-an šadê-e a-si-bi ak-ta-šad*).[183] There, he captured and plundered the city.[184]

Reliefs

The reliefs from the gates installed by Shalmaneser III at Balawat (Imgur-Enlil), depict the king's expeditions in northern Syria.[185] These bands include embossed scenes of Shalmaneser III's campaigns in Syria.[186] The upper frieze of the band depicts the attack against Dabigu in northern Syria.[187] The inscription on the left side of the upper register (A.0.102.68) states: "Battle against the city Dabigu, which belonged to Aḫunu of Bīt-Adini."[188] Meanwhile, the lower register represents another Syrian city,[189] but then shifts to yet another site. In the upper frieze, Assyrian chariots and royal attendants are shown behind the king, who is seated on a throne with attendants. In front of the king, there are sixteen Assyrian archers attacking Dabigu, from the left. A soldier with a shield is scaling a ladder against the city wall, with a sapper below. There are nine archers and five chariots, followed by four soldiers on the right. One defender is shown at each end of the city wall.

The left side of the lower frieze apparently has a representation of an attack of the Assyrian army against another city in Syria.[190] The Assyrian army is leaving their camp to attack the enemy city. Assyrian chariots

181. *RIMA* 3, 218'b–219'a (p. 80).

182. *RIMA* 3, 219'b–220'a (p. 80).

183. *RIMA* 3, 220'b–222'a (p. 80).

184. *RIMA* 3, 222'b–224'a (p. 80).

185. Barnett, *Assyrian Palace Reliefs*, figs. 159–60, 163–64; Strommenger, *5000 Years*, 442.

186. Band VI describes Shalmaneser III's expedition in northern Syria. For a line drawing of the whole band, see Schachner, *Bilder eines Weltreichs*, 296. For the detailed scenes of the band, see Birch, *Bronze Ornaments of the Palace Gates*, plates J1–J7; Strommenger, *5000 Years*, plate 210.

187. Strommenger, *5000 Years*, 442.

188. *RIMA* 3, 142.

189. Schachner, *Bilder eines Weltreichs*, 41–43; King, *Bronze Reliefs from the Gates of Shalmaneser*, 24.

190. Strommenger, *5000 Years*, 442.

and royal attendants follow the king who is seated on a throne. Assyrian archers are shooting at the enemy on the city walls and a six-wheeled siege engine is breaching the wall with a battering ram. On the right side of the city wall, six enemy soldiers are impaled, and several Assyrian soldiers approach the city. The impalement of an enemy outside a city gate was intended to punish and frighten the enemy.[191]

Regarding the relationship between the images and the text (epigraph) of the Balawat gates, Schachner suggests that both of them have a common goal: emphasis on the Assyrian kingship.[192] Even though a comparison between the images and the text of the gates shows their differences in content, both of the media emphasize the power of the Assyrian king.[193] In particular, the scenes and the epigraphs of the military campaigns seem to highlight the controlling power of the king over the enemies.

Adad-nārārī III (810–783 BCE)

Texts: A.0.104.6 and A.0.104.8

Adad-nārārī III advanced against Mari in Damascus during his reign.[194] Two texts describe this military campaign against Mari with details of the tribute. The text is engraved on a stone-stele that was discovered at Saba'a. It states, "I commanded [my troops to march to Damascus]. I [confined] Mari in Damascus. [. . . He brought to me] 100 talents of gold (and) 1,000 talents of silver as tribute. [I received it and took it to Assyria.]."[195] A related text was found by Loftus in 1854 at Calah.[196] According to this text, the Assyrian king marched to Damascus and confined Mari in Damascus, his royal city (*ina āli di-ma-áš-qi āl šarru-ti-šú lu-ú e-sir-šú*).[197] The awesome brilliance of Ashur overwhelmed him and he submitted to the Assyrian king, becoming his vassal.[198] He received "2,300 talents of silver,

191. Strommenger, *5000 Years*, 442.

192. Schachner, *Bilder eines Weltreichs*, 261.

193. Schachner, *Bilder eines Weltreichs*, 261.

194. The exact date of the military campaign has not yet been clearly identified. For a detailed discussion about it, please see Pitard, *Ancient Damascus*, 160–67.

195. *RIMA* 3, A.0.104.6, 19–20 (p. 209).

196. *RIMA* 3, p. 212.

197. *RIMA* 3, A.0.104.8, 15–16 (p. 213).

198. *RIMA* 3, 17–18a (p. 213).

20 talents of gold, 3,000 talents of bronze, 5,000 talents of iron, linen garments with multi-colored trim, an ivory bed, a couch with inlaid ivory, his property (and) possessions without number . . . within his palace in Damascus."[199] Regarding the chronological order and the discrepancy in tribute reports between these texts, Luis Siddall argues that the Saba'a stele pre-dates the Calah text.[200]

The tribute represents the acknowledgment of the rule of the Assyrian Empire through a suzerain and vassal relationship. Bagg agrees that the payment of tribute by Mari is related to his subservience to the Assyrian king.[201] Furthermore, Siddall argues that Adad-nārārī III's subjugation of Mari was his crowning military achievement and is found in every inscription composed after the Saba'a stele.[202]

Ashur-nārārī V (754–745 BCE)

Texts

There is only a fragmentary record of the military campaigns by Ashur-nārārī V. Grayson suggests that this text describes a battle followed by the granting of a territory to Marduk-šarra-uṣur.[203] This text contains some words such as "siege ladders (*si-mi-il/la-te*)" and "siege ramps (*na-bal-kát-te*)."[204] Even though the text is fragmentary, those words indicate that Ashur-nārārī V employed military siege tactics in his military campaigns.

Tiglath-pileser III (744–727 BCE)

Texts

A valuable text referencing the reign of Tiglath-pileser III is the Kalḫu annals, which record his military expeditions. Barely one third, if not less, of the whole text has survived.[205] For example, the record of the siege against

199. *RIMA* 3,18b–21 (p. 213).
200. Siddall, *Reign of Adad-Nīrārī III*, 42–43.
201. Bagg, *Assyrer und das Westland*, 207.
202. Siddall, *Reign of Adad-Nīrārī III*, 41.
203. *RIMA* 3, 246.
204. *RIMA* 3, A.0.107.1, 2 (p. 247).
205. *RINAP* 1, 4.

Arpad and the conquest of northern Syria from 742 BCE to 740 BCE is missing.[206] In addition to the Kalḫu annals, there are also some additional texts which describe the military expeditions of Tiglath-pileser III.

In 739 BCE, Tiglath-pileser III attacked the land Ulluba. In this campaign, the text says "I sur[rounded] . . . like a ring (*kīma kip-pa-ti al?-[me]-ma?*)."[207] Even though this text has lost some sections, it records that the enemy cities were afraid of the Assyrian army led by Tiglath-pileser III.[208] The text also states that the king took booty from the cities.[209]

In 735 BCE, the army of Tiglath-pileser III advanced to the land of Urarṭu. The Kalḫu annals and other annalistic texts record the military campaigns but they do not describe any siege. Instead, they present the results of the campaign—booty from the enemy cities, the capture and destruction of various cities.[210] Meanwhile, some of the "summary inscriptions" describe sieges of cites in the area. One of the texts is inscribed on a stone slab that "might have been used as a pavement slab in the Central Palace at Kalḫu."[211] According to this text, Tiglath-pileser III confined Sarduri to the city of Ṭurušpâ (*i-na āl ṭu-ru-uš-pa-[a] āli-šú [e]-sir-šú-ma*).[212] Through the siege, the Assyrian king defeated Sarduri and erected his own royal image in front of the city.[213] Another summary inscription reporting this military expedition was found "in the northeast corner of the South-West Palace at Kalḫu."[214] This inscription also describes the siege of the city by Tiglath-pileser III and its defeat, followed by the erection of the royal image of the Assyrian king in front of the city.[215] A third report, found in the Nabu temple at Kalḫu likewise describes the campaign against Sarduri.[216] It is notable that these three inscriptions concur, as shown in Fig. 4.10. Even though none of them describe any booty being taken from the city proper,

206. *RINAP 1*, 6.

207. Tadmor, *Inscriptions of Tiglath-Pileser III*, 114–15; *RINAP 1*, No. 37, 37 (p. 92).

208. *RINAP 1*, 38–41.

209. *RINAP 1*, 42–43a.

210. *RINAP 1*, pp. 54–57, pp. 88–89.

211. *RINAP 1*, 95.

212. Tadmor, *Inscriptions of Tiglath-Pileser III*, 124–25; *RINAP 1*, No. 39, 23a (p. 98).

213. *RINAP 1*, 23b–24 (p. 98).

214. *RINAP 1*, No. 41 (p. 101).

215. Tadmor, *Inscriptions of Tiglath-Pileser III*, 134–35; *RINAP 1*, No. 41, 21'b–25'a (p. 103).

216. *RINAP 1*, 128.

they clearly depict a victory of the Assyrian king over Sarduri, but they do not mention his capture or the capture of his city of refuge.

RINAP 1	Terror & Flight	Confine/outside-gates defeat	Statue
No. 39, 20b-24a	After a battlefield defeat	Yes (*ēsiršu*) / Yes	Yes
No. 41, 15'-25'	After a battlefield defeat	Yes (*ēsiršu*) / Yes	Yes
No. 49, 1'-4'	After a battlefield defeat	Yes (*ēsir*[?]*šu*) / Yes	Yes

Fig. 4.10. Texts regarding Tiglath-pileser III's Campaign against Sarduri.

According to a Kalḫu text, in 733 BCE, Tiglath-pileser III besieged Damascus and its king, Rezin (Rahiānu), for forty-five days.[217] This military campaign is also mentioned in 2 Kgs 16:5–8 and Isa 7:1.[218] In the military expedition to Damascus, the warfare between them became severe.[219] Rezin fled from before the Assyrian army into his city and the Assyrian text says, "he entered the gate of his city [like] a mongoose."[220] The Assyrian king confined him to his city "like a caged bird / a bird in a cage (*kīma iṣ-ṣur qu-up-pi e-sir-šú*)."[221] During the forty-five day siege, Tiglath-pileser III cut down his enemy's plantations and orchards.[222] It is notable that the siege did not conclude with the capture or destruction of Damascus. Subsequently, the text states that the Assyrian king surrounded and captured Rezin's ancestral city, [*x x*]-*ḫādara* ([*x x*]-*ḫa-a-da-ra . . . al-me ak-šud*).[223] Then, he took booty from the cities of the land

217. *RINAP 1*, No. 20 (p. 57).

218. *RINAP 1*, 13.

219. Tadmor, *Inscriptions of Tiglath-Pileser III*, 78–79; *RINAP 1*, No. 20, 1'-8'a (pp. 58–59).

220. *RINAP 1*, 9' (p. 59).

221. *RINAP 1*, 11'a (p. 59). There are other comparable similes in the inscriptions of Tiglath-Pileser III: "I overwhelmed the (tribe) Puqudu like a (case) net" (*mpu-qu-du kīma sa-pa-ri as-hu-up, RINAP 1*, No. 47, 13b [p. 118]); "I ensnared Chaldea in its entirety as with a bird-snare" (*mātkal-du a-na si-ḫir-ti-šú ḫu-ḫa-riš as-⌈ḫu⌉-up, RINAP 1*, No. 47, 15a [p. 119]); and "as with a bird-snare, I ensnared the lands" (*ḫu-ḫa-riš ak-tùm-ma, RINAP 1*, No. 47, 29–32 [p. 120]).

222. *RINAP 1*, 11'b–12' (p. 59).

223. *RINAP 1*, 13'–14'a (p. 59).

of Damascus and destroyed 591 Cities of the sixteen districts of the land Damascus.[224] Finally, he killed Rezin (2 Kgs 16:9).

In 731 BCE, Tiglath-pileser III besieged the city of Šapīya.[225] According to the text, the Assyrian king confined Mukīn-zēri to Sapê (Šapīya), his royal city (ᵐ*mukīn-zēri* ᵐ [*a*]-*muk-ka-a-ni ina* ^ālu^*sa-pe-e āl šarru-tí-šú e-sir-šú*) and inflicted a heavy defeat upon him before his city gates.[226] Regarding this military campaign, the text does not describe any conquest or booty. Instead, it states that the Assyrian king burned orchards and *musukkannu*-trees around the city wall.[227] This situation is similar to that of Rezin and Damascus. Even when the king names all of the cities that he destroyed in his campaign against Mukīn-zēri, Sapê (Šapīya) is not in the list of destroyed cities. Therefore, it is possible that the siege of the city did not lead to the conquest or destruction of the city itself.

Reliefs with Epigraphs

Even though many of the reliefs and sculpted slabs from the reign of Tiglath-pileser III are also missing,[228] some sets of reliefs of Tiglath-pileser III regarding military sieges have been recovered from his Central and South-West Palaces at Nineveh. These reliefs provide scenes of the sieges and their results.

224. *RINAP 1*, 14'b–17' (p. 59).

225. *RINAP 1*, No. 47, obv. line 23b (p. 119).

226. *RINAP 1*, 23b (p. 119).

227. *RINAP 1*, 23b–24a (p. 119).

228. *RINAP 1*, 5.

Fig. 4.11. Prisoners and Cattle Leaving a Babylonian City, Central Palace, Nineveh. British Museum, BM 118882. (Photo: © The Trustees of the British Museum.)

This relief (Fig. 4.11), which was found at the Central Palace at Nineveh, depicts a scene after the capture of the city. There are three gateways with double doors and there is a date-palm tree, which indicates that this city is a Babylonian city.[229] There is a siege machine with a battering ram in front of the city wall. Since the city has already been taken by the Assyrian army, this siege-engine is not in action. It has a turret in its front and four wheels under its body. On the upper level of the relief, a beardless officer stands with a short stick in his right hand. It seems that he is counting out the spoil for the two scribes standing opposite him,[230] both of whom seem to be beardless officers, i.e., eunuchs. The first one holds a clay-tablet in his left and a stylus in his right hand. The second one is writing on a roll presumably made of leather.[231] They seem to be scribes for the cuneiform text and for the Aramaic script, respectively.[232] Behind them, the counted spoil is arranged in two rows and driven away by a beardless officer. In the lower level, women and children are driving away from their captured city in carts that have eight-spoked wheels.

229. Barnett and Falkner, *Sculptures of Tiglath-Pileser III*, 11.

230. Barnett and Falkner, *Sculptures of Tiglath-Pileser III*, 11.

231. Barnett and Falkner, *Sculptures of Tiglath-Pileser III*, 11.

232. Barnett and Falkner, *Sculptures of Tiglath-Pileser III*, 11.

Fig. 4.12. Assyrian Officers Shooting at a City, Central Palace, Nineveh. British Museum, BM 118904. (Photo: © The Trustees of the British Museum.)

Date-palm trees and a pomegranate tree on the left side in this relief (Fig. 4.12) indicate that it describes a military campaign against a southern Babylonian city. A notable feature of this relief is that it shows some details of military formation for the siege against a city. While two archers with long garments are shooting at a city, the third solder has a dagger in his right and holds the high shield. This high shield is used only in sieges.[233] The upper square return of the shield is characteristic of the time of Tiglath-pileser III.[234] The city that they are attacking seems to be surrounded by a moat. In this relief, there is only a part of a turret of the city. From the turret, an archer is shooting at the Assyrian attackers.

233. Barnett and Falkner, *Sculptures of Tiglath-Pileser III*, 8.

234. Barnett and Falkner, *Sculptures of Tiglath-Pileser III*, 8.

Another relief from the Central Palace at Nineveh depicts the scene of a siege against a Babylonian city, as indicated by the date-palm trees.[235] Three Assyrian soldiers are standing behind a high shield. While an archer with a fringed tunic, presumably an officer, is shooting at the city, a second soldier next to him is holding a dagger in his right hand and a high shield in his left hand. Its handle is located not on the broad side as usual, but on the narrow edge of the shield. An interesting point is that another soldier is protecting them with a round shield held over their heads. In front of them, a siege-engine is climbing up the ramp to attack the city. This siege-engine is covered with a fringed cloth. An archer is shooting at the city from the turret of the engine.

Fig. 4.13. Assyrian Army Attacking a Babylonian City, Central Palace, Nineveh. British Museum, BM 118902. (Photo: © The Trustees of the British Museum.)

235. Barnett and Falkner, *Sculptures of Tiglath-Pileser III*, plate XXXII.

This relief (Fig. 4.13) records another scene of a military campaign and the date-palm trees indicate that the location of the city is in Babylonia.[236] An Assyrian siege-engine is climbing up a mound to attack the triple-walled city with a battering ram. Two archers on a turret of the engine and one archer behind them are shooting at the city. On the upper level, an Assyrian soldier is killing his fallen enemy. There are two dead bodies below the city wall and two enemies are falling to the ground.

Fig. 4.14. Siege against the City of U[pa?], Central Palace, Nimrud. British Museum, BM 115634+118903. (Photo: © The Trustees of the British Museum.)[237]

Reliefs inscribed with a part of Kalḫu annals (Fig. 4.14) have been recovered from the Central Palace at Nimrud. The reliefs and the texts depict a siege during Tiglath-pileser III's campaign against the city of U[pa?]. In the reliefs, the Assyrian army is attacking a city on a mound from both sides. There is a one-word epigraph, "Upa (^{ālu}*ú-*[*pa*])," just above the wall of the city.[238] On the right side of the reliefs, the Assyrian archers are shooting at the defenders in the city. High shields protect them from the defenders. The archers are wearing helmets of an unusual design.[239] The foremost

236. Barnett and Falkner, *Sculptures of Tiglath-Pileser III*, 12.

237. Barnett and Falkner, *Sculptures of Tiglath-Pileser III*, plate XL.

238. *RINAP 1*, 144.

239. Curtis and Reade, *Art and Empire*, 60.

archer seems to be a senior official, wearing a long robe.[240] In front of the high shield and the archers, a siege engine with four-spoked wheels is breaking through the city wall with its front spears. Curtis suggests that this kind of machine provided platforms from which archers could shoot at defenders.[241] The machine probably had a leather cover and water was kept inside to counter any fire torches from the defenders.[242] The siege machine was presumably moved by men.[243] Step ramps were sometimes built for the machine to advance close to the enemy city wall.[244] The infantry could attack the enemy from behind the cover of the siege-engine.[245]

On the left side of the reliefs, other Assyrian soldiers are attacking the city wall by a ladder which spans the moat. They are meeting no resistance, and at least one Assyrian soldier is already on the wall. Their uniforms are distinctive: they are wearing helmets and straps with round shields and spears. Reade suggests that they are probably from the western half of the empire or from its mountainous fringes.[246]

At the bottom of the relief, an Assyrian soldier in more traditional Assyrian dress and with a pointed helmet is cutting off the head of an enemy. There are fallen enemies on the ground. The literal headcount was a standard way of estimating the number of the enemies dead.[247]

The whole process of the attack from beginning to end seems to be compressed into a single composition in these reliefs, intended to be a "visual equivalent of the written annals."[248] On the upper right side of the relief, three of the enemies are impaled on stakes, a frequent element with representations of captured cities. This impalement intends to punish some defenders and to generally intimidate potential rebels.[249] Two of the enemies are falling down to the ground with their hair loose. The defenders on the battlements are raising their arms in surrender. At the bottom of the city wall, an Assyrian soldier is cutting off the head of an enemy.

240. Curtis and Reade, *Art and Empire*, 60.

241. Curtis and Reade, *Art and Empire*, 60.

242. Curtis and Reade, *Art and Empire*, 60.

243. Curtis and Reade, *Art and Empire*, 60.

244. Curtis and Reade, *Art and Empire*, 60.

245. Curtis and Reade, *Art and Empire*, 60–61.

246. Curtis and Reade, *Art and Empire*, 61.

247. Curtis and Reade, *Art and Empire*, 61.

248. Curtis and Reade, *Art and Empire*, 61.

249. Curtis and Reade, *Art and Empire*, 61.

The inscription that accompanies the relief in Fig. 4.14 does not mention Upa. This text states that, in his ninth year of rule (738–737 BCE), Tiglath-pileser III marched against several lands including Upa. In the military expedition, he captured, plundered, destroyed, and burned the cities.[250] Considering the images on the relief, the text provides the conclusion of the siege: capture, plundering and destruction of the city Upa.

Sargon II (721–705 BCE)

Texts

In the seventh year of Sargon's reign, Rusā of Urarṭu advanced against Ullusunu of the Mannean land, a vassal of Sargon II, and took twenty-two of his fortresses.[251] Speaking words of defamation and abuse against Ullusunu to Dayukku the governor of the Mannean land, he persuaded him and received his son as a hostage.[252] In response, raising his hands to Ashur, Sargon II surrounded and captured those twenty-two fortresses (22 *bi-ra-a-ti šá-a*$^{*!}$*-ti-na al-me akšud*^{ud}) and brought them into the Assyrian realm.[253] He deported Dayukku with his family and "ordered the troubled Mannean land."[254]

In the eighth year of Sargon II, Urzana of the city of Muṣaṣir transgressed against Ashur and Marduk and sent (a letter full of . . .) to Ursā of Urarṭu.[255] With the encouragement of Ashur, the Assyrian king advanced against the city with his army.[256] When Urzana, the ruler, heard about it, he "fled like a bird and went up the steep mountain (*iṣ-ṣu-riš ip-par-riš-ma šadû-ú mar-ṣu e-li*)."[257] Sargon II surrounded the city of Muṣaṣir (*e-li* ^{ālu}*Mu-ṣa-ṣi-ru šu-bat* ^{d}*Ḫal-di-a ni-i-t*[{*u*}] [{*a*}]*l-me-ma*).[258] Then he took captives, including the family members of Urzana and booty from the city.[259]

250. *RINAP 1*, No. 20, 3–6a (p. 72).
251. Fuchs, *Inschriften Sargons II*, Ann. 101 (pp. 105, 318).
252. Fuchs, *Inschriften Sargons II*, Ann. 102a (pp. 106, 318).
253. Fuchs, *Inschriften Sargons II*, Ann. 102b–103 (pp. 106, 319).
254. Fuchs, *Inschriften Sargons II*, Ann. 103b–104a (pp. 106, 319).
255. Fuchs, *Inschriften Sargons II*, Ann. 149 (pp. 113, 321).
256. Fuchs, *Inschriften Sargons II*, Ann. 150–152 (pp. 114, 321).
257. Fuchs, *Inschriften Sargons II*, Ann. 153 (pp. 114, 321).
258. Fuchs, *Inschriften Sargons II*, Ann. 153b–154a (pp. 114, 321).
259. Fuchs, *Inschriften Sargons II*, Ann. 154b–160a (pp. 114–15, 321–22).

He brought Ḫaldia and Bagartu, the gods of the city, to [the temple of] Ashur.[260] After the campaign, he put the land of Urarṭu into mourning and he annexed the city of Muṣaṣir to the Assyrian Empire and put it under the rule of an official.[261] Being overwhelmed by Ashur, Urzana stabbed himself "like a pig (*kīma šaḫî*)."[262] Another record of Sargon's eighth military campaign directed against Ursā of Urarṭu was recovered in a large clay tablet. According to this record, "I (Sargon) shut him up within his whole camp (*ù šá-a-šu i-na pu-ḫur karāši-šú e-sír-šu-ma*)."[263]

In the twelfth year of his reign, Sargon sent his eunuchs and officials against the people of the land of Ḫamarānu, who fled before the arms of Sargon, withdrew to Sippar, and incessantly robbed the Babylonian caravans.[264] They besieged them with a siege ring (*ni-i-ta il-mu-šú*-[{*nu*}]-*ti*-[{*ma*}]) to prevent anyone from escaping and then killed them.[265]

In the thirteenth year of his rule, Sargon II advanced against an enemy whose name is not clearly indicated in the preserved inscriptions. By the command of Ashur, Šamaš and Marduk, the Assyrian king had his soldiers fly over the watercourses "like eagles (*arâniš*)" to defeat him.[266] Sargon II surrounded him with enclosure (*ni*⌋-*i-tú al-me-šu-ma*) and his core troops, and slaughtered them like lambs before his feet.[267] The Assyrian king also killed the warriors and horses.[268] He even pierced the hand of the enemy with the point of a javelin.[269] The enemy king entered his city "like a mongoose (*kīma šik-ke-e ḫal-la-la-niš*)."[270] The Assyrian king continued to attack the city and took booty from it.[271]

In the thirteenth year of the rule of Sargon II, Mutallu of Kummuḫi, who had withheld recognition, sent his messenger to the land of Bīt-Yakin

260. Fuchs, *Inschriften Sargons II*, Ann. 160a (p. 115).
261. Fuchs, *Inschriften Sargons II*, Ann. 161–164a (pp. 115–16).
262. Fuchs, *Inschriften Sargons II*, Ann. 164b–165a (pp. 116–17, 322).
263. Thureau-Dangin, *Relation*, 24–25; Mayer, *Assyrien und Urartu*, 110–11.
264. Fuchs, *Inschriften Sargons II*, Ann. 318–319a (pp. 155–56, 332).
265. Fuchs, *Inschriften Sargons II*, Ann. 319b–320a (pp. 156, 332).
266. Fuchs, *Inschriften Sargons II*, Ann. 341–343 (pp. 160–61, 333–34).
267. Fuchs, *Inschriften Sargons II*, Ann. 343b–344 (pp. 161, 334).
268. Fuchs, *Inschriften Sargons II*, Ann. 344–346a (pp. 161, 334).
269. Fuchs, *Inschriften Sargons II*, Ann. 346–347 (pp. 161, 334).
270. Fuchs, *Inschriften Sargons II*, Ann. 347b–348 (pp. 161–62, 334).
271. Fuchs, *Inschriften Sargons II*, Ann. 349–354 (pp. 162–64, 334).

into the presence of the Assyrian king in order to save his life.[272] Sargon II sent (his) officials, extensive troops and his royal troop against him.[273] Mutallu fled alone at the advance of the Assyrian army, and the army besieged his city (*āla šu-a-tú il-mu-ma*).[274] They took the booty and the people of the land to Kalhu into the presence of Sargon II.[275]

Examples of a military siege by Sargon II can also be found in inscriptions other than annals. According to the Prunkinschrift No. 61, Sargon II besieged and captured Kibaba, governor of Harhar (^{I}*Ki-ba-ba* ^{lú}*bēl āli ša* ^{ālu}*Ḫar-ḫa-ar al-me ak-šud*).[276] After the capture, he restored the city and erected his own royal image in it.[277] He added six districts of the area under his rule.[278] He besieged and captured the cities of Kišešlu, Kindāu, Bīt-Bagaia and Anzaria (^{ālu}*Ki-šeš-lu* ^{ālu}*Ki-in-da-a-ú* ^{ālu}*Bīt-*^{I}*Ba-ga-ia* ^{ālu}*An-za-ri-a al-me akšud*^{ud}).[279] After the siege, he changed their names into Kār-Nabū, Kār-Sin, Kār-Adad, and Kār-Ishtar, respectively.[280] He also besieged and captured the cities around the land of Ba'it-ili (*a-di ālāni ša li-mì-ti-šú ša māt Ba-'i-it-i-li na-gi-i al-me akšud*^{ud}).[281] After the conquest, he took booty from them.[282] He also besieged and captured the city of Dūr-Yakin (^{ālu}*Dūr-*^{I}*Ia-kin*$_7$ *al-me ak-šud*).[283] He took captives and booty from the city.[284] Then, he burned the city with fire, and totally destroyed the city, especially its towering ramparts.[285]

272. Fuchs, *Inschriften Sargons II*, Ann. 398b–403a (pp. 177–78, 337–38).
273. Fuchs, *Inschriften Sargons II*, Ann. 403b–404a (pp. 178, 338).
274. Fuchs, *Inschriften Sargons II*, Ann. 404b–405a (pp. 178, 338).
275. Fuchs, *Inschriften Sargons II*, Ann. 405b–408a (pp. 178, 338).
276. Fuchs, *Inschriften Sargons II*, 61 (pp. 210, 346).
277. Fuchs, *Inschriften Sargons II*, 63a (pp. 211, 346).
278. Fuchs, *Inschriften Sargons II*, 63b-64a (pp. 211, 346).
279. Fuchs, *Inschriften Sargons II*, 64b (pp. 211, 346).
280. Fuchs, *Inschriften Sargons II*, 65 (pp. 211–12, 346–47).
281. Fuchs, *Inschriften Sargons II*, 68a (pp. 212, 347).
282. Fuchs, *Inschriften Sargons II*, 68b (pp. 212, 347).
283. Fuchs, *Inschriften Sargons II*, 132b, pp. 229, 351.
284. Fuchs, *Inschriften Sargons II*, 133–134a (pp. 229, 351).
285. Fuchs, *Inschriften Sargons II*, 134b (pp. 229, 351).

Reliefs

Room 2

Slab 2 of door H in Room 2 at Sargon II's palace at Khorsabad describes an assault against a fortified city.[286] In the upper register, Assyrian soldiers are attacking a fortified city.[287] In the attack, Assyrian archers in different garb are shooting from each side of the city, which is located on a mound. On the left side of the city, a siege-engine is breaching the city wall. On the right side of the city, an Assyrian spearman is attacking the city, holding a round shield in his left hand.

Reliefs with Epigraphs

Room 14

Slabs 1 and 2 in Room 14 at Sargon II's palace at Khorsabad describe a siege against Pazaši (Panziš).[288] On these slabs, the Assyrian army is besieging and attacking the city of Pazaši (Panziš). In the attack, two siege engines are climbing up ramps and breaching the wall of the city. Spearmen and archers are attacking the city. Some archers are shooting at the enemy from behind a high shield. The defenders are counterattacking the advancing Assyrian army and some of them are shooting arrows. Others are falling down from the city wall.

The two-line epigraph states:[289]

Line1: *āl pa!-za-*š[*i*] *ālu ḫal-ṣu šá māt man-na-a-a*

Line 2: *šá īn n*[*i-ri*]*-be šá māt! zi-kir-ta-a-a*

Translation:

Line 1: The city of Pazashi (Panzish), a fortified city of the land of Mannea

Line 2: which is in front of the pass (entrance) to the land of Zirkitu

286. Botta and Flandin, *Monument de Ninive*, plate 77; Albenda, *Palace of Sargon*, plate 124.

287. Albenda, *Palace of Sargon*, 147.

288. Botta and Flandin, *Monument de Ninive*, plate 145; Albenda, *Palace of Sargon*, plate 136.

289. Albenda, *Palace of Sargon*, 112.

Slab 12 in Room 14 describes a siege against Kisheshlu.[290] On this relief, the Assyrian army is besieging and attacking the city of Kisheshlu. In the attack, three siege engines are climbing up ramps and breaching the wall of the city. Spearmen and archers are attacking the city. Some spearmen are holding round shields. The defenders are counterattacking the advancing Assyrian army.

This relief has a one-line epigraph:[291]

Line 1: *āl! ki!-šeš-lu al-me akšud*^{ud}

Translation:

Line 1: The city of Kisheshlu I besieged (and) captured.

Sennacherib (704–681 BCE)

Texts

Sennacherib's military campaigns are well represented in his preserved inscriptions, although the internal chronology is not always clear. The extant texts describe twelve campaigns between his accession year (704 BCE) and sixteenth regnal year (689 BCE).[292] Eight of these campaigns are specifically enumerated in the preserved texts while the other four are not.[293] Events from his seventeenth regnal year (688 BCE) to his death in his twenty-fourth regnal year (681 BCE) are basically unknown.[294]

In the military campaigns of Sennacherib, his strategy often includes a siege of a resistant city. Two hexagonal clay prisms and various fragments from Nineveh describe his first campaign against Marduk-apla-iddina (Merodach-baladan) and the troops of Elam (704–702 BCE).[295] In the campaign, the Assyrian king "besieged, conquered and plundered 75 of the fortified cities, fortresses of Chaldea, and four hundred small(er) settlements in their environs (75 *ālānī-šú dan-nu-ti bīt dūrānī ša* ^{māt}*kal-di*

290. Botta and Flandin, *Monument de Ninive*, plate 147; Albenda, *Palace of Sargon*, plate 138.

291. Albenda, *Palace of Sargon*, 112.

292. *RINAP 3/1*, 9.

293. *RINAP 3/1*, 9.

294. *RINAP 3/1*, 9.

295. *RINAP 3/1*, 172–73.

ù 4 me'at 20 ālānī ṣehrānī ša li-me-ti-šú-nu al-me akšud^{ud} *áš-lu-la*)."[296] After the conquest, he took auxiliary forces and citizens as booty from the conquered cities (i.39–42).[297]

In his second military campaign, Sennacherib advanced against the Kassites and Yasubigallians in the Zagros Mountains and then against Ispabāra in the land of Ellipi (702 BCE).[298] In the campaign, he surrounded and conquered the cities including Bīt-Kilamazaḫ, Ḫardišpu and Bīt-Kubatti which were located in the Zagros Mountains (^{ālu}*bīt-*^{m}*ki-lam-za-aḫ* ^{ālu}*ḫa-ar-diš-pi* ^{ālu}*bīt-*^{m}*ku-bat-ti ālānī-šú-nu dūrānīn*^{i} *dan-nu-ti al-me akšud*^{ud}).[299] After the conquest, he took booty from the cities and burned "their smaller settlements."[300] Then, the Assyrian king had one of his eunuchs rule over them.[301]

After the conquest of the Kassites and Yasubigallians, he turned against Ispabāra in the land of Ellipi.[302] In this campaign, he besieged, conquered, destroyed, devastated, (and) burned with fire Mar'ubištu and Akkuddu where the royal house of Ispabāra was located (^{ālu}*mar-ú-biš-ti* ^{ālu}*ak-ku-ud-du ālāninibīt šarru-ti-šú a-di 34 ālānī ṣehrānī ša li-me-ti-šú-nu al-me akšud*^{ud} *ap-pul aq-qur i-na girri aq-mu*).[303] The strategic details of the siege are not provided, but he took booty from the cities, punished Ispabāra, and made his land smaller and annexed it to the territory of the Assyrian Empire.[304]

In the third military campaign that occurred in 701 BCE,[305] Sennacherib marched to the land of Ḫatti. "Fear of my (Sennacherib's) lordly brilliance (*pul-ḫi me-lam-me be-lu-ti-ia*)" overwhelmed Lulî, the king of the city Sidon.[306] He fled afar, into the sea and disappeared.[307] "The awesome terror of the weapon of the god Ashur (*ra-šub-bat kakki* ^{d}*aš-šur*)" overwhelmed

296. *RINAP 3/1*, No. 22, i.35–38 (p. 172).
297. *RINAP 3/1*, i.39–42 (pp. 172–73).
298. *RINAP 3/1*, 10.
299. *RINAP 3/1*, i.72–74a (p. 173).
300. *RINAP 3/1*, i.74b–80a (pp. 173–74).
301. *RINAP 3/1*, i.80b–ii.10a (p. 174).
302. *RINAP 3/1*, ii.10–14 (p. 174).
303. *RINAP 3/1*, ii.16–19a (p. 174).
304. *RINAP 3/1*, ii.19b–27a (p. 174).
305. There are duplicate records regarding his third campaign: text nos. 4, 6, 14–19, 21–23, 26, 34 (*RINAP 3/1*, pp. 10–11).
306. *RINAP 3/1*, No. 22, ii. 38–39a (p. 175).
307. *RINAP 3/1*, ii.39b–40a (p. 175).

the cities of Great Sidon, Lesser Sidon, Bīt-Zitti, Ṣarepta, Maḫalliba, Ušû, Akzibu and Acco and they submitted to the Assyrian king.[308]

In his campaign, Sennacherib "surrounded, conquered (and) plundered Bīt-Daganna, Joppa, Banayabarqa, and Azuru, the cities of Ṣidqâ, king of Ashkelon, that had not submitted to me (Sennacherib) quickly (^{ālu}*bīt-da-gan-na* ^{ālu}*ia-ap-pu-ú* ^{ālu}*ba-na-a-a-bar-qa* ^{ālu}*a-zu-ru ālāni*^{ni} *ša* ^{m}*ṣi-id-qa-a ša a-na šēpē-ia ár-ḫiš la ik-nu-šú al-me akšud*^{ud} *áš-lu-la šal-la-su-un*)."[309] The details of the booty that he took from the cities are not provided. In this campaign against Ṣidqâ, the order of the military strategy was siege, conquest and plunder of the cities, as is common in siege warfare descriptions.

In the course of his third campaign, Sennacherib also surrounded, conquered, and plundered the cities of Eltekeh (and) Tamnâ (^{ālu}*al-ta-qu-ú* ^{ālu}*ta-am-na-a al-me akšud*^{ud} *áš-lu-la šal-la-sún*).[310] Then, he advanced against the city Ekron and killed the rebellious governors and nobles, hanging their corpses on towers around the city.[311] He took rebellious citizens as booty, while setting free others judged not guilty.[312] Finally, he retrieved Padî from his confinement in Jerusalem and reinstalled him over Ekron, reestablishing tribute from him.[313]

After the conquest of Eltekeh and Tamnâ, he turned to the land of Judah. In the report of his military campaign, he "surrounded (and) conquered 46 of his fortified cities[314] as well as fortresses and small settlements in their environs . . . (46 *ālānī-šu dan-nu-ti bīt dūrānī ù ālānī ṣeḫrātī ša li-me-ti-šú-nu . . . al-me akšud*^{ud})."[315] When he attacked those cities, he employed siege-ramps (*šuk-bu-us a-ram-me*), battering ramps (*qit-ru-ub šu-pi-i*), infantry (*mit-ḫu-uṣ zu-uk šēpē*), sapping (*pil-ši*), breaches (*nik-si*) and siege-engines (*kal-ban-na-te*).[316] After the conquest of the lesser

308. *RINAP 3/1*, ii.41–46 (p. 175).

309. *RINAP 3/1*, ii.68b–72 (p. 175).

310. *RINAP 3/1*, iii.6b–7a (p. 176).

311. *RINAP 3/1*, iii.7b–10a (p. 176).

312. *RINAP 3/1*, iii.10b–14a (p. 176).

313. *RINAP 3/1*, iii.14b–17 (p. 176).

314. John Russell argues that, even though Lachish was not mentioned by name in Sennacherib's annalistic account of the third campaign, it was among Hezekiah's forty-six strong and walled cities (Russell, *Sennacherib's Palace*, 161).

315. *RINAP 3/1*, No. 22, iii.19–23 (p. 176).

316. *RINAP 3/1*, iii.21b–23a (p. 176).

cities, he took booty from them, including, reportedly, 200,150 people as well as animals.[317]

Furthermore, Sennacherib finally "confined Hezekiah inside Jerusalem, his royal city, like a caged bird / a bird in a cage (*kīma iṣṣur qu-up-pi qé-reb* ālu*ur-sa-li-im-mu e-sír-šú*)"[318] He set up blockades against him (*birāti elišu ú-rak-kis-ma*) so that he could not exit from the besieged city.[319] With the blockade in place, he detached the conquered cities from the land of Hezekiah and imposed more payment (tribute) upon them.[320] No military step against Jerusalem beyond the confinement is mentioned on the inscriptions, which turn to an account of the tribute sent by Hezekiah to the Assyrian capital, Nineveh, apparently after the Assyrian withdrawal.[321]

Sennacherib's fourth military campaign does not include any siege against enemy cities, but it has an interesting report regarding his military campaign against Marduk-apla-iddina (II) (Merodach-baladan) of Babylon. In the military campaign, Sennacherib advanced against the land of Bīt-Yakīn.[322] Marduk-apla-iddina (II) became frightened by the noise of Sennacherib's mighty weapons and fierce battle array.[323] He "flew away like a bird to the city of Nagīte-raqqi, which was located in the midst of the sea (*a-na* ālu*na-gi-te-raq-qí ša qa-bal tam-tim iṣ-ṣu-riš ip-pa-riš*)."[324] The Assyrian king brought people, including the family of the rebel, out of the land.[325] He also destroyed (and) devastated (*ap-pul aq-qur*) the cities and turned (them) into ruins (*ú-še-me kar-meš*).[326]

The fifth military campaign of Sennacherib records a military siege against Maniye of Ukku in a difficult, mountainous area. Sennacherib advanced against the rebellious king, who abandoned his city and fled.[327] He

317. *RINAP* 3/1, iii.24–27a (p. 176).

318. *RINAP* 3/1, iii.27b–29a (p. 176).

319. *RINAP* 3/1, iii.29–30a (p. 176).

320. *RINAP* 3/1, iii.30b–37a (p. 176).

321. *RINAP* 3/1, iii.37b–49 (p. 176). Various scholars, including Hayim Tadmor, John Russell, and Ariel Bagg, have evaluated Sennacherib's military campaign against Hezekiah of Judah, which is discussed in chapter 5.

322. *RINAP* 3/1, iii.57b–58 (p. 177).

323. *RINAP* 3/1, iii.61–62 (p. 177).

324. *RINAP* 3/1, iii.64b–65a (p. 177).

325. *RINAP* 3/1, iii.65b–69a (pp. 177–78).

326. *RINAP* 3/1, iii.69b–70a (p. 178).

327. *RINAP* 3/1, iv.24b–25a (p. 179).

surrounded, conquered, and plundered the city (^{ālu}*uk-ku al-me akšud*^{ud} *áš-lu-la šal-la-su*).[328] He also took booty from the city and from thirty-three cities bordering that district, which he destroyed and burned.[329]

Sennacherib's military campaign against Kirūa of the city of Illubru in his ninth regnal year (696 BCE) is inscribed on an octagonal clay prism that was found at Nineveh.[330] According to the text, Sennacherib sent out the Assyrian army to deal with rebels such as Kirūa, who was in his fortified city, Illubru. So, "they besieged him and . . . cut off his escape route (*ni-tum il-mu-šu-ma iṣ-ba-tu mu-ṣu-šu*)."[331] In the siege, the army brought up "battering rams (*šu-pe-e*), siege-machines (lit. '*nimgallus* of the wall,' i.e., *nim-gal-li dūri*), and siege-engines (*kal-ban-na-e*) (and) the assault of foot soldiers," and they defeated him.[332] After the attack, the army took booty and Kirūa, the city ruler, to Sennacherib.[333] Sennacherib reorganized the city of Illubru under the rule of the Assyrian Empire.[334]

In Sennacherib's military campaign to Gurdî of Urdutu in the following year, his tenth regnal year (695 BCE), he sent out the army, and they carried out a military siege. According to the text, Sennacherib sent his army against the rebellious king of Urdutu.[335] They besieged the city and seized it by piling up earth, bringing up battering rams, (and) the assault of foot soldiers (*āla šu-a-[tum] ni-i-tum il-mu-ma i-na ši-pik e-pe-ri ù qur-ru-ub šu-pi-i mit-ḫu-uṣ zu-uk šēpī iṣ-ba-tu*).[336] After gaining control of the city, they took booty and destroyed the city.[337] The Assyrian king claims to have conscripted fifty thousand soldiers for his own army from the captives and distributed other possessions to his officials and people.[338]

Sennacherib's sixth military campaign does not have any record of a siege, but, in his seventh military campaign, he surrounded, conquered, plundered, destroyed, devastated, and burned with fire thirty-four cities,

328. *RINAP 3/1*, iv.25b–26a (p. 179).
329. *RINAP 3/1*, iv.26b–31 (p. 179).
330. *RINAP 3/1*, p. 125.
331. *RINAP 3/1*, No.17, iv.77b–78a (p. 136).
332. *RINAP 3/1*, iv.79–80a (p. 136).
333. *RINAP 3/1*, iv.82–86 (p. 136).
334. *RINAP 3/1*, iv.87–91 (p. 136).
335. *RINAP 3/1*, v.1–8 (p. 136).
336. *RINAP 3/1*, v.9–11 (p. 136).
337. *RINAP 3/1*, v.12–14 (p. 136).
338. *RINAP 3/1*, v.15–22 (p. 136).

together with the small(er) settlements in their environs, which were without number (34 *ālānī dan-nu-ti a-di ālānī ṣeḫrātī ša li-me-ti-šús-nu ša ni-ba i-šu-ú al-me akšud*[ud] *áš-lu-la šal-la-sún ap-pul aq-qur i-na girri aq-mu*).[339]

The eighth campaign (691–689 BCE) employed a military siege which seems to be the last siege reported for Sennacherib. When Šūzubu (Mušēzib-Marduk), the king of Babylon, rebelled against Sennacherib, the Assyrian king advanced to the enemy city.[340] In the military campaign, he "besieged him (*a-na-ku ni-tum al-me-šu*)."[341] The report of the siege does not mention conquest, destruction, or booty but the flight of Mušēzib-Marduk to the land of Elam and subsequently back to Babylon.[342] Sennacherib's campaign continued until he defeated Babylon, Elam, and their allies at Ḫalulê.[343]

Reliefs

Reliefs illustrating military sieges are included among the reliefs from Sennacherib's palace at Nineveh. The band of text which was often found with the reliefs of previous kings, however, is not a feature of the reliefs of Sennacherib.[344] Russell notes that the only texts included in the wall reliefs were brief epigraphs.[345] In other words, the reliefs of Sennacherib primarily focus on the pictorial description through visual images rather than communication in both written and visual languages.

339. *RINAP 3/1*, No. 22, iv.69–81a (p. 180).
340. *RINAP 3/1*, v.17–24a (p. 181).
341. *RINAP 3/1*, v.24b (p. 181).
342. *RINAP 3/1*, v.25–28a (p. 181).
343. *RINAP 3/1*, v.28b–vi.35 (p. 181).
344. Russell, *Sennacherib's Palace*, 32–33.
345. Russell, *Sennacherib's Palace*, 33.

Fig. 4.15. Siege of Alammu(?), Drawing of Slabs 8–11. Room XIV, Southwest Palace, Nineveh. British Museum (Drawn by Sir Austen Henry Layard). (Photo: © The Trustees of the British Museum.)[346]

In Room XIV, a damaged epigraph (Fig. 4.15) records the siege(?) or attack against a city whose name could be read as Alammu(?).[347] The siege against this city is not mentioned in the annals or any other annalistic inscription of Sennacherib.[348] Therefore, the military campaign to this city is known only from this set of reliefs. There are two damaged lines of the epigraph on this set of reliefs. The first line states: "[The city of] Alammu, I besieged [I conquered] ([^{ālu}]*al-am-mu al-me* [*akšud*^{ud}])."[349] The second line states: "[I] carried off [its spoil] ([*aš*]-*lu-la šal-l*[*a-su*])."[350]

Some parts of the group of reliefs are missing and it is difficult to get an overall grasp of the scene. In this set of reliefs, many Assyrian archers are shooting at the defenders on the city wall. Some of them are shooting from behind high and curved shields for their protection. No siege instruments are shown in the Alammu(?) reliefs.

346. See Russell, *Sennacherib's Palace*, 29, 220 for other parts of the relief of Room XIV.

347. Russell, *Sennacherib's Palace*, 156, 158.

348. Alammu is mentioned in one of Sargon II's letters (136.5). See Lanfranchi and Parpola, *Correspondence of Sargon II*, 105–6.

349. Russell, *Sennacherib's Palace*, 275.

350. Russell, *Sennacherib's Palace*, 275.

Among the Sennacherib reliefs illustrating a siege, the Lachish reliefs are very important. They illustrate the details of a military siege as employed by Sennacherib. Among the reliefs regarding the third campaign of Sennacherib, only the Lachish reliefs bear an epigraph identifying a captured city (Slab VI).[351] This set of reliefs was located in Room XXXVI at the South Palace of Sennacherib at Nineveh.[352]

Fig. 4.16. Sennacherib's Campaign against Lachish. Room XXXVI, South Palace, Nineveh. British Museum, BM 124904 (Slab 1). (Photo: © The Trustees of the British Museum.)[353]

The whole scene is composed of twelve slabs, which show the process of the campaign against the city including the attack on the city, the deportation of the residents, and the royal camp of Sennacherib. In Slab I (Fig. 4.16), the Assyrian army is advancing against the city wall of

351. Russell, *Sennacherib's Palace*, 160. Russell also comments that two fragmentary epigraphs from Room I (the throne room) originally contained the names of cities captured during the third campaign, but these names are now too badly damaged for restoration.

352. Russell, *Sennacherib's Palace*, 200–201.

353. Ussishkin, *Conquest of Lachish*, 78.

Lachish. The army consists of archers and slingers who are advancing from the left side to the city wall to the right.

The archers seem to use composite bows with their recurved shape.[354] The composite bows were made of several strips of wood for resiliency, along with sections of animal horns, tendons and sinews, and glue.[355] It was usually used with metal-tipped arrows.[356] Since it had a range of over two hundred meters, the archers were the most formidable warriors in the infantry.[357]

The slingers are advancing behind the archers to the city wall of Lachish. The stones found at Lachish were smooth and rounded, often of flint, measuring six or seven centimeters in diameter and weighing about 250 grams.[358] They were usually carried in a bag suspended from the shoulder of the soldiers.[359] The slingshots seemed to have great accuracy.[360]

354. King and Stager, *Life in Biblical Israel*, 227.
355. King and Stager, *Life in Biblical Israel*, 227.
356. King and Stager, *Life in Biblical Israel*, 227.
357. King and Stager, *Life in Biblical Israel*, 227.
358. King and Stager, *Life in Biblical Israel*, 228.
359. King and Stager, *Life in Biblical Israel*, 228.
360. King and Stager, *Life in Biblical Israel*, 228.

Fig. 4.17. Sennacherib's Campaign against Lachish. Room XXXVI, South Palace, Nineveh. British Museum, BM 124904 (Slab II). (Photo: © The Trustees of the British Museum.)

In this slab (Fig. 4.17), lancers, spearmen, and archers are attacking the city wall of Lachish. The spearmen are holding shields in their left hands. In the top register, there is a high shield for protection. This slab shows an artificial ramp to assist the siege on the bottom right. Assyrian archers and spearmen are climbing up this ramp to attack the city defenders.

Fig. 4.18. Sennacherib's Campaign against Lachish. Room XXXVI, South Palace, Nineveh. British Museum, BM 124906 (Slab III). (Photo: © The Trustees of the British Museum.)

This slab (Fig. 4.18) depicts the central scene of the siege against the city of Lachish and a part of the results from the siege. It depicts the brutality of the warfare between the Assyrian army and the Judean warriors of Lachish, along with the peaceful exit of many refugees. In particular, this relief shows the siege at several stages. Siege ramps are constructed around the city wall. Siege-engines with battering rams, followed by Assyrian solders, are climbing the ramp and attacking the city wall from two sides. In the attack, Assyrian archers are shooting from behind high shields and spearmen are attacking with shields in their left arms for their protection. In the middle part of the slab, deportees or captives are coming out of the city gate. At the bottom of the relief, three naked prisoners are impaled on stakes; two others are shown being flayed.

The siege-engine used in the attack against the city of Lachish is well displayed on the slab. It has wheels that are partly covered by the body of the engine. The securing pins on the body of the engine show that it was transported from Assyria in sections and assembled on the spot before the attack on the city.[361] The body has a turret with a rectangular window in its front. The battering ram seems to have a metal head for breaking through the city wall.[362] It is possible that the Assyrian soldiers inside the engine pushed it backwards and forwards to pound at the wall until it was finally breached.[363] Behind the turret, a soldier seems to pour water over the front of the machine with a huge ladle as a defense against the flaming torches being thrown down by the defenders.

Fig. 4.19. Sennacherib's Campaign against Lachish. Room XXXVI, South Palace, Nineveh. British Museum, BM 124906 (Slab IV). (Photo: © The Trustees of the British Museum.)

Slab IV (Fig. 4.19) shows a part of the siege ramp together with a scene of booty-takers and deportees, describing several stages of the assault and capture. On the left side of the relief, there are siege ramps on

361. Ussishkin, *Conquest of Lachish*, 101.
362. Ussishkin, *Conquest of Lachish*, 101.
363. Ussishkin, *Conquest of Lachish*, 101.

which the Assyrian army are climbing to attack the defenders of Lachish. A siege-engine is also attacking the city wall with a battering ram. On the wall, some Judean soldiers are raising their hands in surrender. Together with the scene of the siege, the slab depicts the booty-taking of the Assyrian army on the right middle row. In the bottom row, Judean deportees are heading for exile.

These four slabs provide a comprehensive visual depiction of a military siege by the Assyrian army along with the other eight slabs that describe the captives (Slab V–VII), Sennacherib on his throne (Slab VIII), and the royal camp (Slab IX–XII). In particular, this set of reliefs provides details regarding various stages of the campaign including the military siege. Based on the reliefs, Sennacherib's campaign against Lachish began with a military advance and concluded with the capture of the city, followed by booty and deportation.

Esarhaddon (680–669 BCE)

Texts

As the successor of Sennacherib, Esarhaddon was active in military campaigns.[364] Some strategies of military siege can be found in his inscriptions written on the hexagonal clay prisms from Nineveh, Ashur, and Susa.[365] In his campaign against Abdi-Milkūti, king of Sidon, the text describes "by the command of Ashur, my lord, I (Esarhaddon) caught him like a fish from the midst of the sea and cut off his head (*ina qí-bit* ^{d}*aš-šur bēli-ia ki-ma nu-u-ni ul-tu qé-reb tam-tim a-bar-šu-ma ak-ki-sa qaqqad-su*)."[366]

In his military campaign against Sanda-uarri, who was a king of the cities of Kundi and Sissû, and an ally with Abdi-Milkūti, the text reports that "I . . . besieged him (Sanda-uarri), caught him like a bird from the midst of the mountains and cut off his head (*ni-i-tu al-me-šu-ma ki-ma iṣ-ṣu-ri ul-tú qé-reb šadê-i a-bar-šu-ma ak-ki-sa qaqqas-su*)."[367] Though the beheadings were on different occasion during the same campaign,

364. *RINAP* 4, 2.

365. *RINAP* 4, 9. Esarhaddon's text reports an incident in which Marduk-apla-iddina (II) (Merodach-baladan) "besieged Ningal-iddin, the governor of Ur, a servant who was loyal to me, and cut off his escape route (*ni-i-tu il-me-*šu*-ma iṣ-ba-tu mu-ṣa-a-*šú)" (No. 1, ii.44–45 [p. 15]).

366. *RINAP* 4, No. 1, ii.72–74 (p. 16).

367. *RINAP* 4, iii.30–31 (p. 17).

upon return to Nineveh, Esarhaddon reports that he hung (the heads) around the necks of their nobles and paraded them in the squares of Nineveh with singer(s) and lyre(s).[368]

A third example of a siege on the same inscription can be found in the military campaign of Esarhaddon against the people of Cilicia. In this campaign, he "besieged, conquered, plundered, demolished, destroyed, (and) burned with fire twenty one of their fortified cities and small cities (21 *ālānī-šú-nu dan-nu-ti ù ālānī ṣeḫrātī šá li-me-ti-šú-nu al-me akšud*[ud] *áš-lu-la šal-lat-sún ap-pul aq-qur ina girri aq-mu*)."[369] He also imposed additional duties upon them.[370] In this campaign, he tried to prevent any further possibility of continuing rebellion through the destruction of fortified cities and imposition of special duties.

Another example of a military siege can be found in Esarhaddon's "Letter to the God (Ashur)." In the military campaign against the city of Uppume, located on the top of a mountain, Esarhaddon built a siege ramp (*a-ram-mu*) against the city, by piling up dirt, wood, and stones.[371] He "made (it) taboo for his enemy (to stand) atop the wall of his city."[372] The people of the city sprinkled with naphtha the ramp that he constructed against Uppume, . . . and set fire (to it),[373] but the fire did not burn it.[374] Instead, blown by the wind, the flames burned the city wall.[375] Then, the army of Esarhaddon crossed over the siege wall (*da-a-a-i-qu ib-bal-kit-u-ni*).[376] The Assyrian army defeated the city, and punished the rebels.[377]

A poorly preserved clay tablet from Nineveh mentions a military campaign against the Medes and references Egypt. In the campaign, Esarhaddon [be]sieged and plundered ([*al*]*-me-ma aś-lu-la šal-lat-su*) the city of Partukka.[378] After the siege, the people of the city kissed the feet of the

368. *RINAP* 4, iii.37–38 (p. 17).
369. *RINAP* 4, iii.52–53 (p. 18).
370. *RINAP* 4, iii.54–55 (p. 18).
371. *RINAP* 4, No.33, Tablet 2, Obv. i.37–38 (p. 82).
372. *RINAP* 4, i.37–38 (p. 82).
373. *RINAP* 4, ii.2–4 (p. 82).
374. *RINAP* 4, ii.7 (p. 83).
375. *RINAP* 4, ii.7 (p. 83).
376. *RINAP* 4, ii.8 (p. 83).
377. *RINAP* 4, ii.10–11 (p. 83).
378. *RINAP* 4, No. 35, Obv. 2–3 (p. 89).

Assyrian king.[379] Then, he took booty from the city.[380] Even though many parts of the text are missing, it indicates that the siege led to a military victory with submission and booty from the city.

Ashurbanipal (668–626 BCE)

Texts

The annals of Ashurbanipal mention military campaigns by the Assyrian king that sometimes specifically included a reference to the siege of a resistant city. According to the Rassam cylinder, Ashurbanipal advanced against Šamaš-šum-ukīn in his sixth campaign.[381] In Sippar, Babylon, Borsippa, and Kutha, he shut up (*e-si-ir-ma*) the enemy and his warriors, and prevented their escape (*ú-ṣab-bi-ta mu-uṣ-ṣa-šú-un*).[382] He defeated them and the rest of them died from plague and hunger.[383]

In his ninth campaign, Ashurbanipal advanced against the area ranging from Azalla to the city of Quraṣiti. He encircled the tribe of Atarsamain, and the Qedarites of Uaite', son of Bir-Dadda, king of Arabia (^{amēlu}*a'-lu šá* ^{ilu}*a-tar-sa-ma-a-a-in ù* ^{amēlu}*qid-ra-a-a šá* ^{I}*ú-a-a-te-' apil* ^{I}*bir-*^{ilu}*dada šar māt a-ri-bi al-me*).[384] The text does not provide any detailed information about the encirclement or the battle scene. Instead, it reports only that the Assyrian king surrounded and took captives from their cities.[385]

According to Cylinder B, in his fourth campaign, Ashurbanipal besieged, conquered, and plundered the city of Kirbit ([^{ālu}*kir-bít al-me ak-*] *šú-ud aš-lu-la šal-lat-su*).[386] In his fifth campaign, he marched against Aḫšēri, king of Mannai.[387] In the military campaign, he besieged his cities including Izirtu, Urmēte, and Uzbia, and he shut up the people of the

379. *RINAP* 4, Obv. 6 (p. 89).

380. *RINAP* 4, Obv. 10 (p. 89).

381. Streck, *Assurbanipal*, iii.128–129 (pp. 2:32–33).

382. Streck, *Assurbanipal*, iii.130–132 (pp. 2:32–33).

383. Streck, *Assurbanipal*, iii.133–135 (pp. 2:32–33).

384. Streck, *Assurbanipal*, viii.124–ix.2 (pp. 2:72–73).

385. Streck, *Assurbanipal*, ix.3–8 (p. 2:73).

386. Streck, *Assurbanipal*, iii.11 (pp. 2:98–99); Piepkorn, *Historical Prism Inscriptions of Ashurbanipal*, 48–49; Borger, *Beiträge*, 99.

387. Streck, *Assurbanipal*, iii.16–17 (pp. 2:98–99); Piepkorn, *Historical Prism Inscriptions of Ashurbanipal*, 50–51; Borger, *Beiträge*, 16–17.

cities (ālu*i-zir-tu* ālu*ur-me-e-te* ālu*uz-bi-a ālānī dan-nu-ti-šu al-me nišê a-ši-bu-ti ālānī ša-a-tu-nu e-si-ir-ma*).[388] The campaign involved surrounding of the city and then total destruction of a number of besieged cities: "I captured, demolished, destroyed, and burned with fire (*ak-šu-ud ap-pul aq-qur ina išāti aq-mu*)."[389] In his campaign against Elam, Ashurbanipal besieged (*ni-i-tu il-mu-u*) the city of Šapîbêl and prevented any escape by Dunanu (*ú-ṣab-bi-tú mu-ṣa-a-šu*).[390]

Reliefs

Fig. 4.20. Ashurbanipal and His Troops Attacking the Elamite Royal City of Hamanu. Room H, North Palace, Nineveh. British Museum, BM 124931. (Photo: © The Trustees of the British Museum.)

388. Streck, *Assurbanipal*, iii.46b-49a (pp. 2:100–101); Piepkorn, *Historical Prism Inscriptions of Ashurbanipal*, 52–53.

389. Streck, *Assurbanipal*, iii.50 (pp. 2:100–101).

390. Streck, *Assurbanipal*, K.2674, 41 (pp. 2:328–29); cf. Borger, *Beiträge*, 329.

This relief (Fig. 4.20) was discovered in Room H in the North Palace of Ashurbanipal at Nineveh.[391] It depicts the military campaign of Ashurbanipal against the city of Hamanu. As the epigraph on the relief states, Ashurbanipal "besieged, captured, plundered, demolished, destroyed, and burned the city (*al-me akšud^ud aš-lu-la šal-lat-su ap-pul aq-qur ina išāti aq-mu*)."[392] The Assyrian spearmen and archers are climbing a ladder to the double walled city. There is a stream (or a moat) around the city and three fallen enemies are floating in it. At the bottom of the city wall, four Assyrian soldiers are holding round shields in their left hands over their heads for protection with daggers in their right hands. The enemy archers are shooting from the city wall. Four enemies are falling to the ground.

Strategic Stages and Patterns of the Military Campaigns (Sieges)

Military sieges and their related strategies have been reported and illustrated as a widely used strategy based on the inscriptions, the epigraphs, and the reliefs of the Neo-Assyrian Empire. A siege can be defined as a military strategy in which military forces surround a town or building with multiple options, such as negotiations, tribute, total surrender, or even destruction. On the Assyrian reliefs, the besiegers and the attackers are the Assyrian army while the defenders are Assyria's enemies.

In the military campaigns of the Assyrian Empire, the ultimate goal is the consolidation or extension of the rule of the empire over the wide-ranging territory envisioned as the Assyrian Empire. The Assyrians usually gained victory and booty from the campaigns against those who did not follow the rule of the empire. This military and economic achievement was the major goal of the campaign. However, the overarching goal of these military campaigns was the (re)establishment of controlling power over the neighbors. Military victories and economic achievements represent the power of the empire.

This achievement of the controlling power of the Assyrian Empire through military power and warfare as needed, even though it sounds ironic, meant that the peace or the "pacification" was the highest goal of the Assyrian king.[393] When the military warfare was completed, the conclusion should be recovery and reconfirmation of the unequal power relationship

391. Strommenger, *5000 Years*, 451.

392. Streck, *Assurbanipal*, χ. 1b–2 (pp. 2:318–19).

393. Fales, *Guerre et paix en Assyrie*, 227.

between the empire and its subject kingdoms. The empire established order over any disorder caused by the enemies. This type of order would be the peace or "pacification" of the empire as a whole.

Based on the Assyrian records regarding the military campaigns, there are stages in the warfare, and these stages are flexibly applied to the battlefield. The process could include the full isolation (enclosure) of a city, the conquest of the city through siege works, the relocation of the people, the carrying off of booty from the city, and the destruction or devastation of the city.[394] In the field, however, this process varies according to the military-diplomatic situation. Therefore, it is necessary to understand the process stage by stage.

The initial stage was advance of the Assyrian force against the city. At this stage, some cities might submit to the Assyrian army without any actual confrontation or attack, as in Asshurnasirpal II's campaign against the city of Suru.[395] In such a case, an actual assault by the Assyrian army did not take place. Instead, the Assyrian king achieved a victory without any loss and gained controlling power over the city.

The second stage was the active containment/blockade. In the Assyrian inscriptions, *esēru* or *labû/lamû* is used to describe the "surrounding" by the Assyrian army. In the case of *labû/lamû* (*lawû*), *nītum* is often added to describe the "encircling with a siege" of the city. A siege has two types in its process: blockade and break-through.[396] In the case of a blockade, it intends to cut off any means of reinforcement, to prevent further forces and supplies from entering the city, and to block the evacuation of the population out of the city.[397] This type of siege is a persistent, continuous, and prolonged strategy. Meanwhile, the break-through includes the actual assault against the resistant city. In this case, the siege is not a static blockade but a more aggressive way of surrounding the city in the process, preventing any possible escape by the defenders. This siege aims at the conquest of the city, should negotiations fail.

The third stage, which usually occurs simultaneously with the siege, is a verbal intimidation or a negotiation, such as that which can be found in the biblical record of 2 Kgs 18:17–36.[398] Such negotiations might be

394. Campbell, *Besieged*, 9.

395. *RIMA* 2, A.0.101.1, i.80–81 (p. 199).

396. Eph'al, "Ways and Means," 49.

397. Eph'al, "Ways and Means," 49.

398. Yadin, *Art of Warfare in Biblical Lands*, 2:319–20.

conducted at almost any stage of the siege.[399] Yadin notes that the negotiations included threats, psychological warfare, and insinuations.[400] The purpose of the negotiation was "to try and reach agreement without the need for actual fighting."[401] The negotiation appealed to humanitarian measures such as the declaration of a truce, or the security of a more favorable outcome for both sides.[402] In particular, the negotiations might occur when the defenders felt that "the capture was inevitable," or when the attackers realized that "the city could not be subdued by force and preferred partial success to absolute failure."[403]

The final stage of a military campaign is an active assault and destruction of a city. In this stage, the Assyrian force usually made simultaneous use of several methods and techniques to break through the city wall and conquer the city.[404] The possible methods included storming the ramparts, a breach of the walls and gates, scaling and tunneling.[405] The attackers attacked the enemy city through the wall, under it or over it.[406] They broke through the city wall or gates with the aid of battering rams, penetrating under the wall by tunneling and going over the wall with ladders.[407]

The outcomes of the military campaigns which included sieges are reported in the inscriptions of the Neo-Assyrian kings, but they have one thing in common: the achievement of Assyrian control over the enemy. The sieges often do not include the invasion of the enemy cities. Instead, they often concluded with taking the booty from the cities and/or imposing tribute upon the city. Even though the Assyrian army conquered the cities, they sometimes spared those cities from destruction and devastation. Also, the Assyrian kings sometimes changed the names of the cities and annexed them as part of the territory of the empire. They also appointed their own governors over many of the cities including the Syria-Palestinian cities such as Damascus, Megiddo, Samaria, and Tyre.[408]

399. Eph'al, "Ways and Means," 49.
400. Yadin, *Art of Warfare in Biblical Lands*, 2:319.
401. Eph'al, "Ways and Means," 49.
402. Eph'al, "Ways and Means," 49–50.
403. Eph'al, "Ways and Means," 50.
404. Eph'al, "Ways and Means," 49.
405. Yadin, *Art of Warfare in Biblical Lands*, 2:313.
406. Eph'al, "Ways and Means," 49.
407. Eph'al, "Ways and Means," 49.
408. Millard, *Eponyms of the Assyrian Empire*, 55–62.

Meanwhile, reliefs illustrating the military sieges tend to conclude with the conquest of the enemy cities. They seldom describe any kind of variation such as can be found in the inscriptions as described above. In the reliefs, the Assyrian army always conquers the enemy city or they, at least, overwhelm the city. In the scenes of sieges and conquests, they may provide details about the siege that are not mentioned in the inscriptions.[409] Above all, the detailed description in the military warfare scenes shows the ultimate desire for sustaining the supremacy of the empire over the local powers.

Through the inscriptions, the epigraphs, and the reliefs relating to military campaigns, the military sieges of the Assyrian Empire portray some general ideological or propagandistic patterns with many variations. First, the siege represents the *control of the situation* on the battlefield. The location for the siege is usually an enemy city, though some opposing forces are encircled on the field. In the texts, the main figure is an Assyrian king, while in the reliefs, the main figure is usually the Assyrian army, sometimes with the king present or stationed nearby in a protected area, as in the Lachish reliefs. Since the siege itself requires surrounding of the enemy city, the employment of a siege means that the Assyrian Empire has overwhelming power and will be able to control the situation on the battlefield. Along with this, it is notable that the Assyrian reliefs do not show wounded or dead Assyrian soldiers.

With the *control of the situation* clearly established by the Assyrian army, the military siege also represents the *confinement of the rebellious or resistant enemy*. Based on the inscriptions and the reliefs, the enemy or their city is cut off by the Assyrian army. In a siege by the Assyrian army, their enemy cannot easily exit the city. Some individuals, such as Rezin of Damascus and Aḫunu, may have managed to escape. Even though the people could preserve their lives within their city walls for a short term, any long-term survival depended normally on negotiations with the Assyrian army which was surrounding them.

Finally, the general conclusion of the siege is the *victory (conquest or submission), i.e., the dominance or rule of the Assyrian king*. As noted above, the inscriptions sometimes do not mention a military conquest after a siege. Instead, they may describe the receipt or taking of booty or tribute from the enemy city. Even in this case, taking booty or tribute

409. Millard, *Eponyms of the Assyrian Empire*, 50–51.

signifies the dominance of Assyria and the expectation of the continuing rule of the Assyrian Empire.

Critical Discourse Analysis of Assyrian Military Campaigns (Sieges): The Ideology of Power

As in the case of the royal lion hunt, a key contribution of Critical Discourse Analysis to the study of military campaign records—especially reports of successful sieges—lies in its comparative and integrative ideological analysis of written and visual languages. This sociolinguistic approach reveals that the military siege texts and reliefs function together as effective media for Assyrian ideology regarding the power relations of the king with his subjects.

Since the records of the sieges include both written and visual languages, it is necessary to consider what and how the siege is represented in each type of language to understand the ideology embedded in the texts and the reliefs. First, the military siege texts and reliefs seem to be in complementary interrelationship in describing the general patterns of the military campaigns, including the sieges. Even though both describe the military sieges by the Assyrians, their contents do not overlap with each other. For example, the texts provide information on when and where the military campaigns occurred, how they concluded, and what their achievements were, including the booty and spoils the Assyrian kings gained, together with other details about the military siege. Meanwhile, the reliefs show how the actual assault with the siege occurred, with detailed scenes, including the formation of the army and the appearances of the siege-engines, as well as scenes of the outcome—booty and deportation. The reliefs do not convey all the details regarding the full process of the campaign or the spoils, but the texts may describe them more thoroughly. Therefore, the general idea of the military campaigns including the sieges becomes more manifest through the combination of the related inscriptions and reliefs.

Through the general patterns that are reconstructed based on the military siege texts, epigraphs, and reliefs, the siege records clearly represent Assyrian ideology regarding the power of the king and the achievement of divine order over against chaos. As a representative of the gods, the Assyrian king has a duty to establish and defend the divine order against chaos and to expand that order over the world.[410] In this regard, Bustenay Oded

410. Machinist, "Kingship and Divinity," 186–87.

suggests that the military campaign inscriptions often justify warfare as an effort of the king to impose peace and divine order over the chaos caused by a rebellious king.[411] The text of VA 8248 describes Sennacherib's construction of the *akītu*-house at Ashur.[412] According to this text, the festival of the feast of Ashur and the *akītu*-house had been forgotten due to "chaos (disorder) and disruption (unrest) (*e-ša-a-ti u saḫ-ma-šá-a-ti*)."[413] The military achievement of Sennacherib against Babylon brought about order, with the restoration of the festival and the reconstruction of the temple.[414] Similarly, Pongratz-Leisten points to the interrelationship between military strategy and the cultic practice of the *akītu*-festival.[415] The symbolic ceremony of the fight of Ashur against Tiamat has been attested in the cities such as Ashur, Arba'il with Milqia, Nineveh, Ilizi, Kurba'il, and Ḫarran.[416] Those cities were strategically important cities and the practice of the *akītu*-festival in those cities represents that controlling power of the Assyrian king over the space of the anti-order, all at the command of the gods.[417]

Furthermore, a literary formula, *šubat neḫtu šūšubum* ("to let dwell in peace"), as the outcome of the military campaigns, can be found in other Assyrian military inscriptions. For example, Adad-nārārī II marched to the land of the Qumānu, conquered the land and took Iluia, the king of the Qumānu, by the command of Ashur.[418] In the military warfare, the remainder of the troops of the Qumānu had fled from the weapons of the Assyrian king but then came back.[419] The Assyrian king let them settle in peace (*šu-ub-tu né-e[ḫ-tu ušēšibšunu]*).[420] The inscriptions of Ashurbanipal state that "the countries settled in peace (*aš-ba mātāte šub-tu ni-iḫ-[tu]*)," after the military campaigns of the Assyrian king.[421]

In considering the imbedded ideology, it is also important to consider the audience of the discourse. As noted, Russell suggests twelve potential

411. Oded, *War, Peace and Empire*, 101–20.
412. *RINAP* 3/2, 246.
413. *RINAP* 3/2, No. 168, 25–28 (p. 248).
414. *RINAP* 3/2, 36b–44a (p. 248).
415. Pongratz-Leisten, "Interplay of Military Strategy and Cultic Practice," 245–52.
416. Pongratz-Leisten, "Interplay of Military Strategy and Cultic Practice," 246.
417. Pongratz-Leisten, "Interplay of Military Strategy and Cultic Practice," 252.
418. *RIMA* 2, A.0.99.1, Obv, 10–13 (pp. 143–44).
419. *RIMA* 2, 17–19a (p. 144).
420. *RIMA* 2, 19b (p. 144).
421. Streck, *Assurbanipal*, K3050+K2694, i.23a (pp. 2:260–61).

groups of the actual audiences based on various original Assyrian resources including texts, epigraphs, and reliefs.[422] Even though it is difficult to identify the *actual* audiences or the *intended* audiences of the military campaign records, it is still possible to conjecture regarding who might have seen the military records.[423] The possible audience of the annalistic and summary texts would be basically limited to the royal scribes.[424] Meanwhile, the possible audiences for the visual and written languages of the reliefs would include a wider audience including kings, royal family, courtiers, servants, foreign employees, foreign prisoners, future kings, gods, Assyrians, provincials, subject foreigners, and independent foreigners.[425] Fales provides a similar range of audiences for the Assyrian reliefs with four categories, which are outer/non-palatial, inner/palatial, gods, and the king himself.[426]

The discourse of the Assyrian military campaigns in written and visual languages is intended to convey the ideology of the power of the Assyrian kings over the empire and the enemy to the multiple audiences as described above. The general patterns of the military warfare that includes a siege demonstrate the dominant power of the Assyrian Empire over its enemies to the audience. Whenever the audiences read or saw the military records, the royal ideology of the empire was transmitted to them. Through the transmission, the ideology of the Assyrian power was confirmed or reestablished among the audience. This representation and the transmission of the ideology through the discourse contributed to the maintenance of the unequal power relations between the Assyrian Empire and its subject kingdoms.

422. Russell, *Sennacherib's Palace*, 223–40.

423. Holloway, *Aššur Is King!*, 74–76.

424. Russell, *Sennacherib's Palace*, 239–40.

425. Russell, *Sennacherib's Palace*, 238–40.

426. Fales, "Art, Performativity, Mimesis," 281.

Chapter 5

A CAGED BIRD VERSUS YHWH'S PROTECTED CITY

The usage of the simile in the phrase, "shut up/enclosed like a caged bird / a bird in a cage (*kīma iṣṣur quppi qereb esiršu*)," in Sennacherib's inscriptions regarding his siege against Hezekiah requires some comments on the interrelationship between royal hunting, especially the lion hunt, and military campaigns. As described in chapter 3, the simile used with Hezekiah was used earlier in the lion (and ostrich) hunting inscriptions of Ashurnasirpal II. In the military inscriptions of Tiglath-pileser III, it is used for an opponent who is surrounded by an Assyrian military force.

Along with the analysis of Sennacherib's siege based upon the interrelationship between the royal lion hunt and the military campaigns, it would be worthwhile of comparing the Assyrian records to the related biblical passages including 2 Kgs 18:13—19:37; Isa 36:1—37:38; and 2 Chr 32:1–23. In the comparison, this chapter highlights contrasting perspectives of the Assyrian and the biblical resources.

One of the different and even contrasting features in the Assyrian records and the biblical traditions is their respective ideologies. From a sociolinguistic approach or perspective, ideological issues are deeply related to the power conflict between a dominant group and a dominated group. This power conflict is usually reflected in both written and visual languages. Whereas the dominant group may seek to maintain its power through the ideology in these languages as well as through physical pressure, the dominated group tries to resist the control of the dominant group, even occupying a dominant ideological position. In the case of Sennacherib's siege of Hezekiah, the records from each side provide contrasting ideologies. The featured simile in Sennacherib's inscriptions is a crucial literary device that represents the Assyrian ideology regarding Hezekiah.

Assyrian Records and Biblical Traditions Describing Sennacherib's Siege of Jerusalem

The Goal of Sennacherib's Military Campaigns: Dominance

As discussed in chapter 4, the goal of the Assyrian military campaigns is political and economic dominance; sieges contribute to the goal but are not required to be followed by assault and destruction. The reports of a siege by the Assyrian forces involve various stopping points, as determined by other factors, representing flexible and diverse strategies with an identical aim, which is Assyrian dominant power over others. The detailed strategies of the military campaigns seem to be planned and employed with flexibility, according to the conditions of the campaigns, including the status of the land and the military statistics of the opponents. Regardless of the various military tactics, the conclusions of the military campaigns are the same: the dominance of the Assyrian power over allies and opponents.

This dominance of the Assyrian power through military campaigns represents the political dominance of the Assyrian Empire over its subjects. The dominance is expressed not only in terms of conquest and destruction of a city but also in terms of receiving tributes and booty from a subject. The inscriptions and the reliefs of the Assyrian Empire do not miss the point: repetition and reconfirmation of the dominant status of the Assyrian Empire through the military campaign. The successful military campaigns of the Assyrian kings include either conquest of the target subjects or booty from them. Either result represents and conveys the dominant power of the Assyrian king.

Regarding this ideological implication or intention, it is clear that Sennacherib's inscriptions and reliefs were also carefully planned and designed to represent the rule of the Assyrian power over all of its subjects. They explicitly represent the effective rule of Sennacherib over the rebellious subjects, even apart from any other conquest or destruction.

Critical Issues in Sennacherib's Third Campaign

Lachish

The siege, the destruction, and the exile of Lachish in Sennacherib's third campaign are depicted in reliefs. The reason that the Assyrian army attempted to besiege and consequently destroy the city can be found in its military and geographical importance. Ussishkin suggests that Lachish was the most formidable citadel in Judah, and it was an important task for Sennacherib to crush the military power of Hezekiah.[1] Furthermore, the city was important for the control of trading routes as well as for Judah's defense.[2] Tiglath-pileser III founded a main route following the highland plateau leading down toward Southern Damascus, then crossing into the coastal plain from Megiddo South.[3] Later, this route was used for the military campaigns of Esarhaddon and Ashurbanipal against Egypt. Therefore, the conquest of Lachish by Sennacherib meant Assyria's winning control of the southern route through Judah leading to Egypt, as well as the economic control of the trading routes. Meanwhile, Jerusalem itself was not on the routes. From an Assyrian perspective, the conquest and the destruction of Jerusalem would not be considered an essential task for Sennacherib. Judah needed only to be neutralized.

Padî

Regarding Sennacherib's campaign against Judah and his control over the kingdom of Hezekiah, it is important to consider the case of Padî, who had been the loyal Assyrian vassal king of Ekron, as well as the long list of tribute from Jerusalem. Except for the abbreviated editions, all the military inscriptions describe the recovery of Padî by Sennacherib from his imprisonment in Jerusalem and the restoration of Padî to the throne of Ekron during the third campaign of Sennacherib.

Regarding the order of the events, there are various ways to reconstruct the sequence, as the Assyrian and biblical accounts are not chronologically arranged. All the Assyrian inscriptions, which contain the record of Padî, place the recovery of Padî from Jerusalem and his reinstallation in

1. Ussishkin, *Conquest of Lachish*, 17.

2. Rainey, "Biblical Shephelah of Judah"; Monson and Provan, *1 and 2 Kings*, 339.

3. Kuan, *Neo-Assyrian Historical Inscriptions*, 186–92.

Ekron, prior to Sennacherib's siege of Hezekiah in Jerusalem. According to the sequence of these inscriptions, Sennacherib advanced against the city of Ekron and killed the rebellious governors of the city and counted the citizens of the city as booty. Then, he brought out Padî, the king of the city, from Jerusalem, and restored him to the throne of Ekron, and reinstated the tribute due from Ekron to the Assyrian Empire.

Some of Sennacherib's inscriptions indicate why Padî had been taken to Jerusalem. According to the Rassam Cylinder, the governors, the nobles, and the people of the city of Ekron who rebelled against Assyria sent Padî in iron fetters to Hezekiah of Judah.[4] Through the military campaign against the rebels, Sennacherib quelled the rebellion of the city, brought Padî out of Jerusalem, and restored him to his kingship over Ekron. Here, the restoration of the kingship of Padî means the restoration of the Assyrian control over the city of Ekron.[5]

William Gallagher provides an alternative interpretation of the sequence of events regarding the restoration of Padî by Sennacherib. Instead of the sequence as it is written in the Assyrian inscriptions, he suggests that the restoration of Padî to kingship happened after Sennacherib began the siege against Hezekiah in Jerusalem.[6] According to him, the Assyrian inscriptions are more concerned about "topical arrangements" rather than the chronological order of the events.[7]

Gallagher's rearrangement of the order of events seems to make sense in that the siege could have led to the restoration of Padî and the (re) establishment of the controlling power of the Assyrian Empire over Hezekiah. The return of Padî is connected not only to the city of Ekron but also to Jerusalem under Hezekiah. Since Padî had been sent by the rebels of Ekron to Jerusalem for imprisonment, the return of Padî is an indication that Ekron was restored under the rule of the Assyrian Empire, while the release of Padî from Jerusalem suggests that Hezekiah acknowledged the authority of the Assyrian Empire.

The return of Padî supports Ariel Bagg's argument about Sennacherib's successful siege of Jerusalem. As noted earlier in chapter 4, Bagg describes Sennacherib's siege of Jerusalem as successful, based on

4. *RINAP 3/1*, No. 4, 42–43 (p. 64).
5. *RINAP 3/1*, 44–48 (pp. 64–65).
6. Gallagher, *Sennacherib's Campaign to Judah*, 123.
7. Gallagher, *Sennacherib's Campaign to Judah*, 123.

the Assyrian and biblical records that tribute was sent by Hezekiah to Nineveh.[8] The conquest of Jerusalem was not necessary because of the tribute and the "release" of Padî, which signified Hezekiah's acknowledgment of Assyrian dominance. The tribute represents a capitulation of Hezekiah to the Assyrian king. In other words, it reveals the establishment of the power of the Assyrian Empire over Jerusalem. In addition to the tribute, the return of Padî is evidence that Hezekiah of Jerusalem acknowledged Assyrian dominance over his city.

Afterwards: Esarhaddon and Ashurbanipal's Campaigns Against Egypt

The political and military status of Jerusalem under the Assyrian Empire after Sennacherib's third campaign became incidental in the record of his successors. Since Sennacherib took control of the prime areas of Judah including the major trade routes, Judah was under the control of the Assyrian Empire. Jerusalem might have had a political value, but it had no special economic value. If Sennacherib's military campaign against the kingdom of Judah had been unsuccessful, it should have been an important issue for the succeeding kings. Any failure in control of the subject kingdoms would presumably have led to rebellion or revolt. The Assyrians would have had to employ military campaigns to those kingdoms for the reestablishment of their dominant power. However, further military campaigns against the kingdom of Judah are not found in the royal inscriptions of Esarhaddon and Ashurbanipal. Although both were also involved in military campaigns against rebellious kingdoms, none of their records describes any campaign against Judah.

It is notable that both Esarhaddon and Ashurbanipal implemented military campaigns against the land of Egypt. If Esarhaddon or Ashurbanipal had considered the kingdom of Judah as a rebellious one, it would have been possible that their campaigns against Egypt would have included a military campaign against the Judaean capital, even though it was located away from the military supply route.

In case of the military campaigns of Esarhaddon, the military inscriptions regarding his military operations against Egypt does not mention the kingdom of Judah which was located on the route toward Egypt,[9] apart

8. Bagg, "Palestine Under Assyrian Rule," 124–25.

9. *RINAP* 4, Bu 91–5–9, 134; 831–18,836; BM 22465; K 3082 + K 3086 + Sm 2027;

from acknowledging Manasseh as a respectful vassal. In one inscription (82-5-22,13), Esarhaddon even gave orders to Manasseh, the king of Judah, with other kings, for his building project of an armory in Nineveh.[10] Manasseh was also one of the kings of the west to support Ashurbanipal with significant gifts, in connection with his first campaign against Egypt.[11]

Outcome

The inscriptions about Sennacherib's attack against Hezekiah of Jerusalem reveal a pattern distinct from other military siege inscriptions which describe fully fledged warfare.[12] As discussed in chapter 4, the military campaign inscriptions indicate certain general stages in describing the military warfare between the Assyrian army and their enemies. In the case of Hezekiah, no conclusion of the military campaign is specified after Sennacherib encircled (*e-sír-šú*) Hezekiah of Jerusalem "like a caged bird / a bird in a cage (*kīma iṣṣur qu-up-pi*)."[13] Instead, the inscriptions record the booty and the troops that Hezekiah sent to Nineveh. The tribute shows a remarkable subservience by Judah; Hezekiah sent booty and troops, even after the departure of the Assyrian army.

A somewhat similar case is found in Tiglath-pileser III's inscriptions regarding his military campaign against Rezin of Damascus.[14] The Assyrian king with his army encircled (*e-sir-šú*) Rezin in his city like "a caged bird (*kīma iṣ-ṣur qu-up-pi*)."[15] The Assyrian army burnt the enemy's plantations and orchards of Damascus. Later, they surrounded and captured Rezin's ancestral city ([x x]-*ḫādara* ([x x]-*ḫa-a-da-ra . . . al-me akšud*[ud]).[16] Then,

83-1-18, 483; 79-7-8, 196; Rm 284; K 3127 + K 4435; K 13721; VA 2708; Israel Museum 71.74.221; K 8692 (?).

10. *RINAP 4*, No. 1, v. 54–73; No. 6, vi. 6b'–15' (pp. 23, 46).

11. Streck, *Assurbanipal*, Cyl. C, I.25–50 (pp. 2:138–41).

12. *RINAP* 3/1, 176.

13. *RINAP* 3/1, No. 4, 52 (p. 64); No. 15, 18–19 (p. 96); No. 16, col. iv, 8–10 (p. 115); No. 17, col. iii, 52 (p. 133); No. 18, col. iii, 27b–29a (p. 151); No. 22 (the "Chicago" Prism), col. iii, 27b–29a (p. 176); No. 23, col. iii, 33, 24–25 (p. 194).

14. *RINAP 1*, No. 20, 58–59.

15. *RINAP* 1, 11' (p. 59).

16. *RINAP 1*, 13'–14'a (p. 59).

Tiglath-pileser III took booty from the cities of the land of Damascus and destroyed 591 cities of the sixteen districts of the land.[17]

In instances of both Tiglath-pileser III and Sennacherib, the siege did not lead to a full assault and destruction of the city. The Assyrians did not require a fully "triumphant" kind of dominance in the west; some examples, such as Sennacherib and Lachish, would suffice to make the point of Assyrian power. Assyria expected to benefit from the submission of local powers; Sennacherib's successors encountered no resistance from Judah during their invasions of Egypt.

Considering the goal of the Assyrian military campaign as the (re) establishment of the Assyrian dominance, it is necessary to understand that the Assyrian military strategies are flexible. Duncan Campbell notes that the typical process of military campaigns—including siege—involved isolating a city or its walls (through siege or blockade), conquering it using siege works, capturing and relocating the population, carrying off booty, and ultimately destroying or devastating the city.[18] Many of the military campaigns by the Assyrian kings seem to follow this pattern. Regarding the cases of Tigalth-pileser III against Rezin of Damascus and Sennacherib against Hezekiah of Jerusalem, neither describes an actual full-scale assault or conquest but rather a blockade.[19] In the case of Sennacherib, Hayim Tadmor argues, "The truth of the matter is that Jerusalem was not besieged: it was only blockaded without resorting to the usual siege machinery."[20] However, if the goal of the Assyrian army was to attain dominance, further conquest or even destruction might not be needed. Indeed, destruction of a city which already submitted to the empire would reduce the chance to receive tribute or continuing tax from it.

There are two contrasting explanations for the blockade or siege cases with the simile, "like a caged bird / a bird in a cage." First, the usage of the simile might possibly be understood as a face-saving device to cover the "unsuccessful" siege, the failure to capture the enemy's capital and punish the rebellious king after the siege.[21] In the case of Rezin, Tiglath-pileser

17. *RINAP 1*, 14'b–17' (p. 59).

18. Campbell, *Besieged*, 9.

19. Tadmor, *Inscriptions of Tiglath-Pileser III*, 79.

20. Tadmor, "Sennacherib's Campaign to Judah," 75; *With My Many Chariots*, 667–68.

21. Tadmor, *Inscriptions of Tiglath-Pileser III*, 79; *RIANP 1*, No. 39, 23, p. 98; No. 41, 22–23; p. 103; No. 49 obv. 3', p. 129 for Turushpa and No. 47 obv. 23, p. 119; No. 51, 16, p. 136 for Shapiya.

III completed the siege, capturing Damascus in the following year (732 BCE).[22] In the case of Hezekiah, the king of Judah paid a heavy tribute to Nineveh.[23] Tadmor further notes that *ēsiršu* is used in two other cases of "unsuccessful" siege, though without an associated simile: he cites the siege of Tu(ru)shpa in 735 BCE (Summary Inscription 1:23–24) and the siege of Shapiya in 731 BCE (Summary Inscription 7:23).[24]

Yigael Yadin and John Russell suggest problematic arguments regarding Sennacherib's campaign against Hezekiah. Yadin argues that Sennacherib admitted his unsuccessful result in not fully conquering Jerusalem in his inscriptions.[25] As an alternative way of threat, he captured and destroyed Lachish.[26] His conquest of the city was recorded in unusually extensive reliefs.[27] Russell also suggests that Sennacherib's inscriptions describe an unsuccessful siege against Hezekiah of Judah.[28]

Another interpretation of sieges that did not result in an assault or capture—particularly Sennacherib's siege of Jerusalem—is that the campaign was effective without the need for direct conquest. Assyrian dominance was (re)established, as evidenced by the substantial tribute Hezekiah sent to Nineveh.[29] Bagg argues that a full conquest or destruction of Jerusalem was not necessary after Hezekiah's capitulation with a heavy tribute even after the departure of the Assyrian force.[30] The tribute represents submission to the Assyrian Empire. Furthermore, booty is one of the benefits obtained from a military campaign.[31] Therefore, from the viewpoint of the tribute and the imperial control, the military campaign was rather successful and did not need any actual assault with siege-engines, capture, or destruction. David Ussishkin also argues that Sennacherib decided to turn Hezekiah into an Assyrian vassal rather than to conquer and destroy

22. Tadmor, *Inscriptions of Tiglath-Pileser III*, 79.
23. *RINAP 3/1*, No. 4, 55–58 (pp. 65–66); No. 22, col. iii, 35–49 (pp. 176–77).
24. Tadmor, *Inscriptions of Tiglath-Pileser III*, 79.
25. Yadin, *Art of Warfare in Biblical Lands*, 2:320.
26. Yadin, *Art of Warfare in Biblical Lands*, 2:320.
27. Yadin, *Art of Warfare in Biblical Lands*, 2:320.
28. Russell, *Sennacherib's Palace*, 228.
29. Bagg, "Palestine Under Assyrian Rule," 124–25.
30. Bagg, "Palestine Under Assyrian Rule," 125.
31. Fales, *Guerre et paix en Assyrie*, 207–12.

the city of Jerusalem.[32] Sennacherib conquered and destroyed Lachish, the fortified city located on the trading routes, and he besieged Jerusalem. As a result, the Assyrian king achieved his two aims: (1) to disable the military power of Hezekiah, and (2) to demonstrate the overwhelming power of the Assyrian Empire.[33] Sennacherib's controlling power over the Levant including Judah contributed to the successful military campaigns of Esarhaddon and Ashurbanipal against the land of Egypt.[34]

Considering the outcome of the military campaigns of Tiglath-pileser III and Sennacherib, their military campaigns were successful. Their military campaigns contributed to the (re)establishment of the empire over their enemies. Hezekiah apparently sent his tribute to Nineveh after the departure of the Assyrian army. The scribes presented the image of the king and the empire as having powerful and dominant power over the rebels. Hezekiah's successor is also cited as a supportive vassal by Esarhaddon and Ashurbanipal.

Biblical Traditions Regarding Sennacherib's Siege of Jerusalem

The descriptions about the warfare between Sennacherib and Hezekiah can be found in biblical texts such as 2 Kgs 18:13—19:37; Isa 36:1—37:38; and 2 Chr 32:1–23.

2 Kings 18:13—19:37

Second Kings 18 and 19 mainly describe the military conflict between Sennacherib and King Hezekiah of Judah. Second Kgs 18:1 notes the beginning of Hezekiah's rule of the kingdom of Judah. After he began to rule, he removed the high places, broke down the pillars, and cut down the sacred pole (2 Kgs 18:4a). He also broke into pieces the bronze serpent that Moses had made (2 Kgs 18:4b). Some years later, he rebelled against the king of Assyria and refused to serve him (2 Kgs 18:7). He attacked the Philistines as far as Gaza and its territory, from a watchtower to the fortified city (2 Kgs 18:8).

32. Ussishkin, "Sennacherib's Campaign," 353.

33. Ussishkin, *Biblical Lachish*, 277.

34. Ussishkin, *Biblical Lachish*, 277.

Second Kings 18:9—18:12 describes the military campaign of Shalmaneser V against Samaria. In the fourth year of Hezekiah, Shalmaneser V came up against Samaria and besieged it (2 Kgs 18:9). After three years, the Assyrian king took the city and took the people into exile to various Assyrian cities (2 Kgs 18:10–11). This passage concludes with a Deuteronomistic comment on the events (על אשר לא שמעו בקול יהוה אלהיהם ויעברו את בריתו את כל אשר צוה משה עבד יהוה ולא שמעו ולא עשו) (2 Kgs 18:12).[35] A negative attitude toward Israel ruled by Hoshea in the verse makes a sharp contrast with a positive evaluation of Hezekiah in 2 Kgs 18:3–7.

Second Kings 18:13—19:37 deals with the military conflict between Sennacherib and Hezekiah but the narrative does not clearly describe any Assyrian siege. There have been scholarly discussions about the sources of this passage, especially since Bernhard Stade, who suggested that it can be divided into two sources—2 Kgs 18:13–16 (Source A) and 2 Kgs 18:17—19:37 (Source B).[36] In terms of the military conflict and its outcome, such a division would be reasonable. The narrative of 2 Kgs 18:13–16 briefly describes Sennacherib's invasion of Judah and its result. It does not mention the siege against Jerusalem but recounts Sennacherib's attack, Hezekiah's submission to Sennacherib, and his tribute to the Assyrian king. Meanwhile, the narrative of 2 Kgs 18:17—19:37 includes the Rabshakeh's speech, Hezekiah's consultation with the prophet Isaiah, Hezekiah's prayer, the miraculous salvation of Jerusalem by the angel of YHWH, and the later death of Sennacherib at Nineveh. It does not mention Sennacherib's siege against Jerusalem, but it states, "Therefore thus says the LORD concerning the king of Assyria: He shall not come into this city, shoot an arrow there, come before it with a shield, or cast up a siege ramp against it (לכן כה אמר יהוה אל מלך אשור לא יבא אל העיר הזאת ולא יורה שם חץ ולא יקדמנה מגן ולא ישפך עליה סללה) (2 Kgs 19:32)."

A comparison of the two sections shows their different perspectives and conclusions in regard to Sennacherib's campaign. The narrative of 2 Kgs 18:13–16 describes the negotiation in terms of submission and tribute. Hezekiah sent his tribute to Sennacherib to avoid the imminent threat. Meanwhile, the narrative of 2 Kgs 18:17–37 reports the military conflict with additions of dramatic factors including the Rabshakeh's

35. Gray, *I & II Kings*, 658.

36. Stade, "Miscellen," esp. 172–83. His argument was later refined by Brevard Childs. See Childs, *Isaiah and the Assyrian Crisis*, 73–103. For the related past research, see Evans, *Invasion of Sennacherib*, 1–38.

speech, Hezekiah's prayer, and the divine intervention for salvation. It concludes with the withdrawal of Sennacherib, without any mention of any tribute paid to Sennacherib.

Isaiah 36:1—37:38

Isaiah 36:1—37:38 is almost identical to the narrative of 2 Kgs 18:17—19:37 in that it describes the Rabshakeh's speech, the consultation with the prophet, Isaiah, Hezekiah's prayer, the action of the angel of YHWH, and the departure of Sennacherib.[37] There have been ongoing scholarly discussions about the priority between Isa 36–37 and 2 Kgs 18:17—19:37, and it is generally assumed that the stories were originally composed for 2 Kings.[38] As in the narrative of 2 Kgs, the account of Isa 37 does not describe Sennacherib's siege but states, "Therefore thus says the LORD concerning the king of Assyria: He shall not come into this city, shoot an arrow there, come before it with a shield, or cast up a siege ramp against it [לכן כה אמר יהוה אל מלך אשור לא יבוא אל העיר הזאת ולא יורה שם חץ ולא יקדמנה מגן ולא ישפך עליה סללה]" (Isa 37:33). Its conclusion is also identical to the narrative of 2 Kgs: the death of 185,000 Assyrian soldiers and the withdrawal of Sennacherib without any mention of tribute.

2 Chronicles 32:1–23

The account of 2 Chr 32:1–23 seems to be based on 2 Kgs 18–19 and Isa 36–37 but it is significantly shorter and partially rearranged.[39] In this account, Sennacherib invaded Judah and encamped against the fortified cities (2 Chr 32:1). However, the Chronicler does not give any reason for the invasion. Second Chr 32:2–8 describes Hezekiah's preparation for Sennacherib's attack. Then, the account describes the speech by Sennacherib's officers to Hezekiah in a shorter version (2 Chr 32:9–15) and Sennacherib's insulting letter to Hezekiah (2 Chr 32:17). It is notable that 2 Chr 32:10 describes a potential Assyrian siege of Jerusalem in the speech by

37. Gallagher, *Sennacherib's Campaign to Judah*, 143.

38. Gallagher, *Sennacherib's Campaign to Judah*, 143; King and Stager, *Life in Biblical Israel*, 249; Park, *Hezekiah and the Dialogue of Memory*, 255–56. On the contrary, some scholars argue the priority of Isaiah over Kings. See Kahn, *Sennacherib's Campaign against Judah*, 36–37.

39. Klein, *2 Chronicles*, 459.

Sennacherib's officers (כה אמר סנחריב מלך אשור על מה אתם בטחים וישבים במצור בירושלם). The next section describes the angel of YHWH intervening for the salvation of Hezekiah and the people of Jerusalem (2 Chr 32:20–22). In addition, the account says that many people—not identified further—brought gifts to YHWH and precious things to Hezekiah so that he was exalted in all the nations (2 Chr 32:23). Even though it is largely based upon the accounts of 2 Kgs 18–19 and Isa 36–37, it sets more focus on the piety of Hezekiah than the other two passages.[40]

The conclusion of 2 Chr 32:1–23 is similar to that of 2 Kgs 18:17—19:37 and Isa 36:1—37:38 in that the angel of YHWH slayed many of the Assyrian army and the surviving Assyrian army departed following the divine attack. The account of 2 Chr 32 omits any reference to tribute paid by Hezekiah or to his submission to Assyria.

Sennacherib's Siege and Its Outcome in Biblical Traditions

A comparison of the biblical accounts in 2 Kgs 18:13—19:37; Isa 36:1–37:38; and 2 Chr 32:1–23 reveals both similarities and differences in their portrayals of the same historical event: Sennacherib's siege of Judah and the preservation of Jerusalem. Compared to the Assyrian sources—namely, the annals of Sennacherib and the reliefs depicting the siege, capture, and destruction of Lachish—the biblical narratives focus on Sennacherib's military threat against Jerusalem and his departure without conquering or destroying the city. The biblical accounts omit reference to Padî and downplay Hezekiah's tribute, except for 2 Kgs 18:13–16. The Assyrian annals clearly describe that the governors, the nobles, and the people of the city of Ekron handed Padî over to Hezekiah.[41] They continually describe Sennacherib as bringing out Padî from Jerusalem.[42] Regarding the tribute, Sennacherib's annals describe that Hezekiah sent his tribute together with auxiliary forces and elite troops to Nineveh. While 2 Kgs 18:13–16 describes Hezekiah's submission and payment of tribute to Sennacherib, the other biblical accounts remain silent on the matter.

Alongside the similarities, the biblical accounts also reveal differences or variations in their descriptions of the same incident. Ehud Ben-Zvi suggests that such variations of the biblical texts show flexibility or malleability

40. Klein, *2 Chronicles*, 459.

41. *RINAP 3/1*, No. 17, iii.5–9 (p. 132).

42. *RINAP 3/1*, iii.33–37.

in describing the past.[43] In other words, the accounts of the past often were written or edited from different perspectives, none of which would necessarily be "objective." The flexibility or malleability of the biblical texts is related to the socio-historical context or situation of the editor/scribe. Each of the biblical texts has its own author(s)/editor(s)/scribe(s) in its own social or historical setting. Consequently, even though those texts describe the "same" past, they have differences in the way the events are interpreted.

Regardless of the flexibility of the texts, Gallagher argues that the narrative of 2 Kgs 18:13—19:37 and Isa 36–37 reflects historical value in general.[44] Kalimi argues that the narrative of 2 Chr 32:1–23 contains features distinct from the accounts of 2 Kgs 18:13—19:37 and Isa 36–37, but it also has historical value regarding the invasion and threat of Sennacherib against Hezekiah of Judah.[45] According to Kalimi, 2 Chr 32 has "some additional historical data."[46] For example, only the account of the Chronicler describes the preparation of Hezekiah for Sennacherib's attack (2 Chr 32:2–8). The author of the text (the Chronicler) seems to reflect his own historical, social, and religious context in describing the past events of Sennacherib's time, while providing some important information. Each of the biblical accounts presents its own historiographical approach, demonstrating a selective attitude in recording past events. This selective perspective reflects the ideology of the author or redactor within their specific sociopolitical context.

43. Ben-Zvi, "Malleability and Its Limits."

44. Gallagher, *Sennacherib's Campaign to Judah*, 160–254.

45. Kalimi, "Placing the Chronicler"; "Sennacherib's Campaign to Judah."

46. Kalimi, "Sennacherib's Campaign to Judah," 14.

Sennacherib's Annals	2 Kgs 18:13–16	2 Kgs 18:17—19:37	Isa 36:1—37:38	2 Chr 32:1–23
1) The land of Hatti:				
—Lulî of Sidon fled				
—Min(u)ḫimmu of Samsimuruna, Tu-Ba'lu of Sidon, Abdi-Li'ti of Arwad, Ūru-Milki of Byblos, Mitinti of Ashdod, Būdi-il of Bīt-Ammon, Kammūsu-nadbi of Moab, Aya-rāmu of Edom, all of the kings of Amurru:				
submission with many gifts				
2) Ṣidqâ of Ashkelon:				
Šarru-lū-dāri as a new king with tribute and gifts				
3) Surrounded, conquered and plundered the cities Bīt-Daganna, Joppa, Banayabarqa, Azuru and the cities of Ṣidqâ that had not submitted quickly.				

Sennacherib's Annals	2 Kgs 18:13–16	2 Kgs 18:17—19:37	Isa 36:1—37:38	2 Chr 32:1–23
4) Defeated the rebellions of Ekron and the kings of Egypt in the plain of Eltekeh.				
5) Surrounded, conquered, and plundered the cities of Eltekeh and Tamnâ				
Approached Ekron and killed the rebellions of the city.				
6) Brought out Padî from Jerusalem and placed him on the throne of Ekron with payment.				
7) Surrounded and conquered forty-six of Hezekiah's fortified cities. 200,150 people, young and old, male and female, horses, mules, donkeys, camels, oxen, sheep, and goats as booty.	1) Sennacherib captured all the fortified cities of Judah (18:13).		1) Sennacherib captured all the fortified cities of Judah (36:1).	1) Sennacherib's advance against Judah and its fortified cities (32:1)
				2) Hezekiah's preparation for Sennacherib's attack (32:2–8)

Sennacherib's Annals	2 Kgs 18:13–16	2 Kgs 18:17—19:37	Isa 36:1—37:38	2 Chr 32:1–23
8) Confined Hezekiah in Jerusalem : detached the cities of Hezekiah and gave them to Mitinti, Padî, Ṣilli-Bēl with the added payment of gifts.		1) The speech of Rabshakeh (18:17–37) 2) Hezekiah consulted Isaiah (19:1–7). 3) The speech of Rabshakeh (19:8–13) 4) Hezekiah's Prayer (19:14–34)	2) The speech of Rabshakeh (36:2–36:22) 3) Hezekiah consulted Isaiah (37:1–7). 4) Speech of Rabshakeh (37:8–13) 5) Hezekiah's prayer (37:14–35)	3) The speech of Sennacherib's servants (32:9–19) 4) Hezekiah and Isaiah's prayer (32:20)
	2) Hezekiah sent to Sennacherib at Lachish for his submission and Sennacherib demanded three hundred talents of silver and thirty talents of gold. (18:14).	5) The angel of YHWH slayed the Assyrian army (19:35). 6) The departure of Sennacherib (19:36)	6) The angel of YHWH slayed the Assyrian army (37:36). 7) The departure of Sennacherib (37:37)	5) The angel of YHWH slayed the Assyrian army (32:21a). 6) The departure of Sennacherib (32:21b)

Sennacherib's Annals	2 Kgs 18:13–16	2 Kgs 18:17—19:37	Isa 36:1—37:38	2 Chr 32:1–23
9) Hezekiah sent the auxiliary forces and his elite troops with 30 talents of gold, 800 talents of silver, choice antimony, large blocks of . . . ivory beds, armchairs of ivory, elephant hide(s), elephant ivory, ebony, boxwood, every kind of valuable treasure, as well as his daughters, his palace women, male singers, (and) female singers into Nineveh.	3) Hezekiah sent all the silver of the house of YHWH and the treasuries of the king's house and the gold from the doors of the temple of YHWH and from the door posts (18:15–16).			
		7) The assassination of Sennacherib at Nineveh (19:37)	8) The assassination of Sennacherib at Nineveh (37:38)	7) The assassination of Sennacherib (32:21c) 8) Salvation of YHWH (32:22) 9) Gifts and exaltation to Hezekiah (32:23)

Fig. 5.1. Comparative Sequences of Sennacherib's Third Campaign.

The capture of forty-six fortified cities of Judah by the Assyrian army of Sennacherib was one of the major concern in the Assyrian and the biblical accounts. Sennacherib army attacked and subdued forty-six fortified cities of Judah. Lachish is not individually mentioned in the Assyrian annals, but it is clearly identified in an epigraph on the extensive reliefs of the capture of Lachish that were displayed at Nineveh.[47] The excavation of Level III at Lachish provides abundant evidence of fire and demolition, doubtless from the time of Sennacherib's third campaign in 701 BCE.[48] Houses and shops were turned into ruins and ashes, and the domestic pottery vessels were smashed.[49] Four adjoining caves were discovered in the northwest corner of Lachish and they contained fifteen hundred disarticulated human skeletons.[50]

The account of 2 Kgs 18:13—19:37 needs to be considered for the rearrangement of the events for a proper chronology. Second Kings 18:13–16 raises a chronological question about when Hezekiah sent a tribute to Sennacherib. Second Kings 18:14 states that Hezekiah sent a message of submission to Sennacherib, who was then at Lachish after having "seized all the fortified cities of Judah (v. 13)." Hezekiah said, "I have done wrong; withdraw from me; whatever you impose on me I will bear (v. 14a)." So, Sennacherib imposed a tribute of "three hundred talents of silver and thirty talents of gold" (v. 14b). Hezekiah took silver from the temple and the treasuries of the king's house (v. 15) and gold from the doors of the temple and the doorposts to send to Sennacherib (v. 16). According to the annals of Sennacherib inscribed on the Taylor Prism, Sennacherib advanced to Judah because Hezekiah had not submitted to the yoke of Sennacherib (*la ik-nu-šú a-na ni-ri-ia*).[51] Hezekiah sent his tribute to Nineveh only after Sennacherib's attack against Jerusalem.

Regarding the chronological issue, Mark Chavalas—and the vast majority of scholars—argue that the annals of Sennacherib describe one invasion to Judah during his third military campaign to the west.[52] For some scholars, the relevant biblical texts such as Isaiah and 2 Chronicles apart from 2 Kings never mention two separate campaigns by Sennacherib against Judah. Based upon his suggestion, the passage of 2 Kgs 18:13—19:37 should be separated into two different sources: 2 Kgs 18:13–16 and 2 Kgs 18:17—19:37.

47. *RINAP 3/1*, 15, n33.

48. King and Stager, *Life in Biblical Israel*, 250.

49. King and Stager, *Life in Biblical Israel*, 250.

50. King and Stager, *Life in Biblical Israel*, 250.

51. *RINAP 3/1*, No. 22, iii.19 (p. 176).

52. Chavalas, "Historian's Approach," 7; Gallagher, *Sennacherib's Campaign to Judah*, 147, 255–62.

Marvin Sweeney points out the limitation of the source criticism of 2 Kgs 18:13—19:37 and suggests that the account should be read as a whole narrative.[53] He refers to the whole narrative of 2 Kgs 18:13—19:37 as "a typical prophetic confrontation narrative"[54] which describes an indirect confrontation between Isaiah, a prophet of YHWH, and Sennacherib, his opponent. According to him, the account of 2 Kgs 18:13–16 is placed at the beginning of the narrative to highlight an "arrogant and unjust" aspect of Sennacherib, which is followed by the salvation of YHWH.[55]

Simon Parker argues that the account of 2 Kgs 18:13—19:37 should be understood as a theological and ideological arrangement of three separate units of 2 Kgs 18:13–16 (A); 18:17—19:9a, 36–37 (B); and 19:9b–35 (C).[56] The long narratives of B and C trivialize Hezekiah's surrender and tribute to the Assyrian Empire and highlight the divine deliverance from Sennacherib's siege.[57] The present sequence of the narratives also features an increase in the piety of Hezekiah.[58]

Gallagher suggests a rather elaborate rearrangement of the account of 2 Kgs 18:13—19:37 for a proper chronological order.[59] He argues that 2 Kgs 18:13–16 and 18:17—19:37 have different genres and they were not arranged in a chronological order.[60] According to him, a possible rearrangement would be as noted below:[61]

1. 2 Kgs 18:13–14a:	Sennacherib captured all the fortified cities of Judah and Hezekiah sent to him for submission.
2. 2 Kgs 18:17—19:35:	Rabshakeh's speech, Hezekiah's consultation with Isaiah, Rabshakeh's second speech, Hezekiah's prayer, the angel of YHWH
3. 2 Kgs 18:14b:	Sennacherib's demand for tribute (Silver and gold)

53. Sweeney, *I & II Kings*, 411–12.
54. Sweeney, *I & II Kings*, 412.
55. Sweeney, *I & II Kings*, 412.
56. Parker, "Stories of Miraculous Deliverance," 113–20.
57. Parker, "Stories of Miraculous Deliverance," 120.
58. Parker, "Stories of Miraculous Deliverance," 120.
59. Gallagher, *Sennacherib's Campaign to Judah*, 262.
60. Gallagher, *Sennacherib's Campaign to Judah*, 262.
61. Gallagher, *Sennacherib's Campaign to Judah*, 262.

4. 2 Kgs 19:36:	The departure of Sennacherib
5. 2 Kgs 18:15–16:	Hezekiah's tribute (Silver and gold)
6. 2 Kgs 19:37:	The assassination of Sennacherib and the succession of Esarhaddon

One feature that distinguishes the biblical tradition from the Assyrian record is its detailed portrayal of the Assyrian emissaries, who were sent with a large force from Lachish to Jerusalem to speak with Hezekiah, his representatives, and the residents of Jerusalem—none of which is mentioned in the Assyrian annals. According to 2 Kgs 18:17a, the Assyrian king sent the Tartan, the Rabsaris, and the Rabshakeh with a force to meet with Hezekiah at Jerusalem. The Assyrian officials directly confronted three officials of Judah—Eliakim son of Hilkiah, Shebnah the scribe, and Joah son of Asaph. In Isa 36:2a, Sennacherib sent only the Rabshakeh to Jerusalem. Sweeney explains that the Isaian version intends to portray the confrontation between the Rabshakeh as a lone Assyrian representative of Sennacherib, and Hezekiah as a lone representative of YHWH.[62] Second Chronicles 32:9 states that Sennacherib sent his servants to Jerusalem. They addressed a message similar to that of 2 Kgs 18, to Hezekiah and the people. The message of 2 Chr 32 has an explicit reference to "sitting in/enduring a siege (וישבים במצור) (2 Chr 32:10)." The officials sent by Sennacherib communicate their propaganda not only to the king but also to the people of Jerusalem.

Some scholars have explored the historical aspect or possibility of the Rabshakeh and his speeches. Tadmor suggests that he might have been of Israelite extraction, from a noble family exiled to Assyria.[63] Cogan and Tadmor suggest that a reason for the Rabshakeh to address the Judaeans would be his fluency in the language of Judah.[64] Yigal Levin suggests that the Rabshakeh was "a low-level Israelite officer or official who was exiled in 722 or 720 BCE."[65] Peter Machinist suggests that the Rabshakeh's speech seems to have historical authenticity as an element of "psychological warfare" against Judah.[66] Machinist further suggests that the addresses of the Rabshakeh with

62. Sweeney, *I & II Kings*, 414.

63. Tadmor, "Rabshaqeh, Rab-Shaqeh." *Bavli Sanhedrin* 60a: "The *rab šāqēh* was an apostate Israelite (*rab šāqēh yiśrā'ēl mûmar hāyâ*)."

64. Cogan and Tadmor, *II Kings*, 230.

65. Levin, "How Did Rabshakeh Know," 333.

66. Machinist, "Rab Šāqēh at the Wall of Jerusalem," 159.

responses from Judaeans and Hezekiah in the biblical accounts function as a literary tool for the self-identification of the Judaean people. Peter Dubovský suggests an aspect of psychological warfare by the Neo-Assyrian intelligence services behind the Rabshakeh's speech.[67] His argument is important in that it makes more plausible that Sennacherib's army sought to negotiate with Hezekiah along with their military siege of Jerusalem. Tamás Dezsö suggests that the Rabshakeh was involved in the structure of the Assyrian intelligence.[68] He also argues that one of the types of information collected by the intelligence services was military information.[69] Based upon the rearranged sequence of the biblical account of 2 Kgs 18–19 as written above, it is very possible that the Rabshakeh's speech made a significant impact on Hezekiah's decision to send tribute to Nineveh.

Gallagher suggests a possible parallel between the address by the Rabshakeh in the biblical text and Sargon's relief.[70] In the relief, Yadin points to an Assyrian official peering out from the turret of a siege engine with a scroll in hand, and suggests that the official is presumably reading out a summons for the people of the city to surrender.[71] Since Assyrian reliefs of military campaigns often portray several stages of the siege process in the same scene, it would be feasible to include a representation of an official message to the defenders as a part of the process of the conduct of a siege.[72]

Another distinct feature of the biblical texts is that they do not offer any detail of the Assyrian siege or blockade of Jerusalem, though 2 Chr 32 offers details of Hezekiah's preparations for resisting a siege (2 Chr 32:2–8) and the speech of Sennacherib's servants to the people of Jerusalem who were "sitting in/enduring a siege (וישבים במצור) (2 Chr 32:10)." Other than those details, the biblical accounts only cite the Assyrian camp outside of Jerusalem. According to 2 Kgs 18:17a, Sennacherib sent a large force (חיל כבד) with his three officials. They went up and came to Jerusalem (ויעלו ויבאו ירושלם) (2 Kgs 18:17b). According 2 Kgs 19:35 and Isa 37:36, the Assyrians set up a camp (מחנה אשור) outside the city walls of Jerusalem,

67. Dubovský, *Hezekiah and the Assyrian Spies*.

68. Dezsö, "Neo-Assyrian Military Intelligence," 223.

69. Dezsö, "Neo-Assyrian Military Intelligence," 228.

70. Gallagher, *Sennacherib's Campaign to Judah*, 171–72. For the image of the relief, see Albenda, *Palace of Sargon*, plate 136.

71. Yadin, *Art of Warfare in Biblical Lands*, 2:425.

72. Gallagher, *Sennacherib's Campaign to Judah*, 172.

which was itself eventually destructively visited by the angel of YHWH.[73] In 2 Chr 32:2, Sennacherib had come and he intended to fight against Jerusalem (literally, "his face was [set] for warfare against Jerusalem").

The biblical texts focus on how Hezekiah and Isaiah responded to the critical situation posed by Sennacherib's attack on Judah and Hezekiah from within the city walls. They depict Sennacherib's departure as the resolution of the crisis. The narrative in 2 Kgs 18:13–16 attributes this outcome to Hezekiah's submission and payment of tribute to Sennacherib. Meanwhile, other accounts offer a theological perspective on Sennacherib's withdrawal, emphasizing divine intervention that resulted in the death of 185,000 Assyrian soldiers and the retreat of the Assyrian army.

Sociolinguistic Approaches: Contrasting Ideologies of Power

Contrasting Descriptions of the Military Situation

Assyrian Records: Hezekiah Shut up/Enclosed Like a Caged Bird / a Bird in a Cage

When the phrase, *kīma iṣṣūr quppi*, is used in lion (and ostrich) hunting and in military inscriptions, its literal meaning would be "like a caged bird / a bird in a cage," but its contextual implication would be "completely vulnerable (to the attacker)." The usage of the simile in a lion hunt inscription is found in the inscriptions of Ashurnasirpal II. In the hunt, he killed 370 lions "like caged birds with the spear (370 *nēšī kīma iṣṣūrī qu-up-pi ina* ^{iṣu}*pu-aš-ḫi a-duk*)."[74] Examples of the same simile occur in the military campaign inscriptions of Tiglath-pileser III against Rezin of Damascus[75] and those of Sennacherib against Hezekiah of Judah. In the 13th year of his reign (733 BCE), Tiglath-pileser III besieged the capital city of Rezin and "shut him up like a caged bird / a bird in a cage (*kīma iṣṣūr quppi ēsiršu*)."[76] The simile with *ēsiršu*, "I enclosed him," occurs again in the inscriptions of Sennacherib regarding his campaign against Hezekiah. The Assyrian king

73. Cf. מחנה מלך אשור (2 Chr 32:21).

74. *RIMA* 2, A.0.101.2, 42 (pp. 226–27).

75. Gallagher, *Sennacherib's Campaign to Judah*, 133.

76. *RINAP 1*, No. 20, iii.27–28, 11'a (p. 59).

shut Hezekiah up (*e-sír-šú*) in Jerusalem "like a bird in a cage / a caged bird (*kīma iṣṣūr qu-up-pi*)."[77]

Assyrian Records: Sennacherib's Military Campaign as a "Royal Lion Hunt"

Sennacherib's inscriptions and reliefs regarding his third military campaign against Hezekiah of Judah describe the (re)establishment of dominant controlling power over the dominated subjects of the empire, and the reinforcement of the ideology of imperial power for the audiences and readers. Antti Laato argues that the rhetorical studies on the Assyrian inscriptions and reliefs of Sennacherib reveal an ideological manipulation of the record of his third campaign, which targeted, inter alia, Hezekiah of Judah.[78] The historical record of the Assyrian king employs specific literary devices to emphasize the important achievements of the king. The Assyrian inscriptions and the reliefs were intended for variety of audiences to enhance the royal ideology of the Assyrian king. Accordingly, one expects some intentional manipulation in describing what happened during Sennacherib's military campaign against Hezekiah of Judah. Likewise, one expects similar manipulation in the biblical traditions, which is intended to serve Judaean interests.

The phrase, "shut up/confined like a caged bird / a bird in a cage (*kīma iṣṣūr quppi ēsiršu*)," is well-articulated rhetoric in that it combines the language of the royal lion (and ostrich) hunt with the treatment of subject kings who rebel against Assyrian rule. This rhetorical simile was earlier used in connection with the royal lion hunt to describe the power of the Assyrian king as a lion hunter. The simile in military campaign reports underscores the extreme vulnerability of the subject—being caged parallels being fully encircled or enclosed—and thereby, the clear dominance of the Assyrian king. One may assume that Tiglath-pileser III's and Sennacherib's scribes were familiar with the earlier usage in royal hunting inscriptions. Using this expression in the campaign reports, they applied the hunting image of encirclement/enclosure to the military image of siege.

The language of encirclement and the associated vulnerability expressed by the simile are important for establishing the ideological interrelation between royal lion hunt and siege warfare. As noted in chapter

77. *RINAP* 3/1, No. 22, iii.27–28 (p. 176).

78. Laato, "Assyrian Propaganda," 199.

3, various scholars have already noted the relationship between hunting and warfare. André Parrot suggested a rather practical interrelationship as well, arguing that hunting was the best type of training for the battle.[79] Elnathan Weissert emphasized a strong ideological interrelationship through his observation that the number of the lions—eighteen—being hunted down in an arena as shown in the reliefs of Ashurbanipal equals the number of the gates—eighteen—of greater Nineveh.[80] The lions were a threat to both people and animals in the plain outside the city of Nineveh.[81] The hunting competence of the king is an important aspect of the king's role as the protector of the city. As described in the reliefs, the spectators of the hunt would realize and recognize his power to secure the city from any threat including lions and other enemies.[82]

Behind the usage of the phrase, "shut up/confined like a caged bird / a bird in a cage," there are notable affinities between the royal lion hunting and a military siege. First, the texts and the reliefs focus on the Assyrian kings' actions. The text is written from the first-person perspective of the king who is a representative of the central deity, Ashur, the Assyrian army, and/or the hunting group. In the reliefs where the king is present, he is commonly depicted in an image that is larger than any other person and he is often located in the center of the scene.

Second, there is a strategic affinity between military campaigns and royal lion hunting: "confinement" or "blockade." Even though the royal lion hunt texts do not explicitly describe the situation of confinement (apart from the cages), the related reliefs describe the hunting as being conducted in a controlled or even "blocked off" place with the help of the royal attendants, all supporting the king's successful hunt. In the campaigns of Tiglath-pileser III and Sennacherib, their tactics included the isolation of their enemy cities through a blockade. In other words, they sought to "confine" their enemies to their cities (cf. Fig. 5.2).

79. Parrot, *Arts of Assyria*, 54.

80. Weissert, "Royal Hunt and Royal Triumph," 355.

81. Weissert, "Royal Hunt and Royal Triumph," 343.

82. Weissert, "Royal Hunt and Royal Triumph," 356.

Fig. 5.2 Huntsmen Trapping Deer in Nets. Ashurbanipal's North Palace, Nineveh. British Museum, BM 124871. (Photo: © The Trustees of the British Museum.)

Based on these affinities, the campaigns present many parallels with the king's hunting expeditions, the best documented of which are the lion hunts. During the campaigns, the Assyrian army surrounded their enemy cities as "caged birds." The simile, "like a caged bird / a bird in a cage," with the supplementary word, *esēru*, "to enclose," highlights the confinement. In Ashurnasirpal II's lion hunting inscriptions, the king put lions into cages (*bīt e-sir*), which means literally "a structure of confinement."[83]

Given this overlap of the image of the king as a hunter with the description of the king besieging a city, it is rather likely that the scribes of the military siege inscriptions, who described Sennacherib's siege intended to represent the power of the Assyrian king with an image of "a hunter." Even though the siege was not followed up by an actual assault or a conquest, the booty was enough. The simile unambiguously represents the unequal power relationship established between the overwhelmingly powerful and victorious hunter, and the confined and powerless bird in a cage, far from being a dangerous opponent.

Based on the sociolinguistic approach, the royal lion hunt record reinforces the political ideology of power in the report of such a successful siege that the rebellious king is only like a bird in a cage. In each lion-hunting scene, the Assyrian king is depicted as an active participant in the hunt, leading his royal attendants and personally confronting lions, even

83. *RIMA* 2, A.0.101.2, 33–34 (p. 226).

engaging them in direct hand-to-claw combat. In most of the military scenes, on the contrary, the kings, apart from Ashurnasirpal II, are not shown as personally participating in the attack. Instead, they sit apart on their thrones and receive the submission of their enemies or booty from them. Through the expression, "like a caged bird / a bird in a cage," the powerful aspect of the king is inserted in the military campaign. In other words, this literary metaphor applies the imagery of successful lion hunts to representations of military activity, especially sieges.

Sennacherib's inscriptions regarding his siege against Hezekiah of Jerusalem and his Lachish reliefs include political propaganda about the royal ideology of power directed at the intended audiences. The maintenance of the ideology is crucial for the maintenance of the power relations between the Assyrian Empire and the subject kingdoms, including the kingdom of Judah. One of the most important functions of the inscriptions and the reliefs is the presentation and reinforcement of the overwhelming power of the empire. To that end, the scribes employed the expression, "shut up/enclosed like a caged bird / a bird in a cage (*kīma iṣṣūr quppi ēsiršu*)," to project a mighty and powerful image of the Assyrian king, who represents the Assyrian Empire as a whole.

Biblical Texts: The Rabshakeh's Speeches

The Rabshakeh's speeches are recorded in 2 Kgs 18–19; 2 Chr 32; and Isa 36–37. In his speeches, the Rabshakeh asserted that YHWH stood against Hezekiah because he had removed *bamôt* (2 Kgs 18:22), which were related to religious practice of Israel (2 Kgs 17:7–13).

An important question about his speeches is how and why his speeches were recorded in the biblical texts, whereas there is no mention in any comparable Assyrian sources. The rhetorical structure of the speeches shows a mixed or combined form of biblical prophetic formulas and the Assyrian letter-address. Dominic Rudman suggests that his speeches in 2 Kgs 18:17–35 employ biblical "prophetic" languages for threats, admonitions, and promises toward the defenders of Jerusalem.[84] Meanwhile, Machinist suggests that his speeches contain aspects of the Assyrian letter-address.[85] The rhetorical structure of the speeches seems to aim at the intimidation of the defenders of Jerusalem.

84. Rudman, "Is the Rabshakeh Also Among the Prophets?," 110.

85. Machinist, "Rab Šāqēh at the Wall of Jerusalem," 151–68.

Why then were the Rabshakeh's speeches recorded in the biblical texts? Regarding the authorship and the date of the speeches, Ehud Ben-Zvi suggests that it was written based upon the Isaianic tradition or the Deuteronomistic tradition.[86] Based upon his suggestion, the speeches from a possible Israelite exile[87] would not only represent intimidation by the Assyrian official but also theological and political ideologies of Judaean traditions.

First, the speeches show a sharp contrast between the Northern Kingdom of Israel and the Southern Kingdom of Judah, regarding the "the high places (*bamôt*)." The cultic practice of the "high places" in the Northern Kingdom was described with other cultic objects in 2 Kgs 17:11. The cultic practice in the kingdom resulted into the fall of the kingdom by the Assyrian Empire (2 Kgs 17:22–23). Meanwhile, Hezekiah removed "the high places" together with other cultic objects in his religious reform (2 Kgs 18:4). The fall of Samaria is described again (2 Kgs 18:9–12), followed by Sennacherib's military campaign against Judah (2 Kgs 18:13—19:37). In the crises of Israel and Judah created by Assyria, a critical difference between those two kingdoms was their religious reform or Yahwism. The Deuteronomist reiterates and highlights the religious reform of Hezekiah ironically through the Rabshakeh, an assumed Israelite deportee. Cogan and Tadmor suggest that the reform program of Hezekiah is closely related to the Deuteronomic School.[88]

Biblical Texts: The Angel of YHWH

According to the biblical tradition, the prophet Isaiah announced, "I (YHWH) will put a spirit in him (Sennacherib), and he shall hear a rumor and return to his own land; I will cause him to fall by the sword in his own land" (2 Kgs 19:6–7//Isa 37:6–7)[89] in the situation of the military confrontation between the Assyrian army of Sennacherib and the besieged Hezekiah. Meanwhile, according to 2 Kgs 19, Sennacherib had shifted from the defeated Lachish to Libnah, and had learned that the Egyptian forces, under king Tirhakah, were approaching to resist Assyrian advances toward Egypt. In this situation, Hezekiah sought YHWH's intervention.

86. Ben-Zvi, "Who Wrote the Speech," 85.

87. Levin, "How Did Rabshakeh Know," 336.

88. Cogan and Tadmor, *II Kings*, 220.

89. Sennacherib died in 681 BCE, twenty years after the "siege" of Jerusalem.

Again, the prophet speaks a word from YHWH, imitating the Assyrian practice (Fig 5.3) in which Esarhaddon is holding two captives with hooks in their noses: "I will put my hook in your nose and my bit in your mouth; I will turn you back on the way by which you came" (2 Kgs 19:28b// Isa 37:29b). YHWH even adds that Sennacherib will not enter Jerusalem or even actively besiege it (2 Kgs 19:32//Isa 37:33).

Fig. 5.3. Esarhaddon Holding Two Royal Captives. Zinjirli. Staatliche Museen zu Berlin-PK, Vorderasiatisches Museum. (Photo: © Staatliche Museen zu Berlin-PK, Vorderasiatisches Museum, Foto: Olaf M. Teßmer).

At the climax of the confrontation between Sennacherib and Hezekiah, the angel of YHWH (מלאך יהוה) broke the tension and concluded the military confrontation between Sennacherib and Hezekiah. In 2 Kgs 19:35, the angel of YHWH went forth and struck (ויצא מלאך יהוה ויך) 185,000 in the Assyrian camp; all of them were dead when morning dawned. Then, Sennacherib and any remaining forces went back to Nineveh (2 Kgs 19:36//Isa 37:37). The biblical accounts in 2 Kgs 19:37 and Isa 37:38 describe the assassination of Sennacherib right after his retreat to the city, although Sennacherib lived on another twenty years, with many more campaigns.

Sennacherib's annals make no mention of a direct assault on Hezekiah or Jerusalem, referring instead to a blockade, the transfer of former Judean cities to groups centered in Ashkelon, Ekron, and Gaza, and an increased tribute imposed on these regions.[90] According to the annals, Hezekiah sent to Nineveh a wide range of tribute as well as personal representatives to do obeisance.[91] There is no description of further military action against the city, only of subsequent tribute.

Noting the agreement between the Assyrian and the biblical sources that there was no direct assault on the city, there have been continuous discussions and debates about the identification of the disruptive "spirit" that YHWH sent against Sennacherib (2 Kgs 19:7//Isa 37:7) and the radically destructive effect by the messenger/angel of YHWH. Even though there is no further information on the angel in 2 Kgs 18–19// Isa 36–37, there are other comparable references to such a messenger/angel of YHWH. In 2 Sam 24:15–17, YHWH sent a pestilence (דבר) on Israel, killing 70,000, by means of the messenger/angel of YHWH (2 Sam 24:16). In the case of 2 Kgs 18–19//Isa 36–37, one could suggest that the vague reference might refer to a plague striking the Assyrian camp. Herodotus describes that mice invaded an Assyrian camp in the time of Sennacherib and ate "the quivers, the bow(string)s and the shield handles," which effectively disarmed the soldiers and led them to flee and even fall (II, 141).[92] The damage by the mice resulted into the unexpected withdrawal of the Assyrian army. Josephus also describes a breakout of a pestilence among the Assyrian army (*Antiquities*, X, §§1–23).[93] Although there has been doubt about the historical value of Herodotus and Josephus, their accounts provide a possible

90. *RIANP 3/1*, No.22, iii. 30–37a (p. 176)

91. *RIANP 3/1*, iii. 37b–49 (p. 177).

92. Herodotus, *Herodoti Historiae*, 1:141. It is notable that the Assyrian sources do not mention any campaign into Egypt during the reign of Sennacherib; see Strassler, *Landmark Herodotus*, 182–84.

93. Josephus, *Flavii Iosephi Opera*, 2:328–29. Josephus is almost entirely dependent on 2 Kgs and Herodotus. The account of 2 Kgs describes the Assyrian intention was to destroy the land of Judah (18:25) and to deport the people of Jerusalem (18:32), which Assyria did not do.

reason for the withdrawal of the Assyrian army from the siege of Jerusalem. Regarding the expression of the "messenger/angel of YHWH," Millard suggests that the historical event of the withdrawal of the Assyrian army could be only understood and described by the author of the biblical text as the result of the divine intervention.[94] In other words, the "messenger/angel of YHWH" might be a metaphorical expression to account for an actual historical event—the Assyrian withdrawal—which could have been prompted by a plague.[95]

Regarding the expression the "messenger/angel of YHWH," it is important to consider its military aspect in 2 Kgs 19//Isa 37. As noted above, most of the scholarship on the phrase has emphasized its possible association with a plague (of mice) as an actual historical event. Considering the context of 2 Kgs 19:35//Isa 37:36, it is possible to think about a military aspect of the "messenger/angel (מלאך)" as the army (צבאות) of YHWH, which is mentioned in 2 Kgs 19:31[96]//Isa 37:32. The "messenger/angel of YHWH" also occurs in 2 Sam 24:16 but the context (2 Sam 24:10–17) is associated with the divine punishment of the people of Israel due to the mistake by King David, not the enemy of Israel. David had numbered the people, which is described as sin against YHWH (2 Sam 24:10). Meanwhile, the context of the action of the "angel of YHWH" in 2 Kgs 19:35 is the military confrontation between the Assyrian forces and Jerusalem (2 Kgs 18:13—19:37//2 Sam 36:1—37:38). This military tension was resolved when the "angel of YHWH" struck the Assyrian army in their camp, such that they withdrew from Jerusalem. The "victory" of the "angel of YHWH" over the Assyrian army represents a triumph of YHWH on behalf of the kingdom of Judah.

This alleged rescue of Jerusalem through the "angel of YHWH" is tied to the religious and political ideology of Jerusalem/Zion. First, it reinforces the Zion theology in which the city of Jerusalem, the city of YHWH, is regarded as invincible.[97] The city remained essentially intact under the threat of the Assyrian army. Even though the Assyrian and biblical sources refer to Hezekiah's tribute handed over to the Assyrians, Jerusalem, itself, unlike much of Judah, was not conquered or destroyed by Sennacherib's forces.

94. Millard, "Sennacherib's Attack on Hezekiah," 75–76.

95. Laato, "Assyrian Propaganda," 222.

96. Qere, mss. and versions (Isa 37:32) add צבאות (Cogan and Tadmor, *II Kings*, 227).

97. Roberts, "Davidic Origin."

The survival of Jerusalem could be taken as confirmation of the Zion theology of an invincible Jerusalem.

This survival of Jerusalem reinforces the political aspect of the Zion theology. The invincibility of the city of Jerusalem, represented by the "angel of YHWH," implies the preservation of the capital city of the kingdom because of divine protection. The city was a central place not only religiously but also politically. The safety of the city is related not only to the preservation of the temple but also to the preservation of the kingship and the royal court. Therefore, the affirmation of divine intervention by the "messenger/angel of YHWH" reinforces the political ideology of the divine protection of the royal court.

Contrasting Perceptions of the City Walls of Jerusalem

Assyrian Records: A Cage of Limitation

Along with the conclusion of the power struggle between Sennacherib and Hezekiah, there is another contrast between those two sides regarding the city (walls) of Jerusalem. The annals of Sennacherib and the biblical record describe the same event but their perceptions of the city and its walls are quite distinct. In Sennacherib's annals, the walled city is described as a "cage," within which Hezekiah was enclosed. In Sennacherib's annals, Sennacherib says that "I made him dread exiting his city gate.[98] Hezekiah was shut up in the city like a "bird in a cage." To the Assyrian scribes, the city walls constituted a boundary which enclosed Hezekiah. The king of Judah had to stay inside the city without any exit.

Biblical Texts: A Boundary of Protection

In a contrary way, the biblical record seems to consider the city (walls) as a boundary that marks a safety zone for Hezekiah and the people of Jerusalem. The prophecy of Isaiah in 2 Kgs 19:32–34//Isa 37:33–35 proclaims the word of YHWH that Sennacherib will not be able to come into the city and ravage it. YHWH will defend the city from any attack by Sennacherib's army. For King Hezekiah and the people inside the city, the walls can be understood not as a cage but as a boundary, marking out and establishing a safe place for the insiders under the protection of YHWH.

98. *RINAP 3/1*, No. 22, iii.30 (p. 176); cf. "târu," *CAD*, *T*, 277.

Sennacherib's Military Tactics, Outcome, and Ideologies

The Flexibility of Military Tactics in Sennacherib's Third Campaign

Sennacherib's military tactics during his third campaign were flexible, adapting to the actual military situation. In his campaign, Sennacherib quelled rebellious cities including Ḫatti, Ekron, and Eltekeh as well as Jerusalem. In the case of the land of Ḫatti, Lulî, the king of Sidon fled at the mere advance of Sennacherib's army.[99] Sennacherib did not have to conquer or even destroy the city. The Assyrian king replaced the king of Sidon and imposed tribute and payment.[100] In the case of Ekron, Sennacherib had a battle with the confederation forces including the army of Ekron in the plain of Eltekeh and defeated them.[101] Sennacherib brought out Padî, their king, from Jerusalem and imposed payment upon him.[102] In this case, the battle outside of the city of Ekron was enough for Sennacherib to regain controlling power over the city. In the case of Eltekeh, Sennacherib surrounded, conquered, and plundered the city.[103] He killed the rebellious governors and nobles, and hung their corpses on towers around the city.[104] He counted other rebels as booty while freeing other people of the city who were judged to be innocent of rebellion.[105]

In the case of Jerusalem, Sennacherib besieged the city without any assault, conquest, or destruction.[106] In this siege, Sennacherib did not conquer the city.[107] As noted above, Sennacherib brought Padî out of the city. Furthermore, he imposed tribute on Hezekiah.[108] Even though it is not described in Sennacherib's annals, Sennacherib's forces withdrew from the city, possibly leaving a small force that continued to harass the defenders of city.[109] Later, Hezekiah sent a large amount of tribute to Nineveh.[110]

99. *RINAP 3/1*, No. 22, ii.37–40a (p. 175).
100. *RINAP 3/1*, ii.47–49 (p. 175).
101. *RINAP 3/1*, ii.73–iii.6a (pp. 175–76).
102. *RINAP 3/1*, iii.14b–17 (p. 176).
103. *RINAP 3/1*, iii.6b–7a (p. 176).
104. *RINAP 3/1*, iii.8b–11a (p. 176).
105. *RINAP 3/1*, iii.11b–14a (p. 176).
106. *RINAP 3/1*, iii.27b–34 (p. 176).
107. Fuchs, "Assyria at War," 391.
108. *RINAP 3/1*, No. 22, iii.35–37a (p. 176).
109. Fuchs, "Über den Wert," 57.
110. *RINAP 3/1*, iii.43b–49 (p. 176).

The Goal and the Outcome of Sennacherib's Third Campaign

The flexible tactics of Sennacherib's army are guided by the ultimate goal: the establishment of controlling power over the subject kingdoms in the Southern Levant, the staging area for any advance into Egypt. Not all of the military campaigns of Sennacherib required conquest and destruction.[111] Rather, they often omitted those steps of annihilation. When possible, the Assyrian king quelled the rebellions and regained the controlling power over his subjects without resorting to conquest or destruction.

In the case of Jerusalem, Sennacherib chose to besiege the city. He had conquered the fortified cities of Judah including Lachish, located on the route to Egypt, apart from the city of Jerusalem. Instead of conquest and destruction of the city, he surrounded it, enclosing Hezekiah within the city wall.

Based upon the Assyrian records and the biblical accounts, the major results of Sennacherib's campaign against Judah include the destruction of the cities of Judah, the return of Padî of Ekron from Jerusalem to his throne in Ekron, and Hezekiah's tribute to Nineveh. On the Assyrian side, Sennacherib's achievements represent his reestablishment of the dominant power relationship of the Assyrian Empire over the Judaean area. He did not need to conquer or destroy Jerusalem with possible heavy losses.[112] Some scholars suggest that the preservation of the capital city of Judah meant a failure of Sennacherib.[113] However, the military siege against Jerusalem was enough for him to attain his goal of the dominance and tribute. In other words, Sennacherib's military campaign against Judah was considered successful from the Assyrian perspective.[114]

From Judah's perspective, Sennacherib's siege of Jerusalem resulted in the city's preservation under the protection of YHWH, which was seen as a victory for Judah. Even though other cities of Judah had been conquered, destroyed, or given to other kingdoms, the capital city remained

111. Related to the flexibility of military strategies, Jack Sasson stresses the emphasis in the classic work by Sun Tzu on the importance of avoiding sieges of well-defended cities with an example of the siege of Razama by Atamrum from a Mari text (Sasson, "Siege Mentality").

112. Fuchs, "Assyria at War," 391.

113. For example, Tadmor, *Inscriptions of Tiglath-Pileser III*, 79; Matty, *Sennacherib's Campaign*, 492; Liverani, *Assyria*, 128–29.

114. Bagg, "Palestine Under Assyrian Rule," 125; Elayi, *Sennacherib*, 88; Kahn, *Sennacherib's Campaign Against Judah*, 290.

intact. The city was neither conquered nor destroyed. Hezekiah still held on to his kingship over a diminished Judah, and he was soon successfully succeeded by his son.

Therefore, the outcome of Sennacherib's campaign was perceived as victorious for both Sennacherib and Hezekiah.[115] In his third campaign, Sennacherib achieved or reestablished his sovereignty over the Syro-Palestine area. In particular, he reconfirmed his controlling power over Hezekiah of Judah. Even though his military siege of Jerusalem did not include conquest or destruction, he apparently attained what he aimed at through his siege. The preservation of the capital city of Judah was not Sennacherib's failure. It was not necessary for the Assyrian king to conquer and destroy it.[116] The kingdom of Judah was reduced with a major loss of its territory, but Jerusalem, the capital city, remained intact under the kingship of Hezekiah. The related biblical texts emphasize the preservation of Jerusalem while downplaying the territorial losses and subsequent Assyrian dominance over Judah.

Ideologies in the Assyrian Records and the Biblical Texts

The Assyrian records preserved in inscriptions and reliefs, and the biblical accounts of 2 Kgs 18:13–19:37; Isa 36:1—37:38; and 2 Chr 32:1–23 present conflicting ideologies in their accounts of Sennacherib's relationship with Hezekiah in 701 BCE.

There is a fundamental difference between the Assyrian records and the biblical accounts: Sennacherib's third campaign is not centered on Jerusalem, whereas the biblical texts focus primarily on Jerusalem. The Assyrian records describe his campaigns against several rebellious cities and Jerusalem was one of them. Meanwhile, the biblical texts are mainly concerned about Jerusalem, the capital city of Judah.

As noted earlier, the Assyrian annals include important elements that are not taken up in the biblical texts. One important element that is mentioned only in Sennacherib's annals is Padî, an Assyrian approved king of Ekron. The Padî affair sheds great light on the relationship between Sennacherib and Hezekiah, though in the annals no connection is made between Padî and the actual siege of Jerusalem. According to the annals, Sennacherib "brought out" Padî from Jerusalem and put him back on his

115. Evans, *Sennacherib and the War of 1812*, 195.

116. Cf. Evans, *Sennacherib and the War of 1812*, 195.

throne in Ekron. His restoration of Padî in Ekron means that the Assyrian Empire reestablished its control over the coastal plain. It is mentioned before the description of the siege of Sennacherib against the city of Jerusalem. It is not clear how Sennacherib brought him out of Jerusalem or whether this happened before or during the siege. Regardless, the Padî affair in Sennacherib's annals reflects Sennacherib's superior power over Hezekiah. Sarah Melville points out that the fundamental purpose of royal inscriptions and texts is to demonstrate the king's success in fulfilling divine imperatives, not to explain a military strategy or report objective facts.[117]

At the same time, the biblical narrative affirms the religious and political ideology of divine protection over Jerusalem, and thus over Hezekiah, even though his kingdom was significantly diminished and weakened by Sennacherib, to whom he became subservient once more.

Here, it is important to consider the ultimate goal of the political propagandas of each side: reinforcement of the ideology and power for the audiences of the Assyrian inscriptions and reliefs that would include Assyrian kings, officials, subject kings, and other foreigners. Meanwhile, the audience and the readers of the biblical writings would include a limited number of literate members of the elite in ancient Judah.

The Assyrian records and the biblical accounts reflect different sociopolitical contexts and readers. In their propaganda, they reflect their own cultural contexts. In the case of Sennacherib's inscriptions, the scribes used the phrase, "like a caged bird / a bird in a cage," which was used earlier in royal lion and other hunting inscriptions, to describe Sennacherib's military siege. The phrase symbolizes and reinforces the power of the Assyrian kings over their subjects. The helplessness of the subjects, who are described as "birds," is clearly shown in the use of a parallel phrase by Rib-Addi of Byblos to describe himself or his peasants in his letters.[118] Faced by the threat of Abdi-Aširta, king of Amurru, the phrase, "like a bird/birds in a snare/a net," describes Rib-Addi's helpless situation of being enclosed. According to William Moran, he suffered for his loyalty to Egypt.[119] He was betrayed by his peasantry and his brother and even

117. Melville, "Win, Lose, or Draw?," 535.

118. Knudtzon et al., *El-Amarna-Tafeln* 74.45–48 (pp. 376–77); 78.13–16 (pp. 386–87); 79.35–38 (pp. 390–91); 81.34–36 (pp. 394–95); 90.39–42 (pp. 426–29); 115.8–10 (pp. 500–501); 116.18–20 (pp. 502–3).

119. Moran, "Rib-Hadda," 173.

isolated by other rebellious local vassals of Egypt.[120] Compared to the use of the same simile in the inscriptions of Ashurnasirpal II, Tiglath-pileser III, and Sennacherib, the simile shows the helplessness that the ones who are enclosed or shut up would feel.

The biblical authors turned to another image—the power of the "angel of YHWH"—to emphasize that they have access to a power greater than Assyria or any king, and thereby reaffirm the Zion theology of Psalms, prophets (especially, Isaiah), as well as the Deuteronomistic History.[121] The "angel of YHWH" is important in that it symbolizes the preservation of Jerusalem.

The contrasting—or even conflicting—ideologies between the ruling group and the ruled group result in differing perceptions and descriptions of the same military conflict. While the authorship of the dominant Assyrian Empire articulated their ideology in records intended for both internal and external audiences, the authorship of the subjugated Judah expressed their own political and religious ideologies in texts aimed at their specific audience.

120. Moran, "Rib-Hadda," 173.

121. Na'aman argues that Hezekiah's rebellion was a total failure, but it was treated favorably by the Deuteronomistic historian. See Na'aman, "Deuteronomist and Voluntary Servitude," 51–52.

CONCLUSION

In this book, I have sought to understand the outcome of Sennacherib's campaign against Hezekiah in 701 BCE and its conflicting perceptions and related ideologies in Assyrian royal lion hunting and military inscriptions and reliefs, as well as the biblical accounts of 2 Kgs 18:13—19:37; Isa 36:1—37:38; and 2 Chr 32:1–23 through Critical Discourse Analysis. In chapter 1, I introduced and analyzed the relevant Assyrian and biblical accounts regarding Sennacherib's campaign against Hezekiah of Judah. I also analyzed the interrelationship between history and ideology in these sources. Chapter 2 showed that Critical Discourse Analysis (CDA) is applicable to Assyrian and biblical sources, based upon a relational theory that depicts the interrelationship between ideology and society. In chapter 3, I analyzed the Assyrian royal lion hunting inscriptions and reliefs, and the use of the simile, "like a caged bird / a bird in a cage," in hunting reports, so as to understand the general patterns and tactics of the hunt. In chapter 4, I explored various Assyrian military campaign inscriptions and reliefs to determine the general military patterns and tactics. In particular, I set my focus on Assyrian military sieges and the use of the simile "(shut up/enclosed) like a caged bird / a bird in a cage." In chapter 5, I compared and analyzed the outcomes of Sennacherib's military campaign against Hezekiah and the ideologies represented in the relevant Assyrian and biblical accounts.

Based upon Critical Discourse Analysis of the sources in regard to Sennacherib's campaign against Hezekiah, I have concluded that the Sennacherib's military campaign was successful but the outcome of the military campaign was perceived and described as victorious in both Assyrian and biblical records from their separate perspectives. Sennacherib's inscriptions describe that Sennacherib "shut up Hezekiah in Jerusalem like a caged bird / a bird in a cage." The simile symbolically represents Sennacherib's achievement of dominance over the king of Judah. Sennacherib conquered and destroyed the cities of Judah, including Lachish. He also brought Padî out of Jerusalem and Hezekiah reportedly sent tribute to Nineveh either before or even after Sennacherib's army left Jerusalem. Therefore, Sennacherib's military campaign can be viewed by him as successful in that it (re)established the controlling power of the Assyrian Empire over the Kingdom of Judah and prepared the way for future Assyrian campaigns into Egypt.

From the perspective of the Kingdom of Judah, the outcome of the military conflict between Sennacherib and Hezekiah was also regarded as a victory. Although the kingdom lost territory and paid tribute to Assyria, the preservation of Jerusalem symbolizes and reaffirms YHWH's divine protection over the kingdom and the Davidic kingship. The omission of the Padî affair and the reduced list of tribute paid to Nineveh—both of which could be seen as signs of Hezekiah's submission to Sennacherib—serve to downplay Judah's concessions. Instead, the biblical accounts portray Sennacherib's campaign as a victory for Hezekiah as well.

Sennacherib's campaign against Judah lends itself to multiple avenues of analysis. This book focuses on reevaluating the outcomes and analyzing the conflicting perceptions and ideologies found in Assyrian and biblical sources, using Critical Discourse Analysis as its primary method. However, there remains much more to investigate. The sociolinguistic theory opens the door to additional perspectives, including ethical and postcolonial approaches, which can shed new light on the unequal power relations and military confrontation between the Assyrian Empire and the Kingdom of Judah. These alternative frameworks will hopefully contribute to a deeper understanding of Sennacherib's campaign and offer further avenues for discussion.

Bibliography

Albenda, Pauline. "Ashurnasirpal II Lion Hunt Relief BM124534." *Journal of Near Eastern Studies* 31.3 (1972) 167–78.

———. *The Palace of Sargon, King of Assyria: Monumental Wall Reliefs at Dur-Sharrukin, from Original Drawings Made at the Time of Their Discovery in 1843–1844 by Botta and Flandin.* Synthèse 22. Paris: Editions Recherche sur les Civilisations, 1986.

Amiet, Pierre, et al., eds. *Art in the Ancient World: A Handbook of Styles and Forms.* Translated by Valerie Bynner. New York: Rizzoli, 1981.

Aruz, Joan, et al. *Assyria to Iberia at the Dawn of the Classical Age.* New York: Metropolitan Museum of Art, 2014.

Aynard, Jeanne-Marie. *Le prisme du Louvre AO 19.939.* Paris: H. Champion, 1957.

Bagg, Ariel M. *Die Assyrer und das Westland: Studien zur historischen Geographie und Herrschaftspraxis in der Levante im 1. Jt. v.u. Z.* Leuven: Uitgeverij Peeters en Departement Oosterse Studies, 2011.

———. "Palestine Under Assyrian Rule: A New Look at the Assyrian Imperial Policy in the West." *Journal of the American Oriental Society* 133.1 (2013) 119–44.

Bahrani, Zainab. *The Graven Image: Representation in Babylonia and Assyria.* Archaeology, Culture, and Society. Philadelphia: University of Pennsylvania Press, 2003.

———. *Rituals of War: The Body and Violence in Mesopotamia.* New York: Zone, 2008.

Baines, John. *High Culture and Experience in Ancient Egypt.* London: Equinox, 2013.

Barnett, Richard David. *Assyrian Palace Reliefs and Their Influence on the Sculptures of Babylonia and Persia.* London: Bathchworth, 1960.

———. *Assyrian Sculpture in the British Museum.* Toronto: McClelland and Stewart, 1975.

———. *Sculptures from the North Palace of Ashurbanipal at Nineveh (668–627 BC).* London: Trustees of the British Museum, 1976.

Barnett, Richard David, et al. *Sculptures from the Southwest Palace of Sennacherib at Nineveh.* 2 vols. London: Trustees of the British Museum, 1998.

Barnett, Richard David, and Margaret Falkner. *The Sculptures of Tiglath-Pileser III (745–727 BC) from the Central and South-West Palaces at Nimrud.* London: Trustees of the British Museum, 1962.

Bauer, Theo. *Das Inschriftenwerk Assurbanipals.* 2 vols. 1933. Leipzig: Zentralantiquariat der Deutschen Demokratischen Republik, 1972.

Ben-Zvi, Ehud. "Who Wrote the Speech of Rabshakeh and When?" *Journal of Biblical Literature* 109, no. 1 (1990): 79–92.

———. "Malleability and Its Limits: Sennacherib's Campaign Against Judah as a Case-Study." In *"Like a Bird in a Cage": The Invasion of Sennacherib in 701 BCE*, edited by Lester Grabbe, 73–105. Journal for the Study of the Old Testament Supplement Series 363. London: Sheffield Academic, 2003.

Biggs, Robert D., and Erica Reiner, eds. "Quppu." In *The Assyrian Dictionary of the Oriental Institute of the University of Chicago*, 13:307–10. Chicago: The Oriental Institute, 1982.

Birch, Walter de Gray, ed. *The Bronze Ornaments of the Palace Gates of Balawat [Shalmaneser II. BC 859–825]*. Translated by Theophilus Goldridge Pinches. London: Offices of the Society, 1880.

Blenkinsopp, Joseph. *Isaiah 1–39: A New Translation with Introduction and Commentary*. New York: Doubleday, 2000.

Blommaert, Jan, and Chris Bulcaen. "Critical Discourse Analysis." *Annual Review of Anthropology* 29 (2000) 447–66.

Borger, Rykle. *Beiträge zum Inschriftenwerk Assurbanipals: Die Prismenklassen A, B, C*. Wiesbaden: Otto Harrassowitz, 1996.

———. *Die Inschriften Asarhaddons, Königs von Assyrien*. Archiv für Orientforschung Beiheft 9. Osnabrück: Biblio, 1956.

Botta, Paul Émile, and Eugène Flandin. *Monument de Ninive*. Osnabrück: Biblio, 1972.

Buss, Martin J. *The Changing Shape of Form Criticism: A Relational Approach*. Sheffield, UK: Sheffield Phoenix, 2010.

Campbell, Antony F., and Mark A. O'Brien. *Unfolding the Deuteronomistic History: Origins, Upgrades, Present Text*. Minneapolis: Fortress, 2000.

Campbell, Duncan B. *Besieged: Siege Warfare in the Ancient World*. New York: Osprey, 2006.

Chavalas, Mark W. "An Historian's Approach to Understanding the Accounts of Sennacherib's Invasion of Judah." *Fides et Historia* 27.2 (1995) 5–22.

Childs, Brevard S. *Isaiah and the Assyrian Crisis*. London: SCM, 1967.

Cogan, Mordechai, and Hayim Tadmor. *II Kings*. Anchor Bible 11. Garden City, NY: Doubleday, 1988.

Collins, Paul. *Assyrian Palace Sculptures*. Austin: University of Texas Press, 2008.

Collon, Dominique. *Near Eastern Seals*. Berkeley: University of California Press, 1990.

Cornelius, Izak. "The Lion in the Art of the Ancient Near East: A Study of Selected Motifs." *Journal of Northwest Semitic Languages* 15 (1989) 53–85.

Curtis, John E., and Julian E. Reade, eds. *Art and Empire: Treasures from Assyria in the British Museum*. New York: Metropolitan Museum of Art, 1995.

Curtis, John, and N. Tallis, eds. *The Balawat Gates of Ashurnasirpal II*. London: British Museum, 2008.

Dezsö, Tamás. "Neo-Assyrian Military Intelligence." In *Krieg und Frieden im Alten Vorderasien: 52e Rencontre Assyriologique Internationale, International Congress of Assyriology and Near Eastern Archaeology, Münster, 17–21 Juli 2006*, edited by Hans Neumann et al., 221–35. Alter Orient und Altes Testament 401. Münster: Ugarit, 2014.

Dowd, Garin, et al., eds. *Genre Matters: Essays in Theory and Criticism*. Portland, OR: Intellect, 2006.

Dubovský, Peter. *Hezekiah and the Assyrian Spies: Reconstruction of the Neo-Assyrian Intelligence Services and Its Significance for 2 Kings 18–19*. Roma: Editrice Pontificio Istituto Biblico, 2006.

Elayi, Josette. *Sennacherib, King of Assyria*. Archaeology and Biblical Studies 24. Atlanta: SBL, 2018.

Eph'al, Israel. "Ways and Means to Conquer a City, Based on Assyrian Queries to the Sungod." In *Assyria, 1995: Proceedings of the 10th Anniversary Symposium of the Neo-Assyrian Text Corpus Project Helsinki, September 7–11, 1995*, edited by S. Parpola and R. M. Whiting, 49–53. Helsinki: Neo-Assyrian Text Corpus Project, 1997.

Evans, Paul S. *The Invasion of Sennacherib in the Book of Kings: A Source-Critical and Rhetorical Study of 2 Kings 18–19*. Supplements to Vetus Testamentum 125. Leiden: Brill, 2009.

———. *Sennacherib and the War of 1812: Disputed Victory in the Assyrian Campaign of 701 BCE in Light of Military History*. Library of Hebrew Bible/Old Testament Studies 736. New York: T&T Clark, 2023.

Fairclough, Norman. *Critical Discourse Analysis: The Critical Study of Language*. New York: Longman, 2010.

———. *Language and Power*. New York: Longman, 1989.

Fales, Frederick Mario. "Art, Performativity, Mimesis, Narrative, Ideology, and Audience: Reflections on Assyrian Palace Reliefs in the Light of Recent Studies." *KASKAL* 6 (2009) 235–93.

———. *Guerre et paix en Assyrie: Religion et impérialisme*. Paris: Les Éditions du Cerf, 2010.

Foreman, Benjamin. "What Is Stronger than a Lion? Leonine Image and Metaphor in the Hebrew Bible and the Ancient Near East." *European Journal of Theology* 16.2 (2007) 135–36.

Foster, Benjamin R. "The Beginnings of Assyriology in the United States." In *Orientalism, Assyriology and the Bible*, edited by Steven W. Holloway, 44–73. Sheffield, UK: Sheffield Phoenix, 2006.

Frahm, Eckart. *Einleitung in die Sanherib-Inschriften*. Archiv für Orientforschung, Beihefte. Wien: Institut fur Orientalistik der Universitat, 1997.

———. "Images of Assyria in Nineteenth- and Twentieth- Century Western Scholarship." In *Orientalism, Assyriology and the Bible*, edited by Steven W. Holloway, 74–94. Sheffield, UK: Sheffield Phoenix, 2006.

Fuchs, Andreas. "Assyria at War: Strategy and Conduct." In *The Oxford Handbook of Cuneiform Culture*, edited by Karen Radner and Eleanor Robson, 380–401. New York: Oxford University Press, 2011.

———. *Die Inschriften Sargons II aus Khorsabad*. Göttingen: Cuvillier, 1994.

———. "Über den Wert von Befestigungsanlagen." *Zeitschrift für Assyriologie und vorderasiatische Archäologie* 98.1 (2008) 45–99.

Gallagher, William R. *Sennacherib's Campaign to Judah: New Studies*. Studies in the History and Culture of the Ancient Near East 18. Leiden: Brill, 1999.

Geertz, Clifford. *The Interpretation of Cultures: Selected Essays*. New York: Basic, 1973.

Grabbe, Lester, ed. *"Like a Bird in a Cage": The Invasion of Sennacherib in 701 BCE*. Journal for the Study of the Old Testament Supplement Series 363. London: Sheffield Academic, 2003.

Gray, John. *I & II Kings: A Commentary*. 2nd rev. ed. Old Testament Library. Philadelphia: Westminster, 1970.

Grayson, A. Kirk. *Assyrian Rulers of the Early First Millennium BC I (1114–859 BC)*. Vol. 2 of *Royal Inscriptions from Mesopotamia: Assyrian Periods*. Toronto: University of Toronto Press, 1991.

———. *Assyrian Rulers of the Early First Millennium BC II (858–745 BC)*. Vol. 3 of *Royal Inscriptions from Mesopotamia: Assyrian Periods*. Toronto: University of Toronto Press, 1996.

Grayson, A. Kirk, and Jamie R. Novotny, eds. *The Royal Inscriptions of Sennacherib, King of Assyria (704–681 BC)*. Vol. 3/1 of *Royal Inscriptions of the Neo-Assyrian Period*. Winona Lake, IN: Eisenbrauns, 2012.

———. *The Royal Inscriptions of Sennacherib, King of Assyria (704–681 BC)*. Vol. 3/2 of *Royal Inscriptions of the Neo-Assyrian Period*. Winona Lake, IN: Eisenbrauns, 2014.

Gunkel, Hermann. *Genesis*. Translated by Mark E. Biddle. Mercer Library of Biblical Studies. Macon, GA: Mercer University Press, 1997.

———. *Introduction to Psalms: The Genres of the Religious Lyric of Israel*. Mercer Library of Biblical Studies. Macon, GA: Mercer University Press, 1998.

Herodotus. *Herodoti Historiae*. 2 vols. Scriptorum Classicorum Bibliotheca Oxoniensis. Oxonii: E Typographeo Clarendoniano, 1963.

Hill, Jane A., et al., eds. *Experiencing Power, Generating Authority: Cosmos, Politics, and the Ideology of Kingship in Ancient Egypt and Mesopotamia*. Philadelphia: University of Pennsylvania Press, 2013.

Hobbs, T. R. *2 Kings*. Word Biblical Commentary 13. Waco, TX: Word, 1985.

Holloway, Steven W. *Aššur Is King! Aššur Is King!: Religion in the Exercise of Power in the Neo-Assyrian Empire*. Culture and History of the Ancient Near East. Leiden: Brill, 2002.

Japhet, Sara. *I & II Chronicles: A Commentary*. Louisville, KY: Westminster John Knox, 1993.

Josephus, Flavius. *Flavii Iosephi Opera*. 2nd ed. 7 vols. Berolini: Apud Weidmannos, 1955.

Jowett, Garth, and Victoria O'Donnell. *Propaganda and Persuasion*. People and Communication 18. Newbury Park, CA: Sage, 1986.

Kahn, Dan'el. *Sennacherib's Campaign Against Judah: A Source Analysis of Isaiah 36–37*. Society for Old Testament Study Monographs. Cambridge, UK: Cambridge University Press, 2020.

Kalimi, Isaac. "Placing the Chronicler in His Own Historical Context: A Closer Examination." *Journal of Near Eastern Studies* 68.3 (2009) 179–92.

———. "Sennacherib's Campaign to Judah: The Chronicler's View Compared with His 'Biblical' Sources." In *Sennacherib at the Gates of Jerusalem: Story, History and Historiography*, 11–50. Culture and History of the Ancient Near East. Leiden: Brill, 2014.

Kalimi, Isaac, and Seth Richardson, eds. *Sennacherib at the Gates of Jerusalem: Story, History and Historiography*. Culture and History of the Ancient Near East 71. Leiden: Brill, 2014.

King, L. W. *Bronze Reliefs from the Gates of Shalmaneser, King of Assyria, BC 860–825*. London: British Museum, 1915.

King, Philip, and Lawrence Stager. *Life in Biblical Israel*. Louisville, KY: Westminster John Knox, 2001.

Klein, Ralph W. *1 Chronicles: A Commentary*. Edited by Thomas Kruger. Hermeneia. Minneapolis: Fortress, 2006.

———. *2 Chronicles: A Commentary*. Edited by Paul Hanson. Hermeneia. Minneapolis: Fortress, 2012.

Knierim, Rolf. "Old Testament Form Criticism Reconsidered." *Interpretation* 27.4 (1973) 435–68.

Knoppers, Gary N., and J. G. McConville, eds. *Reconsidering Israel and Judah: Recent Studies on the Deuteronomistic History*. Sources for Biblical and Theological Study 8. Winona Lake, IN: Eisenbrauns, 2000.

Knudtzon, J. A., et al. *Die El-Amarna-Tafeln*. Vol. 1. Vorderasiatische Bibliothek 10. Leipzig: J. C. Hinrichs, 1915.

Kuan, Jeffrey Kah-Jin. "Hezekiah." In *The New Interpreter's Dictionary of the Bible*, edited by Katharine Sakenfeld, 818–21. Nashville: Abingdon, 2007.

———. *Neo-Assyrian Historical Inscriptions and Syria-Palestine: Israelite/Judean-Tyrian-Damascene Political and Commercial Relations in the Ninth-Eighth Centuries BCE*. Hong Kong: Alliance Bible Seminary, 1995.

Kuhrt, Amélie. *The Ancient Near East*. 2 vols. Routledge History of the Ancient World. London: Routledge, 1995.

Laato, Antti. "Assyrian Propaganda and the Falsification of History in the Royal Inscriptions of Sennacherib." *Vetus Testamentum* 45.2 (1995) 198–226.

Lanfranchi, G. B., and Simo Parpola. *The Correspondence of Sargon II, Part 2: Letters from the Northern and Northeastern Provinces*. State Archives of Assyria 5. Helsinki: Helsinki University Press, 1990.

Leichty, Erle. *The Royal Inscriptions of Esarhaddon, King of Assyria (680–669 BC)*. Vol. 4 of *Royal Inscriptions of the Neo-Assyrian Period*. Winona Lake, IN: Eisenbrauns, 2011.

Levin, Yigal. "How Did Rabshakeh Know the Language of Judah?" In *Marbeh Hokmah: Studies in the Bible and the Ancient Near East in Loving Memory of Victor Avigdor Hurowitz*, edited by Shamir Yonah et al., 323–37, Winona Lake, IN: Eisenbrauns, 2015.

Liverani, Mario. *Assyria: The Imperial Mission*. Mesopotamian Civilizations 20. Winona Lake, IN: Eisenbrauns, 2017.

———. "The Ideology of the Assyrian Empire." In *Power and Propaganda: A Symposium on Ancient Empires*, edited by Mogens Trolle Larsen, 297–317. Mesopotamia 7. Copenhagen: Akademisk Forlag, 1979.

———. *Israel's History and the History of Israel*. Translated by Philip Davies and Chiar Peri. Bible World. London: Equinox, 2007.

———. "Rib-Adda, Righteous Sufferer." In *Myth and Politics in Ancient Near Eastern Historiography*, edited by Zainab Bahrani and Marc van de Mieroop, 97–124. Ithaca NY: Cornell University Press, 2007.

Machinist, Peter. "Kingship and Divinity in Imperial Assyria." In *Text, Artifact, and Image: Revealing Ancient Israelite Religion*, edited by Gary M. Beckman and Theodore J. Lewis, 186–87. Brown Judaic Studies 346. Providence, RI: Brown Judaic Studies, 2006.

———. "The Rab Šāqēh at the Wall of Jerusalem: Israelite Identity in the Face of the Assyrian 'Other.'" *Hebrew Studies* 41.1 (2000) 151–68.

Marcus, David. "Animal Similes in Assyrian Royal Inscriptions." *Orientalia* 46 (1977) 86–106.

Matty, Nazek Khaled. *Sennacherib's Campaign against Judah and Jerusalem in 701 BC: A Historical Reconstruction*. Beihefte zur Zeitschrift für die alttestamentliche Wissenschaft 487. Berlin: de Gruyter, 2016.

Mayer, Walter. *Assyrien und Urartu, I: Der achte Feldzug Sargons II. Im Jarhr 714 v. Chr.* Alter Orient und Altes Testament 395/1. Münster: Ugarit, 2013.

———. *Politik und Kriegskunst der Assyrer.* Abhandlungen zur Literatur Alt-Syrien-Palästinas und Mesopotamiens 9. Münster: Ugarit, 1995.

McKenzie, Steven L. "Deuteronomistic History." In vol. 2 of *The Anchor Bible Dictionary*, edited by David Noel Freedman et al., 160–68. New York: Doubleday, 1992.

———. *The Trouble with Kings: The Composition of the Book of Kings in the Deuteronomistic History.* Supplements to Vetus Testamentum 42. Leiden: Brill, 1991.

Melville, Sarah C. "Win, Lose, or Draw? Claiming Victory in Battle." In *Krieg und Frieden im alten Vorderasien: 52e Rencontre Assyriologique Internationale, International Congress of Assyriology and Near Eastern Archaeology, Münster, 17.–21. Juli 2006*, edited by Hans Neumann et al., 527–37. Alter Orient und Altes Testament 401. Münster: Ugarit, 2014.

Meuszyński, Janusz, et al. *Die Rekonstruktion der Reliefdarstellungen und ihrer Anordnung im Nordwestpalast von Kalḫu (Nimrūd).* Baghdader Forschungen 2. 3 vols. Mainz am Rhein: P.v. Zabern, 1981.

Mieroop, Marc van de. *Cuneiform Texts and the Writing of History.* London: Routledge, 1999.

Millard, Alan Ralph. *The Eponyms of the Assyrian Empire 910–612 BC.* Helsinki: Neo-Assyrian Text Corpus Project, 1994.

———. "Sennacherib's Attack on Hezekiah." *Tyndale Bulletin* 36 (1985) 61–77.

Monson, John M., and Iain Provan. *1 and 2 Kings.* Grand Rapids: Zondervan, 2016.

Moran, William L., ed. *The Amarna Letters.* Baltimore: Johns Hopkins University Press, 1992.

———. "Rib-Hadda: Job at Byblos?" In *Biblical and Related Studies Presented to Samuel Iwry*, edited by Ann Kort and Scott Morschauser, 173–81. Winona Lake, IN: Eisenbrauns, 1985.

Myers, Jacob Martin. *II Chronicles.* Anchor Bible 13. Garden City, NY: Doubleday, 1965.

Na'aman, Nadav. "The Deuteronomist and Voluntary Servitude to Foreign Powers." *Journal for the Study of the Old Testament* 20.65 (1995) 37–53.

Nicholson, Ernest W. *Deuteronomy and Tradition.* Oxford: Blackwell, 1967.

Niditch, Susan. "Oral Tradition and Biblical Scholarship." *Oral Tradition Journal* 18.1 (2003) 43–44.

Noth, Martin. *The Deuteronomistic History.* Sheffield, UK: University of Sheffield, 1981.

Novotny, Jamie R. *Selected Royal Inscriptions of Assurbanipal: L3, L4, LET, Prism I, Prism T, and Related Texts.* State Archives of Assyria Cuneiform Texts 10. Helsinki: Neo-Assyrian Text Corpus Project, 2014.

Oded, Bustenay. *War, Peace and Empire: Justifications for War in Assyrian Royal Inscriptions.* Wiesbaden: Ludwig Reichert, 1992.

Olmstead, A. T. *Assyrian Historiography: A Source Study.* University of Missouri Studies. Columbia: University of Missouri, 1916.

Oppenheim, Leo, and Erica Reiner, eds. "Iṣṣūru." In *The Assyrian Dictionary of the Oriental Institute of the University of Chicago*, 7:210–14. Chicago: The Oriental Institute, 1960.

Osten-Sacken, Elisabeth von der. "Netz. B." In vol. 9 of *Reallexikon der Assyriologie*, edited by Gabriella Frantz-Szabo et al., 239–42. Berlin: de Gruyter, 2001.

Park, Song-Mi Suzie. *Hezekiah and the Dialogue of Memory.* Minneapolis: Fortress, 2015.

Parker, Simon B. "Stories of Miraculous Deliverance from a Siege." In *Stories in Scripture and Inscriptions: Comparative Studies on Narratives in Northwest Semitic Inscriptions and the Hebrew Bible*, 105–30. New York: Oxford University Press, 1997.

Parrot, André. *The Arts of Assyria*. Translated by Stuart Gilbert and James Emmons. New York: Golden, 1961.

Person, Raymond F. *The Deuteronomic School: History, Social Setting, and Literature*. Studies in Biblical Literature 2. Atlanta: Society of Biblical Literature, 2002.

Peterson, Brian Neil. *The Authors of the Deuteronomistic History: Locating a Tradition in Ancient Israel*. Minneapolis: Fortress, 2014.

Piepkorn, Arthur Carl. *Historical Prism Inscriptions of Ashurbanipal*. Chicago: University of Chicago Press, 1933.

Pitard, Wayne Thomas. *Ancient Damascus: A Historical Study of the Syrian City-State from Earliest Times until Its Fall to the Assyrians in 732 BCE*. Winona Lake, IN: Eisenbrauns, 1987.

Polak, Frank H. "Sociolinguistics: A Key to the Typology and the Social Background of Biblical Hebrew," *Hebrew Studies* 47 (2006): 115–62.

Pongratz-Leisten, Beate. *Ina Sulmi Irub: Die kulttopographische und ideologische Programmatik der Akitu-Prozession in Babylonien und Assyrien im I. Jahrtausend v. Chr.* Mainz am Rhein: Philipp von Zabern, 1994.

———. "The Interplay of Military Strategy and Cultic Practice in Assyrian Politics." In *Assyria, 1995: Proceedings of the 10th Anniversary Symposium of the Neo-Assyrian Text Corpus Project Helsinki, September 7–11, 1995*, edited by S. Parpola and R. M. Whiting, 245–52. Helsinki: Neo-Assyrian Text Corpus Project, 1997.

Porada, Edith. "*5000 Years of the Art of Mesopotamia* by Eva Strommenger, Christina Haglund, Max Hirmer." *Art Bulletin* 47.4 (1965) 537.

Porter, Barbara N. "Decorations, Political Posters, Time Capsules, and Living Gods." In *Assyrian Reliefs from the Palace of Ashurnasirpal II: A Cultural Biography*, edited by Ada Cohen and Steven E. Kangas, 143–58. New Hampshire: University Press of New England, 2010.

———. *Trees, Kings, and Politics: Studies in Assyrian Iconography*. Orbis Biblicus et Orientalis 197. Gottingen: Vandenhoeck & Ruprecht, 2003.

Pury, Albert de, et al., eds. *Israel Constructs Its History: Deuteronomistic Historiography in Recent Research*. English ed. Journal for the Study of the Old Testament Supplement Series 306. Sheffield, UK: Sheffield Academic, 2000.

Rad, Gerhard von. *The Problem of the Hexateuch and Other Essays*. Edinburgh: Oliver & Boyd, 1966.

Rainey, Anson F. "The Biblical Shephelah of Judah." *Bulletin of the American Schools of Oriental Research* 251 (1983) 1–22.

———. *Canaanite in the Amarna Tablets: A Linguistic Analysis of the Mixed Dialect Used by Scribes from Canaan*. Vols. 2–3. Handbuch Der Orientalistik. Erste Abteilung, Der Nahe und Mittlere Osten 25. Leiden: Brill, 1996.

Raney, Donald C. *History as Narrative in the Deuteronomistic History and Chronicles*. Studies in the Bible and Early Christianity 56. Lewiston, NY: E. Mellen, 2003.

Reade, Julian. *Assyrian Sculpture*. Cambridge, MA: Harvard University Press, 1983.

———. "Ideology and Propaganda in Assyrian Art." In *Power and Propaganda: A Symposium on Ancient Empires*, 329–43. Mesopotamia 7. Copenhagen: Akademisk Forlag, 1979.

———. "Religious Ritual in Assyrian Sculpture." In *Ritual and Politics in Ancient Mesopotamia*, edited by Barbara N. Porter, 7–61. New Haven: American Oriental Society, 2005.

———. "Royal Lion Hunt." In *Art and Empire: Treasures from Assyria in the British Museum*, edited by John E. Curtis and Julian E. Reade, 50–51. New York: Metropolitan Museum of Art, 1995.

Reiner, Erica, ed. "Târu." In *The Assyrian Dictionary of the Oriental Institute of the University of Chicago*, 18:250–79. Chicago: The Oriental Institute, 2006.

Rimbach, James Allen. "Animal Imagery in the Old Testament: Some Aspects of Hebrew Poetics." PhD diss., Johns Hopkins University, 1972.

Roberts, J. J. M. "The Davidic Origin of the Zion Tradition." *Journal of Biblical Literature* 92.3 (1973) 329–44.

———. "Isaiah in Old Testament Theology." *Interpretation* 36.2 (1982) 130–43.

Rogers, Robert William. *A History of Babylonia and Assyria*. 2nd ed. 2 vols. New York: Eaton & Mains, 1901.

Römer, Thomas, ed. *The Future of the Deuteronomistic History*. Bibliotheca Ephemeridum Theologicarum Lovaniensium 1. Leuven-Louvain: Leuven University Press, 2000.

———. *The So-Called Deuteronomistic History: A Sociological, Historical and Literary Introduction*. London: T&T Clark, 2005.

Rudman, Dominic. "Is the Rabshakeh Also Among the Prophets? A Rhetorical Study of 2 Kings XVIII 17–35." *Vetus Testamentum* 50.1 (2000) 100–110.

Russell, John Malcolm. *Sennacherib's Palace without Rival at Nineveh*. Chicago: University of Chicago Press, 1991.

———. *The Writing on the Wall: Studies in the Architectural Context of Late Assyrian Palace Inscriptions*. Winona Lake, IN: Eisenbrauns, 1999.

Sasson, Jack M. "Siege Mentality: Fighting at the City Gate in the Mari Archives." In *Marbeh Hokmah: Studies in the Bible and the Ancient Near East in Loving Memory of Victor Avigdor Hurowitz*, edited by Shamir Yona et al., 465–78. Winona Lake, IN: Eisenbrauns, 2015.

Schachner, Andreas. *Bilder eines Weltreichs: Kunst- und kulturgeschichtliche Untersuchungen zu den Verzierungen eines Tores aus Balawat (Imgur-Enlil) aus der Zeit von Salmanassar III, König von Assyrien*. Brussels: Brepols, 2007.

Schniedewind, William. "Prolegomena for the Sociolinguistics of Classical Hebrew." *Journal of Hebrew Scriptures* 5 (2005). https://doi.org/10.5508/jhs.2004.v5.a6.

Siddall, Luis Robert. *The Reign of Adad-Nīrārī III: An Historical and Ideological Analysis of An Assyrian King and His Times*. Leiden: Brill, 2013.

Stade, Bernhard. "Miscellen: Anmerkungen zu 2 Kö. 15–21." *Zeitschrift für die Alttestamentliche Wissenschaft* 6 (1886) 122–89.

Strassler, Robert B., ed. *The Landmark Herodotus: The Histories*. New York: Anchor, 2007.

Strawn, Brent A. *What Is Stronger Than a Lion?: Leonine Image and Metaphor in the Hebrew Bible and the Ancient Near East*. Orbis Biblicus et Orientalis 212. Gőttingen: Vandenhoeck & Ruprecht, 2005.

Streck, Maximilian. *Assurbanipal und die letzten assyrischen Konige bis zum Untergange Niniveh's*. Vorderasiatische Bibliothek. 3 vols. Leipzig: J. C. Hinrichs, 1916.

Strommenger, Eva. *5000 Years of the Art of Mesopotamia*. Translated by Christina Haglund. London: Thames and Hudson, 1964.

Sweeney, Marvin A. *I & II Kings: A Commentary*. Old Testament Library. Louisville, KY: Westminster John Knox, 2007.

Sweeney, Marvin A., and Ehud Ben-Zvi, eds. *The Changing Face of Form Criticism for the Twenty-First Century*. Grand Rapids: Eerdmans, 2003.

Tadmor, Hayim. *The Inscriptions of Tiglath-Pileser III, King of Assyria: Critical Edition, with Introductions, Translations, and Commentary*. Jerusalem: Israel Academy of Sciences and Humanities, 1994.

———. "Propaganda, Literature, Historiography: Cracking the Code of the Assyrian Royal Inscriptions." In *Assyria, 1995: Proceedings of the 10th Anniversary Symposium of the Neo-Assyrian Text Corpus Project Helsinki, September 7–11, 1995*, edited by S. Parpola and R. M. Whiting, 325–338. Helsinki: Neo-Assyrian Text Corpus Project, 1997.

———. "Rabshaqeh, Rab-Shaqeh." In *Enṣiqlōpēdiâ Miqrā'it*, edited by Benjamin Mazar et al., 323–25. Jerusalem: Mosad Bialik, 1976.

———. "Sennacherib's Campaign to Judah: Historical and Historiographical Considerations." Translated by M. Feinberg-Vamosh. *Zion* 50 (1986) 65–80.

———. *"With My Many Chariots I Have Gone Up the Heights of the Mountains": Historical and Literary Studies on Ancient Mesopotamia and Israel*. Edited by Mordechai Cogan. Jerusalem: Israel Exploration Society, 2011.

Tadmor, Hayim, and Shigeo Yamada, eds. *The Royal Inscriptions of Tiglath-Pileser III (744–727 BC) and Shalmaneser V (726–722 BC), Kings of Assyria*. Vol. 1 of *Royal Inscriptions of the Neo-Assyrian Peirod*. Winona Lake, IN: Eisenbrauns, 2011.

Telfer, Charles K. "Toward a Historical Reconstruction of Sennacherib's Invasion of Judah in 701 BC: With Special Attention to the Hezekiah-Narratives of Isaiah 36–39." *Mid-America Journal of Theology* 22 (2011) 7–17.

Thureau-Dangin, François. *Une Relation de La Huitième Campagne de Sargon (714 Av. J.-C.): Texte Assyrien Inédit, Publié et Traduit*. Paris: P. Geuthner, 1912.

Ussishkin, David. *Biblical Lachish: A Tale of Construction, Destruction, Excavation and Restoration*. Jerusalem: Israel Exploration Society, 2014.

———. *The Conquest of Lachish by Sennacherib*. Publications of the Institute of Archaeology 6. Tel Aviv: Tel Aviv University, Institute of Archaeology, 1982.

———. "Sennacherib's Campaign to Philistia and Judah: Ekron, Lachish, and Jerusalem." In *Essays on Ancient Israel in Its Near Eastern Context: A Tribute to Nadav Na'aman*, edited by Yaira Amit, et al., 339–57. Winona Lake, IN: Eisenbrauns, 2006.

Watanabe, Chikako E. *Animal Symbolism in Mesopotamia: A Contextual Approach*. Wiener Offene Orientalistik 1. Wien: Institut fur Orientalistik der Universität Wien, 2002.

Weinfeld, Moshe. *Deuteronomy and the Deuteronomic School*. Oxford: Clarendon, 1972.

Weissert, Elnathan. "Royal Hunt and Royal Triumph in a Prism Fragment of Ashurbanipal (82-5-22,2)." In *Assyria, 1995: Proceedings of the 10th Anniversary Symposium of the Neo-Assyrian Text Corpus Project Helsinki, September 7–11, 1995*, edited by S. Parpola and R. M. Whiting, 339–58. Helsinki: Neo-Assyrian Text Corpus Project, 1997.

Winter, Irene. "Art *in* Empire: The Royal Image and the Visual Dimensions of Assyrian Ideology." In *Assyria, 1995: Proceedings of the 10th Anniversary Symposium of the Neo-Assyrian Text Corpus Project Helsinki, September 7–11, 1995*, edited by S. Parpola and R. M. Whiting, 359–381. Helsinki: Neo-Assyrian Text Corpus Project, 1997.

———. "The Program of the Throneroom of Assurnasirpal II." In *Essays on Near Eastern Art and Archaeology in Honor of Charles Kryle Wilkinson*, edited by Prudence Oliver Harper and Holly Pittman, 15–31. New York: Metropolitan Museum of Art, 1983.

———. "Royal Rhetoric and the Development of Historical Narrative in Neo-Assyrian Reliefs." In vol. 1 of *On Art in the Ancient Near East: Of the First Millennium BCE*, edited by Irene Winter, 3–70. Leiden: Brill, 2010.

Wolff, Hans Walter. "The Kerygma of the Deuteronomic Historical Work." In *The Vitality of Old Testament Traditions*, by Walter Brueggemann and Hans Walter Wolff, 83–100. Atlanta: John Knox, 1975.

Yadin, Yigael. *The Art of Warfare in Biblical Lands in the Light of Archaeological Study*. 2 vols. New York: McGraw-Hill, 1963.

Younger, K. Lawson. *Ancient Conquest Accounts: A Study in Ancient Near Eastern and Biblical History Writing*. Journal for the Study of the Old Testament Supplement Series 98. Sheffield, UK: Journal for the Study of the Old Testament, 1990.

Author Index

Albenda, Pauline, 63–64, 134–35, 178
Amiet, Pierre, 18
Aruz, Joan, 39
Aynard, Jeanne-Marie, 14

Bagg, Ariel M., 122, 138n321, 161–62, 165
Bahrani, Zainab, 23, 27
Baines, John, 93
Barnett, Richard David, 15, 18–19, 33, 78, 88–89, 120n185
Barnett, Richard David, et al., 19
Barnett, Richard David, and Margaret Falkner, 18, 126–29nn229–37
Bauer, Theo, 14, 68n74, 69n85, 70n89
Ben-Zvi, Ehud, 22, 169–70n43, 184
Biggs, Robert D., and Erica Reiner, 8n28
Birch, Walter de Gray, 120n186
Blenkinsopp, Joseph, 37n212
Blommaert, Jan, and Chris Bulcaen, 52–53n46–47
Borger, Rykle, 10, 11n43, 13–14, 68n75, 69n85, 149nn386–87, 150n390
Botta, Paul Émile, 134n286, 288
Buss, Martin J., 49–50

Campbell, Antony F., and Mark A. O'Brien, 35n188
Campbell, Duncan B., 152n394, 164
Chavalas, Mark W., 175
Childs, Brevard S., 36, 167
Cogan, Mordechai, and Hayim Tadmor, 22, 35–36, 177, 184, 187
Collins, Paul, 20
Collon, Dominique, 39
Cornelius, Izak, 92
Curtis, John E., and Julian E. Reade, 18, 21, 33n181, 39n226, 65nn70–71, 92nn133–34, 136, 106nn92–97, 108–9nn99–106, 129–30nn239–49
Curtis, John, and N. Tallis, 15, 34n183, 39n224, 67nn72–73, 109–14nn107–123

Dezsö, Tamás, 178
Dowd, Garin, et al., 47n17
Dubovský, Peter, 22, 178

Elayi, Josette, 190n114
Eph'al, Israel, 152nn396–97, 153nn399, 401–4, 406–7
Evans, Paul S., 22, 167n36, 191nn115–16

Fairclough, Norman, 43–44, 51–53, 91, 94
Fales, Frederick Mario, 22, 151n393, 157, 165n31
Foreman, Benjamin, 29n159
Foster, Benjamin R., 23n117
Frahm, Eckart, 13, 22

Fuchs, Andreas, 3n9, 7n21, 10, 11n43, 41, 131–33nn251–62, 264–85, 189nn107, 109, 190n112

Gallagher, William R., 22, 41, 161, 168, 170, 175, 176, 178, 179n75
Geertz, Clifford, 24, 44n3
Grabbe, Lester, 22
Gray, John, 167n35
Grayson, A. Kirk, 2n3, 7nn19–20, 24, 10–13, 21n106, 33–34, 58–63nn6–28, 33–34, 36–40, 43–61, 67n72, 97–104nn4–90, 104, 114n124, 115–20nn125–39, 141–84, 188, 121–22nn195–99, 203–4, 152n395, 156nn418–20, 179n74, 182n83
Grayson, A. Kirk, and Jamie R. Novotny, 1n1, 3nn11–13, 11n43, 13, 33n177, 135–140nn292–313, 315–43, 156nn412–14, 161nn4–5, 163nn12–13, 165n23, 169nn41–42, 175nn47, 51, 180n77, 188–189n98–106, 108, 110
Gunkel, Hermann, 45–50

Herodotus, 186
Hill, Jane A., et al., 97n2
Hobbs, T. R, 35
Holloway, Steven W., 97n1, 157

Japhet, Sara, 38nn219–21
Josephus, Flavius, 186
Jowett, Garth, and Victoria O'Donnell, 26n136

Kahn, Dan'el, 168n38, 190n114
Kalimi, Isaac, 38n217, 170
Kalimi, Isaac, and Seth Richardson, 22
King, L. W., 120n189
King, Philip, and Lawrence Stager, 143nn354–60, 168n38, 175nn48–50
Klein, Ralph W., 37n216, 38, 168–169nn39–40
Knierim, Rolf, 47–49
Knoppers, Gary N., and J. G. McConville, 35n188
Knudtzon, J. A., et al., 8–9nn31–32, 35–37, 34nn185–85, 192n118
Kuan, Jeffrey Kah-Jin, 38n217, 160n3
Kuhrt, Amélie, 11–12n51, 13n62

Laato, Antti, 180, 187n95
Lanfranchi, G. B., and Simo Parpola, 141n348
Leichty, Erle, 7n25, 8n27, 10, 13, 54n52–53, 147–49nn364–65, 366–80, 162n9, 163n10
Levin, Yigal, 177, 184n87
Liverani, Mario, 9, 23n118, 24–25, 34n187, 190n113

Machinist, Peter, 155n410, 177, 183
Marcus, David, 2, 53nn50–51, 54n54
Matty, Nazek Khaled, 22, 190n113
Mayer, Walter, 7nn22–23, 40n233, 41, 132n263
McKenzie, Steven L., 35n188
Melville, Sarah C., 192
Meuszyński, Janusz, et al., 15
Mieroop, Marc van de, 23n119
Millard, Alan Ralph, 153–154n408–9, 187
Monson, John M., and Iain Provan, 160n2
Moran, William L., 8nn29–30, 9, 34nn184–87, 192–93n120
Myers, Jacob Martin, 38n218

Na'aman, Nadav, 193n121
Nicholson, Ernest W., 35
Niditch, Susan, 48n24
Noth, Martin, 35
Novotny, Jamie R., 14

Oded, Bustenay, 31, 40, 92nn137–38, 155–56n411
Olmstead, A. T., 14n63
Oppenheim, Leo, and Erica Reiner, 8n30
Osten-Sacken, Elisabeth von der, 38n223, 83n111

Park, Song-Mi Suzie, 168n38
Parker, Simon B., 36–37, 176
Parrot, André, 15, 17–19, 57n1, 71, 75nn104–6, 80, 181
Person, Raymond F., 35n188
Peterson, Brian Neil, 35n188
Piepkorn, Arthur Carl, 14, 149–50nn386–88
Pitard, Wayne Thomas, 121n194
Polak, Frank H., 55
Pongratz-Leisten, Beate, 30n166, 69n83, 156
Porada, Edith, 107n98
Porter, Barbara N., 15n78, 27
Pury, Albert de, et al., 35n188

Rad, Gerhard von, 35
Rainey, Anson F., 9n33, 34n187, 160n2
Raney, Donald C., 35n188
Reade, Julian, 27–28, 39nn225, 227, 58n2, 65n69, 88, 105
Reiner, Erica, 188n98
Rimbach, James Allen, 2n4, 8n26
Roberts, J. J. M., 37, 187n97
Rogers, Robert William, 11n50–12
Römer, Thomas, 35n188
Rudman, Dominic, 183
Russell, John Malcolm, 3–6, 19, 31, 84nn117–18, 86n122–87n123, 88n126, 93–94, 137n314, 138n321, 140, 141–42nn346–52, 156–57nn422–24, 165

Sasson, Jack M., 190n111
Schachner, Andreas, 120nn186, 189, 121
Schniedewind, William, 55
Siddall, Luis Robert, 122
Stade, Bernhard, 36, 167
Strassler, Robert B., 186n92
Strawn, Brent A., 2n4, 14, 29, 39, 61
Streck, Maximilian, 14, 84–88nn117–26, 149–50nn381–90, 151n392, 156n421, 163n11
Strommenger, Eva, 17–18, 26–27, 71–72nn99–103, 75n107, 80n110, 83, 89n130, 120–21nn185–87, 190–91, 151n391
Sweeney, Marvin A., 176–77
Sweeney, Marvin A., and Ehud Ben-Zvi, 49

Tadmor, Hayim, 2, 10–11n44, 12, 25–26, 32–33n180, 40–41n234, 123n207, 123nn207, 212, 215, 124n219, 138n321, 164–65, 177, 190n113
Tadmor, Hayim, and Shigeo Yamada, 2n2, 3n10, 11n43, 12n55, 122–23n205–6, 208–16, 124–25nn224–28, 129n238, 131, 163–64nn14–17, 179n76,
Telfer, Charles K., 37
Thureau-Dangin, François, 7n21, 132n263

Ussishkin, David, 19, 142n353, 146nn361–63, 160, 165, 166nn32–34

Watanabe, Chikako E., 2, 58, 60
Weinfeld, Moshe, 35
Weissert, Elnathan, 14, 15n72, 19–20nn98–99, 21, 29–30, 32, 68nn75–79, 69–70, 71n94, 92, 181
Winter, Irene, 15n78, 17, 28–29, 31, 64
Wolff, Hans Walter, 35

Yadin, Yigael, 152n398, 153, 165, 178
Younger, K. Lawson, 23, 24n122–23

Subject Index

'Abdi-Aširta, 9, 192
Abdi-Li'ti, 171
Abdi-Milkūti 147
Adad-nārāri II/Adad-nirari II, 59, 60, 67–68, 89, 98–99, 112, 121–22, 156
Adiâ, 19
Adinu, 118
Aḫaunu, 114–17, 120, 154
Aḫšēri, 149
akītu festival, 29, 30, 69, 156
akītu-house, 156
Aramu, 116
Araštua, 101–2
Ashur (god), 7, 30, 97, 100–103, 119, 121, 131–32, 136, 147–48, 156, 181
Ashurbanipal, 3, 6, 10–11, 13–15, 19–20, 25–26, 28–30, 33, 57, 61, 68–71, 76–80, 83–90, 92, 98, 149–51, 156, 160, 162–63, 166, 181
Ashur-nārāri V, 122
Ashurnasirpal II, 2, 7, 10–12, 15–18, 21, 28, 31–34, 38–39, 57, 61–67, 90, 98–114, 158, 179, 182–83, 193
Aššur-bēl-kala, 58, 89
Aššur-dan II, 59, 60
Atarsamain, 149
Aya-rāmu, 171
Aziru, 34

Bagartu, 132
Balawat Gates, 15, 18, 39, 66, 109, 116, 121
Bir-Dadda, 149
Būdi-il, 171

Carchemishite, 117
Critical Discourse Analysis (CDA), 43–45, 51–58, 91, 94, 155, 195–96

Davidic kingship, 196
Deuteronomic School, 36, 184
Deuteronomist , 35, 184
Deuteronomistic History (DH), 35, 193
Deuteronomistic tradition, 184
Dunanu, 150

Elamite, 21, 150
Elamites, 3, 21
Esarhaddon, 7–8, 13, 18, 39, 41, 53–54, 147–48, 160, 162–63, 166, 177, 185

Form Criticism, 43, 45–50

Gurdî, 139

Hazael, 119

Hezekiah, 1–2, 10, 12–13, 21–22, 33–34, 36–38, 41–43, 54–56, 138, 158–70, 172–80, 183–92, 195–96
Hunting, ass 62; bulls 17, 54, 59–61, 63, 103; deer 182; elephant 59–60, 62, 174; gazelle 62; lion 43, 57–80, 83–94, 155, 158, 179–83, 192, 195; lioness 21, 66, 79–80, 85; onager 83, 90; ostrich 12, 43, 62–63, 103, 158, 179, 180; ox 12, 62, 172
Ḫaldia (god), 132
Ḫamarānu, 132
Ḫemti-ili, 102
Ḫullāiia, 100

Ilānu, 103
Iluia, 156
Irbibu, 104
Isaiah, 37, 55, 167–68, 173, 175–76, 179, 184, 188, 193
Isaianic tradition, 184
Ishtar, 30, 69, 85
Ispabāra, 136
iṣṣūr(u), 1–2, 6–8, 11, 12, 33, 58, 62, 124, 138, 158, 163, 179–80, 183

Judaean tradition, 184

Kāki, 117
Kalḫu annals, 122–24, 129
Kammūsu-nadbi, 171
Kassites, 136
Kibaba, 133
Kiki, 119
kīma, 1–2, 7–8, 12, 33, 53, 62, 103, 123–24, 132, 138, 158, 163, 179–80, 183
Kirūa, 139
Kudurru, 102, 108

Labṭuru, 102, 104
Lulî, 136, 171, 189

Mamu, Temple of, 113
Manasseh, 163
Maniye, 138
Marduk, 7, 131–32
Marduk-apla-iddina (Merodach-baladan), 3, 135, 138, 147n365
Marduk-bēl-usāte, 118
Marduk-šarra-uṣur, 122
Min(u)ḫimmu, 171
Mitinti, 171, 173
Mukīn-zēri, 125
Mutallu, 132–33

Nabu temple, 123
Nergal (god), 59–62, 87
Ninnu, 117
Ninurta (god), 11, 58–62
Nūr-Adad, 98–99

Padî, 1, 22, 37, 42, 137, 160–62, 169, 172–73 189–92, 196
Pharaoh, 8–9, 34

Qedarites, 149
qupp(u), 1–2, 6–8, 12, 33, 62, 124, 138, 158, 163, 179–80, 183

Rabshakeh, 167–68, 173, 176–78, 183–84
Rezin, 2–3, 12, 33, 124–25, 154, 163–64, 179
Rib-Addi, 8–10, 34, 192
Rusā, 7, 131

Sagara, 110–11
Sanda-uarri, 8, 147
Sangara, 117
Sapalume, 117
Sarduri , 123–24
Sargon II, 2–3, 7, 97, 131–34, 141
Sennacherib, 1–10, 12–13, 15, 19, 21–22, 31–34, 36–39, 41–43, 54–56, 93–94nn146–47, 98, 135–42, 144–47, 156–81, 184–86, 188–93, 196
Shalmaneser III, 60, 65, 89, 98, 114–20n186
Shalmaneser V, 98, 167
Siege, 1–2, 8–9, 12–13, 15, 18–19, 22, 32, 38–39, 41, 43, 54, 56, 64, 96–109, 115–42, 144–55, 157–61, 163–69, 176–85, 187, 189–92, 195

Simile, 1–3, 6–10, 12–15, 32–34, 38–43, 53–54n54, 124n221, 158–59, 164–65, 179–80, 182, 193, 195–96
Ṣidqâ, 137, 171
Ṣilli-Bēl, 173
Šamaš, 132
Šamaš-šum-ukīn, 149
Šarru-lū-dāri, 171
Šuzubu (Mušēzib-Marduk), 3, 140

Tiamat, 156
Tiglath-pileser I, 7, 11, 32, 58, 89, 97–98
Tiglath-pileser III, 2–3, 8, 12, 15, 18, 32–33, 40–41n234, 122–29, 131, 158, 160, 163–66, 179–81, 190n113, 193
Tuatti, 119
Tu-Ba'lu, 171
Tukulti-nirurta II, 98
Tullu, 119
Ṭupusu, 102, 104

Uaite', 149
Ullusunu, 131
Ursā, 131–32
Ūru-Milki, 171
Urzana , 7, 131–32

Yahwism, 184
Yasubigallians , 136
YHWH, 22, 35–37, 158, 167–69, 173–74, 176–77, 179, 183–88, 190, 193, 196

Zion, tradition, 37; theology, 37, 187–88, 193

Geographical Index

Adauš, 7
Aisa, Mount, 97
Akzibu , 137
Alammu(?), 141
Ali[ṣir]/Ali[muš], 117
Amedu , 103–4
Ammali, 101
Amurru, 171, 192
Anzaria (Kār-Ishtar), 133
Arabia, 149
Aramu, 116
Araštua, 101–2
Arba'il, 156
Aridu, 117
Arinu, 97, 98
Arman, 118
Arpad, 123
Arwad, 171
Ashdod, 171
Ashkelon, 1, 137, 171, 186
Ashur, 116, 118, 147, 156
Assyrian Empire, the, 122, 132, 136, 139, 151, 154–55, 157, 159, 161–62, 165–66, 176, 183–84, 190, 192, 196
Azalla, 149
Azuru, 137, 171

Babylon, 138, 140, 149, 156
Ba'it-ili, 133
Balawat, 34, 109–13, 120
Balih, 67–68
Banayabarqa, 137, 171
Baqānu, 118
Bīt-Adini/Bit-Adini, 103, 109–15, 120
Bīt-Ammon, 171
Bīt-Bagaia (Kār-Adad), 133
Bīt-Daganna, 137, 171
Bīt-Dakkuri, 118
Bīt-Kilamazaḫ, 136
Bīt-Kubatti, 136
Bit-Yakin/Bit-Yahiri, 113, 132, 138
Bīt-Zitti, 137
Borsippa, 149
Burmar'ina, 115
Byblos, 8–10, 32, 34, 171, 192

Cairo, 13
Calah, 61–62, 103, 119, 121–22
Chaldea, 124n221, 135
Cilicia, 148

Dabigu, 115–16, 120
Damascus, 2, 12, 33, 119, 121–22, 124–25, 153–54, 160, 163–64, 165, 179
Damdammusa, 100, 103
Danabu, 119
Dayukku, 131
Dūr-Yakin, 133

Edom, 171
Egypt, 1, 9, 13, 41–42, 54, 93, 148, 160, 162–63, 164, 166, 172, 184, 186n92, 190, 192–93, 196
Ekron, 1, 22, 42, 137, 160–61, 169, 172, 186, 189–92
Elam, 85, 135, 140, 150
Ellipi, 136
Eltekeh, 137, 172, 189
Euphrates, the, 102, 108

Gannanate, 118
Gaza, 166, 186

Hamanu, 150–51
Harhar, 133
Hatti/Ḫatti, 110, 119, 171
Hilqian , 114
Hudun, 102
Ḫabḫu, 7
Ḫalulê, 3, 140
Ḫalupe, 100
Ḫanigalbat, 98
Ḫardišpu, 136
Ḫarmiš, 104
Ḫarran, 156
Ḫatti/Hatti, 63, 110–11, 119, 136, 171, 189
Ḫubuškia, 117
Ḫunusu, 98
Ḫuzirina, 98

I[all]igu, 111
Ilizi, 156
Illubru, 139
Izirtu, 149

Jerusalem, 1–2, 12, 22, 33, 35–37, 41–43, 54, 56, 137–38, 159–69, 172–73, 175, 177–80, 183–93, 196
Joppa, 137, 171
Judah, 1, 13, 21–22, 33, 35n188, 37–38n217, 41–42, 54–56, 137–38n321, 160–70, 172, 174–80, 183–84, 186–88, 190–93, 195–96

Kalḫu/Kalhu, 12, 15, 123, 133
Kaprabu, 103
Kašiiari, Mount, 101
Khorsabad, 134
Kinabu, 100–101
Kindāu (Kār-Sin), 133
Kipšuna, 97
Kirbit, 149
Kišešlu/Kisheshlu (Kār-Nabū), 133, 135
Kouyunjik, 40
Kummuḫi, 132
Kundi, 8, 147
Kurba'il, 156
Kutha, 149

Lachish, 1, 19, 22, 36, 38, 54, 137n314, 142–47, 154, 160, 164–66, 169, 173–75, 177, 183–84, 190, 196
Laḫiru, 118
Lamenaš, Mount 120
Laqû, 102
Levant, 166, 190

Madara, 102
Maḫalliba, 137
Malaḫu, 119
Mannai, 149
Mannean land, the, 131
Mari, 121–22, 190n111
Marinâ, 109–10, 113–14
Medes, 148
Megiddo, 153, 160
Memphis, 13, 42
Mê-turnat, 118
Milqia, 156
Moab, 171
Muṣaṣir, 7, 131–32

Nahr el-Kelb, 24
Naṣibina, 98
Neo-Assyrian Empire, the, 14, 23, 53–55, 96–97, 151
Nimrud, 16–18, 63–66, 105–8, 129

Nineveh, 4–6, 14, 19–20, 22, 29–30, 70–72, 74–82, 84, 86, 88–90, 125–28, 135, 138–42, 144–48, 150–51, 156, 162–63, 165–67, 169, 174–75, 178, 181–82, 186, 189–90, 196
Nirbu, 101

Paqaraḫubunu, 119
Partukka, 148
Pazaši/Panziš, 134

Qumānu 97–98, 156
Quraṣiti 149

Rugulutu, 112

Samaria, 153, 167, 184
Samsimuruna, 171
Sapê/Shapiya/Šapīya 125, 164n21, 165
Sappanu, 99
Sazabû, 117
Sidon, 136–37, 147, 171, 189
Sikkur, 99
Simesi, 117
Sippar, 132, 149
Sissû, 8, 147
Sugunia, 116
Suḫu, 102
Sūru/Suru, 100, 102, 108, 152
Syria, 107, 120, 123
Syro-Palestine/Syria-Palestine, 42, 153, 191

Ṣarepta, 137
Ṣumur, 9
Šapîbêl 150
Šilaia, 115, 117
Šītamrat, 116

Tamnâ, 137, 172
Tanakun, 119
Tēla, 101
Tīl-Barsip, 115
Tu(ru)shpa, 165
Tyre, 153

Udu, 104
Ukku, 138
Ulluba, 110–11, 123
Upa/U[pa?], 129, 131
Uppume, 148
Urarṭu/Urartu, 7nn22–23, 40n233, 131–32n263
Urdutu, 139
Urmēte, 149
Urraṭinaš, 7
Ušû, 13
Uzbia, 149

Zagros Mountains, the, 136
Zion, Mount, 37
Zinjirli, 24, 185
Zion 187
Zirkitu, 134

Ancient Document Index

Ancient Near Eastern Documents (RIMA, RINAP, and VAT)

RIMA 2 11n43, 45, 61n43, 62n53, 63n61, 67n72, 104nn83, 85, 87

A.0.87.1 7nn19–20, 11n46–49, 58nn6–10, 97–98nn4–11
A.0.87.2 98nn12–13
A.0.89.2 58n11–59n12
A.0.89.7 59nn13–17
A.0.98.1 59nn18–21
A.0.99.1 156nn418–20
A.0.99.2 59–60nn22–28, 98–99n14–26
A.0.100.5 60nn33–34, 36–37
A.0.101.1 7n24, 100–104nn27–82, 114n124, 152n395
A.0.101.2 12nn53–54, 21n106, 33nn178–79, 34n182, 61–62nn44–52, 179n74, 182n83
A.0.101.19 63n60
A.0.101.21 104nn84, 86–90
A.0.101.30 62–63nn54–59
A.0.102.6 60–61nn38–40

RIMA 3 115nn125, 134, 116nn139, 144, 117n153, 120n188, 122

A.0.102.1 115nn130–32, 117nn145–47, 151–53
A.0.102.2
(the "Kurkh Monolith" text)
115nn126–29, 133–34, 116nn135–38, 117–18nn148–50, 154–60
A.0.102.5 116nn141–43, 118nn161–71,
A.0.102.6 119nn172–74
A.0.102.8 116n138
A.0.102.16 119–20nn175–84
A.0.104.6 121nn195–96
A.0.104.8 121–22nn197–99
A.0.107.1 122n204

RINAP 1 11n43, 122n205, 123nn206, 208–11, 123n216, 124, 125n228, 144, 163n14

No. 20 12n55, 124n217, 124–25n219–24, 131n250, 163–64nn14–17

No. 22 3n10, 180
No. 39 123nn212–14, 124
No. 41 123n215, 124
No. 47 124n221, 125nn225–27
No. 49 124

RINAP 3/1 11n43, 13n59, 135nn292–95, 136n305, 139n330, 163n12, 175n47

No. 4 (the Rassam Cylinder) 1n1, 161, 13n57, 161nn4–5, 163n13, 165n23
No. 15 1n1, 13n57, 163n13
No. 16 1n1, 13n57, 163n13
No. 17 1n1, 139, 13n57, 139nn331–38, 163n13, 169nn41–42
No. 18 1n1, 13n57, 163n13
No. 20 2n2, 179n76
No. 22 (the "Chicago" Prism) 1n1, 3nn11–13, 137–39, 140, 13n57, 33n177, 136–37nn296–304, 306–13, 137–39nn315–29, 140nn339–43, 163n13, 165n23, 175n51, 180n77, 188–89nn98–106, 108, 110
No. 23 1n1, 13n57, 163n13

RINAP 3/2 11n43, 13n59, 156n412

RINAP 4 11n43, 13n61, 147nn364–65, 162n9

No. 1 7n25, 8n27, 147–48nn366–70, 163n10
No. 15–16 13n62
No. 20 13n62
No. 32 54n52
No. 33 148nn371–77
No. 34 54n53
No. 34–39 13n62
No. 35 148–49nn378–80
No. 98 13n62
No. 168 156nn413–14

VAT

9752 104
9782 104

Old Testament/ Hebrew Bible

2 Samuel

24:15–17 186

2 Kings

18:3–7 167
18:9–12 167
18:13—19:37 158, 166–67, 169–78, 183–84, 186, 191, 195
19:7 186
19:32–34 188

Isaiah

36:1—37:38 158, 168, 169–74, 183, 186, 191, 195
37:33–35 188
37:36 178

2 Chronicles

32:1–23 158, 168–74, 183, 186, 191, 195
32:2 179
32:2–8 178
32:10 178

Greco-Roman Writings

Flavii Iosephi Opera

Antiquities X, §§1–23 186

Herodoti Historiae

II, 141 186

www.ingramcontent.com/pod-product-compliance
Lightning Source LLC
Chambersburg PA
CBHW051640230426
43669CB00013B/2383